Chivalry in Westeros

Chivalry in Westeros

The Knightly Code
of *A Song of Ice and Fire*

CAROL PARRISH JAMISON

McFarland & Company, Inc., Publishers
Jefferson, North Carolina

ISBN (print) 978-1-4766-7005-8
ISBN (ebook) 978-1-4766-3316-9

Library of Congress cataloguing data are available

British Library cataloguing data are available

Front cover image © 2018 iStock

Manufactured in the United States of America

*McFarland & Company, Inc., Publishers
Box 611, Jefferson, North Carolina 28640
www.mcfarlandpub.com*

For my son, Jamison, who shares my love of literature; for my daughter, Parrish, who gave me this advice before she left for college: "Don't be sad. Go write a book."

With appreciation to Julia Broyles, my research assistant.

Table of Contents

Preface

In *Travels in Hyper-Reality*, Umberto Eco famously observed, "it seems that people like the Middle Ages."[1] The immense success of George R.R. Martin's *A Song of Ice and Fire* validates Eco's remark, perhaps even proving it to be an understatement. Benjamin Breen explains that "seemingly unwittingly, [Martin has] brought a fairly obscure sub-discipline of academic history—the early modern world—to the masses."[2] Martin has not only made accessible, as Breen notes, the history of the early modern world, but the literature of that time period, as well. Casual readers delight in the pseudo-historical world of Westeros, while scholars and students of medieval literature are fascinated with the many ways the series mirrors familiar works from the Middle Ages.

In the preface to the 1996 edition of *Studies in Medievalism*, the journal's founder Leslie Workman defined medievalism as "the continuing process of creating the Middle Ages." Workman legitimized medievalism, paving the way for the kind of scholarship that will unfold in the subsequent chapters of this book. Acclaimed as a great writer of fantasy, George R.R. Martin is equally a writer of medievalism. Especially in Martin's first novels, magic is largely kept at bay, limited to the regions beyond the boundaries of Westeros and doubted by many Westerosi. The reader is immersed into an alternate medieval world rather than an entirely magical one, Martin's re-creation of the Middle Ages.

In this book, I explore how, through his complex and multi-faceted portrayal of the chivalric code, Martin's novels intersect with and illuminate secular medieval literature. I also discuss the HBO series, but to a lesser extent and generally as comparison to the novels. My goal is to look at Martin's novels as a continuation of medieval themes and tropes. Although rich with literary allusions and historical references, Martin's *A Song of Ice and Fire* does not strive for one-to-one correspondences between his characters and those from medieval literature and history. Rather, Martin's creative inspirations are loosely drawn from history and fiction.[3] Westeros is crafted from a variety of sources, creating what Tom Shippey terms "a permanent anachronistic stew," an expansive and somewhat random incorporation of "the medieval imaginary."[4] Martin's novels explore the complexities and nuances of medieval concepts such as chivalry. Thus, Martin's depiction of chivalry and the institution of knighthood merits scholarly discussion and can also enlighten non-specialists who more casually enjoy the medievalism of Westeros.

Martin's contribution to the ongoing traditions of medieval literature makes newly relevant the themes and tropes from a variety of genres in the Middle Ages, especially those portraying chivalric values. Throughout his series, Martin variously challenges, upholds, overturns, and deconstructs the chivalric code. While readers must wait to see his ultimate response to these codes with the completion of the series, his varied approaches offer a rich new perspective for medievalists and scholars of medievalism. His novels not only intersect with medieval literature, but also serve as a fully visualized reflection of the significance and dissemination of that literature.

I emphasize chivalric aspects that I deem most pertinent to Martin's creation of a (pseudo)medieval world: the creation of literature through oral and written lore and specific chivalric values, particularly franchise, loyalty, prowess, blood ties, and political peace weaving. While Martin may not intentionally borrow from medieval literature, his knowledge of the Middle Ages, and especially of chivalry, is impressive and can be informative. I seek to show how his novels portray many of the same kinds of social influences that shaped medieval works. Martin's Westeros in many respects mirrors medieval western Europe, particularly England.[5] His novels intersect with a variety of genres, but I primarily emphasize Martin's connection with the chivalric literature of England and France. My purpose is to pair Martin's novels with well-known works of medieval literature to illustrate Martin's complex portrayal of the chivalric code. Thus, this book is primarily directed to scholars of medievalism, students of medieval literature, and teachers who are interested in including works of medievalism in their medieval classes or developing courses solely devoted to medievalism. Casual readers of the novels and fans of the HBO series, however, will also gain new insight into Martin's Westeros through this discussion.

Martin's vision of a complex chivalric code aligns most closely with medieval romance. Thus, I bring into the discussion familiar medieval romances such as those by Chrétien de Troyes, *King Horn*, *Sir Gawain and the Green Knight*, and especially Sir Thomas Malory's *Le Morte Darthur*. *A Song of Ice and Fire* might be seen, much like Malory's work, as a commentary on the ambiguities of chivalry, so I refer with particular frequency to the intersections between Martin's novels and this romance.[6] However, Martin uses various kinds of medieval literature, including heroic, to craft a Westerosi chivalric code. In the present tense of Martin's novels, Westeros is a brutal place in the midst of civil war. Many of the salient characteristics of the heroic code overlap with and prefigure those of the chivalric code. For example, Martin's depiction of battlefield etiquette and strategies, as well as much of the political intrigue involved in forming alliances, aligns with heroic works of literature such as *The Battle of Maldon* and *Beowulf*, to which I also make frequent reference.

Chapter One discusses the evolution in medieval literature from the heroic to the chivalric and then explores the origins of Westerosi chivalry. I define chivalry, both as it is conceived by medieval writers and as it is reinterpreted by Martin. I devote considerable attention to Martin's spelling and vocabulary choices as these choices enable him to create a believable medieval world. I examine his use of terms such as "courtesy" and "chivalry" as well as his sometimes-unconventional spellings. My purpose is to show these linguistic details as strategic to Martin's creation of an alternative portrayal of chivalry that simultaneously resonates with modern readers and merits serious attention from medievalists. Finally, I provide an overview of Martin's complex and multi-faceted portrayal of chivalry.

Chapters Two and Three examine Martin's creation of a Westerosi literary tradition that is closely aligned with the literary traditions of the Middle Ages. The lore that was shaped into medieval chivalric literature emerged from "the fog of legends." Martin similarly forms an intricate web of legends that, although they sometimes allude to or are loosely based upon medieval sources, are largely his own creation rather than the collectively owned tropes of an age. Martin layers fiction upon fiction as the characters of Westeros relate the stories of their legendary past. Chapter Two focuses on the origins and the significance of oral lore and storytelling in Westeros, drawing parallels to the oral dissemination of chivalric matter in the Middle Ages. Medieval writers depended on their readers' having knowledge of the legends and tropes that undergird their literary creations, legends that spread through oral narratives: the author of *Beowulf* assumes that his readers are familiar with such characters as Sigemund and Weland; and Chrétien de Troyes, twelfth-century French author who is considered the first writer of romance, assumes that his readers are already familiar with the cast of characters that frequent Arthurian romance. In "The Knight of the Cart," Chrétien delays naming the hero, Lancelot, perhaps because he is "inventing" this character, or perhaps to surprise the reader once an already-familiar character is revealed in a new context. The Westerosi have a similarly rich oral history of legends, tropes, and fictionalized heroes upon which they base their chivalric values.

Chapter Three discusses the reception and dissemination of written literature in Westeros. Written literature functions in Westeros remarkably as it did in medieval England prior to Caxton's introduction of the printing press. Martin references romances, chronicles, chivalric handbooks, and didactic literature in his depiction of Westerosi literature. Though disregarded by many Westerosi, this literature may well hold keys to battling the Others and cannot be discounted. This chapter ends with a brief discussion of Martin's metafiction, references within his texts to other works of medievalism

Chapter Four begins an exploration of specific chivalric attributes. The discussion in this chapter focuses on the concept of *franchise*, one of the most essential traits for the warriors of heroic literature and the knights of romance. Historian Maurice Keen defines *franchise* as "the free and frank bearing that is visible testimony to the combination of good birth and virtue,"[7] an attribute that is requisite for literary knights and warriors. For example, in Malory's *Le Morte Darthur*, knights may be temporarily disenfranchised or initially unaware of their heritage, as with Gareth who upon first entering Arthur's court hides his nobility, or Tor who is raised as a shepherd but learns he is the son of King Pellinore. However, as Felicia Ackerman explains, Malory's fictional world is "fundamentally a world of the aristocracy; it does not have the full range of people found in the actual world."[8] Such a limited fictional world would have appealed to romance audiences, largely composed of aristocracy. However, a world composed entirely of aristocracy would be unlikely to captivate today's general readers. Martin's depiction of Westerosi society is complex and nuanced and puts to the test the concept of *franchise* as a necessary attribute of chivalry.

Martin illustrates the complexities of medieval chivalry and the constraints on chivalric values, particularly when liminal characters attempt to penetrate the nobility. In Westeros, although birthright grants prestige, "rank is not hereditary and it is possible for the baseborn to become knights."[9] Martin's vision of a socially nuanced society in which upward mobility is a possibility appeals to modern readers, but also draws heavily on the real life social situations in the Middle Ages as bourgeois acquired money and sometimes bought titles. Such social changes are evidenced in some medieval literary genres, particularly the fabliau, and serve to complicate further the chivalric code. Thus, this chapter includes discussion of mock-chivalric fabliaux which are often populated by poor, destitute knights and rich peasants who have bought titles. In addition to those of noble birth, Westerosi knights and warriors include the mostly lowborn hedge knights (wandering knights who serve no lord) and sellswords (mercenaries who sometimes earn knightly titles as compensation), and lower-class characters who rise in rank and gain title. These liminal characters further stretch and test the idealized attributes of the chivalric code. As this chapter shows, Martin combines the kinds of chivalric struggles found in Malory's work with the societal changes reflected in fabliaux when lower class characters attain knightly titles.

Chapter Five explores the critical role of vows and the difficulties of juggling conflicting loyalties. Loyalty and remaining true to vows are essential characteristics of the hero in both chivalric and heroic literature. Closest to Martin's portrayal of loyalty is Malory's *Le Morte Darthur*; thus, although I note a number of other works, I use Malory as the main point of reference in this chapter. Like Malory, Martin explores the difficulties of upholding the chivalric code when loyalties conflict. This chapter begins with a brief survey of some of Malory's characters who struggle to maintain conflicting loyalties, from Balin to Arthur himself. The remainder of the chapter shows how Martin's characters wrestle with similar kinds of struggles, including Jon Snow's struggles to keep the vows of the Night's Watch, Jaime Lannister's struggles to uphold conflicting vows of the King's Guard, Robb Stark's torn loyalties between the Freys and his love for Jeyne Westerling, and Brienne of Tarth's struggles to remain simultaneously loyal to Lord Renly, Catelyn Stark, and Jaime.

Chapter Six explores Martin's portrayal of prowess. Martin's comprehensive creation of the Westerosi chivalric code certainly emphasizes prowess over softer aspects of chivalry. This emphasis on battlefield etiquette intersects most closely with heroic literature, although prowess remains a salient quality of romance, as well. Martin portrays the social role of the knight and warrior, and the function of prowess, which entails both possession of weaponry and skills at arms. Chapter Six includes some discussion of weaponry, skill, and training, but my emphasis is literary rather than technical. Thus, I focus on the etiquette of warfare, the standards for determining what constitutes fair play, and the role of mercy. I compare Martin's depiction of battle scenes, duels, and tournaments to those frequently depicted in the corpus of medieval literature. I also examine Martin's portrayals of justice, including trial by combat, again considering his novels alongside medieval genres.

In Chapter Seven, I discuss the significance of the blood feud, prominent in Anglo-Saxon heroic works and romance, and also key to the plot of Martin's novels. In medieval literature as in Westeros, the closest ties are between kinsmen. In order to save personal and familial honor, knights and warriors are obligated to avenge their kin. For many of Martin's characters, this thirst for vengeance is the strongest motive for bloodshed. Martin strongly echoes both heroic and chivalric literature in his portrayal of the tensions that result when loved ones must be avenged. I examine the effects of blood feuds on individuals and families, including the Targaryens, the Starks, and the Martells. The chapter ends with an exploration of two of the biggest taboos in medieval and Westerosi culture: king killing and kin killing. None is more reviled than the king killer, especially when the king is killed by one of his own men. Kin killing is equally vile. As the internecine struggles amongst the Lannisters and the history of internecine struggles of the Targaryens reveal, vengeance goes awry when one family member turns on another.

Chapter Eight focuses on how the politics of Westeros affect a specific element of the population: women. Women are important in both heroic and romance literature not only as objects of affection for whom knights strive, but also as queens, diplomats, and weavers of peace. Though Martin has been condemned by some feminists for his treatment of women, the women of Westeros are integral to his narrative. The main impetus for Martin's novels, in fact, is the Helen of Troy–like abduction of Lyanna Stark, a move that, along with the murder of Mad King Aerys Targaryen, motivates the struggle for the Iron Throne. In order to understand and appreciate Martin's portrayal of women, it is critical to situate them in the context of medieval literature. Particularly, women can have important roles in sealing alliances and forging peace and are thus crucial to winning the game of thrones. This chapter emphasizes the role of females as both queens and peace weavers, but also discusses the role of men and children in forging political alliances. I devote much attention to heroic literature as a point of comparison, *Beowulf* in particular, as this work offers numerous examples of peace weaving.

The conclusion explores the pedagogical possibilities of Martin's Westeros. Martin's novels might be successfully integrated into a college classroom on medieval literature, and they can also be included effectively in a course entirely devoted to medievalism. I offer my own experiences bringing discussions of Martin's Westeros into my medieval literature classroom, and I also discuss my experience teaching a senior seminar which focused solely on Martin's novels. Included is a discussion of the slipperiness of the terminology associated with the field of medievalism and how consideration of that terminology can be fruitful in class discussions. Finally, I speculate about how Martin's portrayal of chivalric and heroic codes might evolve as he brings his series to completion.

Thus, *Chivalry in Westeros* demonstrates how Martin incorporates chivalry throughout his series. He simultaneously evokes chivalric medieval literature, recasts significant chivalric themes and tropes, and duplicates the written and oral traditions of medieval literature. His depiction of Westerosi chivalry includes references to post-medieval representations and thus strongly resonates with contemporary audiences. Martin thereby creates a deeply textured fictional world replete with its own copious tradition of chivalric lore and literature.

ONE

An Introduction to Westerosi Chivalry

*"Chivalry, the code that made a knight
more than any pit fighter."*—D with D 806

Martin's Medievalism

George R.R. Martin has sparked renewed interest in all things medieval. His immensely popular *A Song of Ice and Fire* has inspired an award-winning HBO series and an industry of medieval-themed merchandise, including games, apparel, figurines, and jewelry. Fans have created blogs and websites that are devoted to discussions of characters and loaded with speculation about how the series might end. Martin has created quite a sensation. He is acclaimed as a great writer of fantasy, but Martin is equally a writer of medievalism. As evidenced by the recent appearance of scholarly books and articles as well as sessions devoted to his works at academic conferences, Martin's works merit scholarly discussion.[1] Through his creation of Westeros, he presents a richly textured, faux-medieval world that provides particularly rich material for scholars and students of medievalism.

The relatively new field of medievalism originated with the work of Leslie Workman, founder of the journal *Studies in Medievalism*, in the 1970s. Workman's widow, Kathleen Verduin, describes her husband's conception of medievalism and his battle to legitimize it in scholarly circles. In his journal's first issue, Workman attempted what Verduin calls "his first formal attempt at definition": "*Studies in Medievalism* is concerned with the study of scholarship which has created the Middle Ages we know, ideals and models derived from the Middle Ages, and the relations between them." In other words, medievalism involves an engagement with the medieval past. As Workman explains in his preface to the 1996 edition of the journal, "Medievalism and medieval studies might well be defined as the Middle Ages in the contemplation of contemporary society." It is "the continuing process of creating the Middle Ages."[2]

As the field of medievalism has flourished, subsequent scholars have expanded upon Workman's definition, drawing and sometimes erasing perceived boundaries between the kinds of works that might constitute the genre. However, scholars have yet to settle on an authoritative definition. This fact attests more to the vibrancy and relevancy of the field than to scholarly disagreement, particularly as other subcategories of medievalism are added into the mix (such as, according to the *Medieval Electronic Multimedia Organization*, modernist medievalism, postmodern medievalism, creative medievalism, and neo-medievalism). Some of the top scholars in the field have contributed to the discussion of definition. For example, Tom Shippey writes that

> Medievalism is the study of responses to the Middle Ages at all periods since a sense of the mediaeval began to develop. Such responses include, but are not restricted to, the activities of scholars, historians and philologists in rediscovering medieval materials; the ways in which such materials were and are used by political groups intent on self-definition or self-legitimation; and artistic creations, whether literary, visual or musical, based on whatever has been or is thought to have been recovered from the medieval centuries.[3]

Shippey's definition raises a provocative question: when did "a sense of the medieval" begin? As Louise D'Arcens notes (and as I shall subsequently illustrate), Sir Thomas Malory's *Le Morte Darthur* as well as some other medieval romances might arguably demonstrate medievalism because they look backwards with nostalgia to a golden age of chivalry. Though written in the Middle Ages, these works show a "sense of the medieval" by creating a fictional and glorified medieval past. Further, Edmund Spenser in the sixteenth century, Sir Walter Scott in the eighteenth century, and Alfred Tennyson in the nineteenth century are among other well-known writers who made conscious efforts to recreate medieval pasts. Thus, medievalism actually began in the Middle Ages and has a far-reaching historical background.

Answering this question about when a "sense of the medieval" began becomes further problematized by the fact that the dates scholars use to define the medieval period are themselves rather arbitrary. D'Arcens describes "the scale and the classificatory slipperiness of the period from which it takes its inspiration."[4] As a result of this slipperiness, D'Arcens observes, "several types of medievalism can be distinguished" and "a single text representing the Middle Ages will include people and features which would not have co-existed historically, but which together create an aggregate of 'the medieval.'"[5] Likewise, Pam Clements writes that "There are certain tropes … in works of contemporary medievalism. These are not exactly symbols, but signposts or signifiers of 'the medieval,' sufficient to create enough of a sense of verisimilitude for audiences to accept a work as 'medieval.'"[6] Certainly, this is the case with Martin's medievalism which cannot be pinned down to a specific medieval culture or time, but is rather loosely "medieval." D'Arcens lists some categories of "the medieval" as it is portrayed in works of medievalism including, but not limited to, the two forms which are the focus of my study, "Arthurianism" (more broadly as relating to chivalric romance, for purposes of my discussion) and "Anglo-Saxonism" (more specifically relating to heroic literature).

Martin's medievalism is particularly provocative because it is not limited to his novels but includes the popular HBO series based upon them as well as the industry that has risen around them. Elizabeth Emery's use of the term "creative medievalism" might well apply to the plethora of products inspired by Martin's Westeros: "The term 'creative medievalism' might allow one to encompass a variety of cultural productions (in poetry, painting, literature, music, film, comic books) that may or may not engage directly with historical reality, but have been inspired by it to create new aesthetic products."[7] Further, the HBO series, and the ever-growing industry of *Game of Thrones*–related merchandise, because they are based on Martin's medievalism, might well be classified as neo-medievalism, an even more evasive concept. Carol L. Robinson and Pamela Clements write that neomedievalism is "further independent, further detached, and thus consciously, purposefully, and perhaps even laughingly reshaping itself into an alternate universe of medievalism, a fantasy of medievalisms, a meta-medievalism."[8] The HBO series, games, and products inspired by *A Song of Ice and Fire* qualify as neo-medievalism, according to this definition. Because they are based upon Martin's novels, they may be considered meta-medievalism, or medievalism twice removed. The HBO series, however, is especially problematic in this regard. Initially based on the novels, but now ahead of them, is the HBO series perhaps no longer "meta-medievalism"? This is the kind of provocative question raised by the creation and reception of Martin's Westeros and a primary reason why it inspires scholars in the field of medievalism. The answer depends upon how one draws the parameters of the terminology.

Categorizing Martin's brand of medievalism is a difficult task because his works and the empire around them are complex and multi-faceted. Through his creation of Westeros, Martin layers medievalism upon medievalism, creating the richest of medievalist texts. His contribution to the ongoing traditions of medieval literature makes newly relevant the themes and tropes from a variety of genres in the Middle Ages. Martin creates multilayered medievalisms that engage with the historical Middle Ages and that also reflect various forms of medieval literature. The purpose of this study is an exploration of Martin's medieval literary influences; specifically, how Martin's work provides rich commentary on the themes and motifs common to medieval chivalric literature. Martin recalls a number of sources to create a chivalric code for the fighters in his fictional world, including the heroic code of Anglo-Saxon literature.[9] Thus, an understanding of Martin's chivalric code as a reflection of English and French literature best begins with a consideration of *Beowulf.* This epic poem pre-dates chivalry, but emphasizes heroic attributes such as loyalty, honor, and prowess, attributes that are equally apparent in later chivalric literature.[10]

In *Beowulf,* the hero travels to King Hrothgar's court to uphold familial honor and to gain glory. King Hrothgar took in Beowulf's father, Ecgtheow, after he was exiled for committing a crime. Years later, when Beowulf learns that King Hrothgar's kingdom is plagued by attacks from the monster Grendel, he travels across the sea to repay his father's debt. Beowulf displays his martial abilities in single-handed combat first against Grendel, and then Grendel's mother. In later years when he himself becomes king, the loyalty of his men is tested when Beowulf battles against the savagery of a menacing dragon. Much like Martin's Dothraki leader Khal Drogo and the Unsullied champion Grey Worm, Beowulf is a virtuous leader and a fierce warrior, but not a knight. Martin draws comparisons to other warrior codes, particularly the heroic code, that intersect with the code for knights and serve to both highlight and complicate his portrayal of chivalry. The remainder of this chapter, however, will focus primarily on Martin's adaptation of chivalry, most notably his use of chivalric language and his portrayal of complexities and contradictions that are inherent in the chivalric code.

Chivalric Terminology

The etymology of the term *chivalry* develops from the Old French word for horse, *cheval.* The term originally denoted a fighter on horseback. Westerosi chivalry similarly stems from the martial methodology of men fighting on horseback. Martin traces its inception to the Andals: "The military success of the Andals' mounted knights and their steel armament proved vital to the Andals' conquest of Westeros."[11] For both Martin and medieval writers of romance, chivalry evolves into much more than merely fighting on horseback. Likely an import from Muslim Spain, medieval chivalry developed in the twelfth century from the influence of Troubadours into an ethical and moral code of behavior for knights. Nigel Saul writes about chivalry in medieval England: "chivalry, tempered and refined by the new mood of the twelfth century, transformed the knight from a mere warrior into an idealized figure."[12] Martin's faux history of Westeros implies a similar kind of evolution from warrior to knight. *The World of Ice and Fire*, a compendium of background stories akin to Tolkien's *Silmarillion*, credits John the Oak with bringing chivalry to Westeros, calling him "the First Knight."[13] This compendium contains numerous accounts of knights from the distant past of Westeros, many idealized and praised for possessing the attributes associated with chivalry.

As defined by historian Maurice Keen, chivalry entails *"prouesse, loyauté, largesse, courtoisie,* and *franchise."*[14] Knights should possess superior martial abilities, or *prouesse* (prowess). They should maintain *loyauté* (loyalty) to God, king, country, and lady. They should possess *largesse* (generosity of spirit) by a willingness to serve those in need. *Courtoisie* (or language and behavior, primarily at court) should be impeccable, and knights should possess *franchise* (good breeding and the looks and demeanor that are illustrative of birthright). The chivalric code, though enacted by actual historical knights of the Middle Ages, was largely portrayed through literature. It is prefigured in heroic literature, illustrated in romance, spelled out in handbooks such as those by Ramon Lull and Christine de Pizan, and parodied in other medieval genres such as the fabliau. In a description of the evolution of chivalry, Nigel Saul explains that "the chivalric lifestyle of the aristocracy found its mirror in literature, just as literature found much of its inspiration in chivalry."[15] Westeros is populated with knights and warriors whose motives and ideals can be better understood when placed in the context of the corpus of secular medieval literature, particularly as depicted in medieval romance, a genre that flourished in Europe from the twelfth to the fifteenth centuries.

The term *romance,* descending from *roman,* a reference to the Vulgar Latin in which certain works were written, came to designate a body of literature which served to illustrate ideal behavior for knights, the code of behavior we know as chivalry. Paul Rovang explains the didactic function of Caxton's edition of Malory's *Le Morte Darthur* as *"exempla,* … not only as a code for insiders, but as a how-to book for outsiders who want to enter the game."[16] The chivalric code offered ideals of behavior, and it was thus impossible to attain. One could aspire to perfection, but attainment of perfection is ever elusive. Further, from its inception, the chivalric code was fraught with complications and ambiguities that test the knight who strives to abide by the rules.

For example, a primary feature of earlier heroic literature, prowess remains a critical part of knighthood in romance as it was for the warriors of heroic literature. However, the motives for demonstrating prowess are often more complicated in romance and frequently involve the knight fighting to rescue a lady from harm or to prove his worth to her. In Chrétien de Troyes' "The Knight of the Cart," Lancelot is engaged in combat with Meleagant when, in the midst of the fight, Guinevere gives him orders to "do his worst." His reputation on the jousting field is at stake if he follows this order, yet he is also bound to obey Guinevere. His devotion to his lady proves the higher priority, and Lancelot is shamed in battle until Guinevere releases him to resume his fighting. In order to be chivalric, feats of arms must be paired with other chivalric attributes, a pairing that, as Lancelot's dilemma illustrates, might lead to conflicts of interest.

Other conflicts of interest challenge the chivalric code. For instance, *franchise*, or good birth and noble bearing, is a mandatory attribute of the chivalric code, though one that becomes complicated in the later Middle Ages as bourgeoisie gained the means to buy titles and land. Likewise, generosity, often manifested in the reciprocal relationship between lord and thane, was a necessary component of feudalism but could descend into bribery for unwarranted support. For the knight errant, generosity is also an assurance of shelter while on the road to adventure, yet it might pose challenges to chivalric virtue. Chrétien's Lancelot feels the constraints of this attribute as he is repeatedly offered lodging, but with a challenge attached. One damsel, for instance, offers Lancelot lodging, but only if he will sleep with her. (He escapes with honor, lying beside her but refusing to touch her.)

Courtesy, behavior at court, can entail challenges of honor and integrity, especially when ladies are involved in the narrative. Gawain in *Sir Gawain and the Green Knight* feels the constraints of both generosity and courtesy upon accepting lodging at the castle of Lord Bertilak. He vows to Bertilak that he will obey his rules while in his home, and he makes an agreement that the two will exchange winnings each day. While the lord goes out hunting each morning, Gawain lies in bed and is surprised when the lady of the castle sneaks into his bedroom offering herself to him. Gawain must courteously refuse the advances of the lady while maintaining loyalty to her husband. As a representative of Arthur's court, Gawain is further obligated to behave with courtesy in this difficult situation lest he bring shame on the entire court. Additionally, as a Christian knight, he cannot commit a breach in conduct that might threaten his loyalty to God. As Gawain's dilemma illustrates, loyalty to king, kingdom, God, and lady can be complicated, even impossible, to attain.

Malory's Lancelot, however, epitomizes this conflict in balancing chivalric duties through his love affair with Guinevere. Unlike Chrétien's portrayal of this affair, Malory emphasizes the strain placed upon Lancelot as he attempts to juggle his relationship with his king, his devotion to God, and his adulterous affair with the queen.[17] Kenneth Hodges describes the chivalric conflicts that populate Malory's work as a flaw in the chivalric code itself: "Read dialogically, *Le Morte Darthur* is not simply a tragedy of characters; it is a tragedy of ideas. Chivalry is not intrinsically evil, nor do the best characters fundamentally fail to live up to some true code; rather, chivalry is noble but fatally flawed, fatally unstable, and so too must be its practitioners."[18] Thus, the impetus of the romance is to follow romance heroes through these chivalric difficulties as they aspire to live up to an impossible code.

Chivalry and Knighthood in Westeros

Chivalry in *A Song of Ice and Fire* mirrors medieval works in that maintaining chivalric virtues is similarly complicated for Martin's characters. Martin highlights these complexities and nuances by showing tensions between the various aspects of chivalry. His view of the chivalric ethos is sometimes nostalgic, sometimes sarcastic, and sometimes serious. He does not merely overturn various aspects of chivalry, but in doing so, he provides new insight into medieval literary portrayals.

Martin explores contradictions inherent in medieval chivalric ideals while simultaneously making the chivalric code relevant for his general readers. He problematizes knighthood by the cynical comments and cruel actions of some of his characters. Charles Hackney explains that, in Martin's Westeros, "one must search high and low … to find knights who genuinely embody [chivalric] ideals."[19] In Westeros, there are no perfect knights. However, the same could be said of Malory, if one agrees that Galahad, who abjures worldly love to attain spiritual perfection, and Lancelot, who abjures the spiritual in favor of earthly love, are not perfect. Martin's criticism of knighthood is more obvious and perhaps more biting than Malory's; his characters more noticeably flawed and his villains less easily identified.

Sansa Stark, whose image of knights is drawn from the romance-like works she has read and the songs she has heard, cannot reconcile the harsh reality in which she finds herself with her own idealized view of the world. Sansa's negative encounters with knights serve to illustrate the impossibility of living up to the ideals set forth in the chivalric code. Upon learning from Sandor Clegane (The Hound) that his brother, Ser Gregor, burned him when he was a child, she condemns the cruel act: "he was no true knight" (*G of T* 303).[20] She later repeats these words to Ser Meryn, who has hit her on behalf of Joffrey and tries to justify his actions as obedience to his king (*G of T* 745). When King Joffrey has had his knights disrobe and beat Sansa, she contemplates the chivalric code and determines that, after all, there are no true knights. None of those she has encountered can meet her idealistic expectations. She ponders the role of knights and begins questioning her expectations about them. She has been led to believe that knights protect the weak and defenseless and fight for just causes. She is dismayed that the only knight who seems willing to help her is the drunk and disenfranchised Ser Dontos (*C of K* 490).

Other characters show disdain for the institution of knighthood. The Hound, who detests knights because his cruel brother is among their ranks, questions the status of the rogue knight Beric Dondarrion and his companions, concluding that, since they are liars, they may, in fact, be knights (*S of S* 465). The Hound then gives them his jaded view of knighthood: "A knight's a sword with a horse. The rest, the vows and the sacred oils and the lady's favors, they're silk ribbons tied round the sword. Maybe the sword's prettier with ribbons hanging off it, but it will kill you just as dead" (*S of S* 466). Similarly, Jaime Lannister, member of the Kingsguard, shows cynicism about chivalry when he rescues Brienne of Tarth. When Jaime offers her a position with the City Watch, she declines, claiming that she will not serve a kingdom notorious for bloodshed and failure to keep vows. Jaime, filled with cynicism, thinks to himself, "*Then why did you ever bother putting on a sword?*" (*S of S* 845).

Even with the cynicism of these characters, Martin does depict good characters and at least one "true" knight, Ser Barristan Selmy, whose only apparent flaw seems to be his advanced age. Additionally, the Westerosi know legends of other knights who are, at least in their (doubly) fictionalized depictions, ideal. In the present of his novels, Martin includes characters who are not ideal, but nonetheless admirable in their well-intentioned attempts to adhere to chivalric virtues. The challenges and struggles of these characters give Martin ample opportunity to explore the constraints of the chivalric code.

Medieval chivalry depicted in romance applies solely to knights. Non-nobles may appear along the periphery of the romance but serve simply to move the narrative. Occasionally, the birthright of a chivalric hero may be questioned or not immediately revealed, but by the end of the narrative, his status is established. Martin's chivalric characters, on the other hand, span a broad swath of Westerosi society. The theme of chivalry pervades the novels, not merely providing a code of ideal behavior for knights, but also serving as a moral and ethical code for the inhabitants in Westeros, whether or not they are technically knights. The chivalric ethos encompasses most of Westerosi society, governing not only the ways nobility treat one another, but also the ways lower class characters speak to those ranked above them. Both at court and on the battlefield, chivalry provides a code of ethical behavior for the Westerosi. Thus, any discussion of chivalry in Martin's novels must extend the application of chivalry beyond those who are technically designated knights.

The actual institution of knighthood in Westeros is narrowly defined: "A knight is a member of a warrior tradition that is heavily interwoven in the feudal culture of the Seven Kingdoms and the Faith of the Seven. Knights occupy a social standing between that of lords and smallfolk."[21] Although Martin associates true knighthood with a pseudo-religion, this description of the social function of the knight seems otherwise drawn from the chivalric romance.[22] The worthiest of his characters, like those of medieval romance, aspire to chivalric ideals. They value loyalty, familial and personal honor, birthright, and duty. They strive to achieve heroic acts such as avenging the deaths of loved ones, protecting the realm, showing fealty to one's king, demonstrating prowess and courtly love, and, perhaps most importantly, honoring oaths and vows.

However, the chivalric heroes in Westeros are not necessarily knights. For example, the North, ruled by the Starks of Winterfell, worship the old gods and cannot be granted knighthood, as it is reserved for those who are sworn to the Seven. Nevertheless, they train in chivalry, fight alongside knights, and value such virtues as honor, prowess, courtesy, and loyalty. Eddard Stark (Ned) is clearly a hero, having fought alongside Robert Baratheon at Storm's End and later serving as King's Hand. His sons Jon and Robb have spent their childhoods learning chivalric virtues from their father and training at arms. Although neither becomes a knight, this training prepares Jon to be an excellent leader when he assumes the position of Lord Commander of the Night's Watch and also prepares Robb to lead a series of successful battles when he becomes King of the North. In *A Game of Thrones*, Ser Rodrick, who has been training Rob and Jon at jousting, tells the Lannisters, "I am training knights" (74), confusing the distinction between those who are technically knights and those, like the Starks, who excel at the chivalric code without knighthood. In Ser Rodrick's mind, Robb and Jon are, for all intents and purposes, "knights."

Other warriors of Westeros embody codes of behavior that invite comparison to the chivalric code. The Ironborn, who follow the drowned God rather than the Seven, are also not technically knights. They are known for sea roving and raiding. They wear armor, yet their fighting is done primarily via naval fleet. The Ironborn seem modeled on Vikings more so than knights, yet Martin's portrayal of them alongside knights invites comparison. The Dornish, who dwell in the southernmost region of Westeros, are heavily influenced by Rhoynish customs as opposed to the Andal customs from which Westerosi chivalry originates. The Dornish are set apart from the rest of Westeros not only by their belief that either gender can inherit and by their libertine views, but also by their method of combat. They are known for trickery and subterfuge rather than chivalry, yet again, they are portrayed alongside Westerosi knights and depicted in battle with them.

The other kingdoms of Westeros, all which worship the Seven, would seem to offer a more conventional view of knighthood. Repeatedly, however, Martin portrays scenarios in which non-knights are truer to the chivalric code than actual knights, providing a nuanced and complex view of chivalry. Even beyond the borders of Westeros, across the Narrow Sea, warriors have their own codes of behavior that sometimes overlap with Westerosi chivalry.[23] Occasionally, these warriors, including the Unsullied warrior Greyworm and the Dothraki leader Khal Drogo, seem more ethical than the actual knights of Westeros.

By blurring the distinction between knights and other warriors, Martin exposes the chivalric code to scrutiny. The values of the Starks, for example, are nearly identical to those of the true knights of Westeros. In fact, the Starks, with their emphasis on honor, maintain the chivalric code more consistently than many of the actual Westerosi knights. Their virtuous behavior highlights the frequent bad behavior of actual knights. It is conceivable that Eddard Stark's children might be able to become knights as their mother worships the Seven, the religion of Westerosi knighthood. However, if Robb Stark is ever dubbed knight before becoming King of the North, Martin neglects to tell his readers. Before his injury, Bran Stark's greatest desire is to become a knight, and afterwards, his greatest regret is that he cannot fulfill this dream. At no point is he contradicted that, as a Stark, knighthood might not have been possible. Such portrayals leave Martin's readers to ponder exactly what constitutes knighthood.

Unlike the conventional chivalric heroes that populate medieval romance, Martin's heroes are multi-faceted. Martin often chooses unconventional characters as models of chivalric behavior, such as Brienne of Tarth (a homely woman), Sandor Clegane (who detests the institution of knighthood, but holds true to many aspects of chivalry), and Ser Davos (a lowly smuggler who rises to knighthood). About his controversial portrayal of Jaime Lannister, who models franchise and prowess but commits vile acts at the beginning of the series, Martin writes that "Men are still capable of great heroism. But I don't necessarily think there are heroes." Using Woodrow Wilson as an example, he explains that "You can't make him a hero or a villain. He was both. We're all both."[24] Characters like Jaime may commit heinous, unchivalrous acts, but may also be offered opportunities for redemption, and characters who aren't knights at all may demonstrate chivalric virtue. Thus, Martin's readers learn not to judge characters by their initial appearances; good and evil characters are not always as they initially may appear.

Carol L. Robinson and Pamela Clements note that many works of medievalism subscribe to one of two views of the Middle Ages: either the Merrye Olde England version, or the "life is filthy, brutal and short' version, neither of which provides anything like a realistic picture of the era ... most choose to depict the medievalist Middle Ages either *in bonum* or *in malum*."[25] But Martin breaks many of these rules by refusing to present Westeros as either extreme. Martin's faux medieval world is neither good nor bad but ambiguous, and his inclusion of "medieval values" such as chivalry shows that these values are complex, even impossible, and that these values need not be limited to knights.

The warriors and pseudo-knights that populate the pages of Martin's novels bring into question the institution of knighthood itself. In addition to being of high birth and possessing prowess, true knights have undergone dubbing rituals that sanctify their status and affirm their loyalties. Keen describes the medieval knight as "a man of aristocratic standing and probably of noble ancestry, who is capable, if called upon, of equipping himself with a war horse and the arms of a heavy cavalryman, and who has been through certain rituals that make him what he is—who has been 'dubbed' to knighthood."[26] He then describes some of the rituals associated with becoming a knight, including the presence of an "examiner" who deems the candidate worthy: "Of the examination of the squire who will enter the order of chivalry or knighthood: the examiner should be of high repute and should seek to raise to knighthood only those who are worthy."[27] The twelfth-century chivalric handbook *Ordene de Chevalrie* describes the ceremony conferring knighthood on Saladin, which includes the gift of a sword, "whose two sharp edges are to remind the new knight that justice and loyalty go together."[28] The edges of the sword are to become, for Saladin, reminders of his vows. Other works reference that the candidate to knighthood spends an evening in prayer and fasting, and is struck lightly upon the shoulders with a sword in a ceremony that includes the swearing of oaths. Together, these rituals comprise the dubbing ceremony associated with knighthood.

Dubbing is requisite to becoming a knight, yet Martin almost entirely omits references to this important rite of passage in his series. One of the few references to dubbing is made by the sellsword Bronn (newly titled Ser Bronn of the Blackwater) who tells Tyrion Lannister that Tyrion's father, Lord Tywin, has granted him knighthood. He describes the dubbing process for those non-knights who were rewarded after the Battle of Blackwater Bay: "Them of us survived ... got ourselves dabbed by the High Septon and dubbed by the Kingsguard" (*S of S* 54). Similarly, one of the other references to dubbing is briefly mentioned when Ser Davos, formerly a smuggler, recalls that he loses his fingertips (penance for his crimes against Stannis) on the very day he is dubbed knight (*S of S* 72). By referencing the dubbing ceremonies of a sellsword and a former smuggler, Martin complicates, and even occasionally makes parodic, his portrayal of the chivalric code. His depiction of chivalry opens up the concept of chivalry as applicable to a broader array of society which might include such characters as Bronn and Davos rising up the social ladder and attaining titles traditionally reserved for the nobility.

Martin does not dwell on dubbing ceremonies. He does, however, emphasize the significance of vows, knightly and otherwise, and he does so in ways that align with medieval romance. The whole of Malory's concept of chivalry is revealed through the struggles and triumphs of Arthur's knights. The Round Table, or Pentecostal, Oath articulates some of the most important vows:

> never to do outerage nothir mourthir and allwayes to fle treson, and to gyff mercy unto hym that askith mercy, uppon payne of forfiture of their worship and lordship of Kyng Arthure for everimore, and allwayes do ladyes, damesels, and jantilwomen and wydowes [sucour].[29]

Martin has not fully articulated the oaths of Westerosi knights, but he includes some parts of them in his graphic novel *The Hedge Knight*. These vows are similar to the Pentecostal Oath in content: "In the name of the Warrior I charge you to be brave.... In the name of the Father I charge you to be just.... In the name of the Mother I charge you to defend the young and innocent.... In the name of the Maid I charge you to protect all women...."[30] They mirror some of the same priorities as the Pentecostal Oath: mercy, justice, defense of women.

Martin also articulates the oath of the men of the Night's Watch. Although the Night's Watch originally consisted of knights, this is no longer a requisite in the present tense of Martin's novels (many, in fact, are former criminals), yet they also take oaths that mirror many of the requisites of chivalry. The men of the Night's Watch vow to forgo family, land, and love in order to fulfill their primary duty: defense of the kingdom. Even with their disparate backgrounds, most of them take their vows seriously. In addition to these formalized vows, Martin's knights and pseudo-knights repeatedly make lesser vows of intent, as well. Typically, these are vows of loyalty or vows of vengeance that may sometimes conflict, creating interesting narrative tension and illustrating the complexities of Westerosi chivalry.

Martin's Terminology and Spelling

In creating a re-interpretation of medieval chivalry that resonates with both specialists and non-specialists, Martin is challenged by the fact that knighthood has ceased to be a relevant social institution and that most of his readers are unfamiliar with the works of Chrétien de Troyes and other medieval authors. Through creative linguistic choices and carefully drawn models of chivalry, he carefully navigates receptive general readers into a fully visualized, alternate medieval world that also satisfies scholars and students of medieval literature. Writers of medievalism, some with no knowledge of medieval language, frequently use archaic-sounding language to convey a sense of the medieval. Edmund Spenser did exactly this when he wrote *The Shepheardes Calender* in the sixteenth-century. Although scholars today mostly admire his efforts, he received mixed reviews from his contemporaries for his creative and experimental use of language. More recent writers of medievalism sometimes make this attempt, as well, and their efforts are often more annoying than effective. Thankfully, Martin limits such language, which scholars of medieval literature might easily find irritating and fake. He does, however, seem to make subtle and thoughtful linguistic choices that guide his readers through his medieval re-creation.

Since the term "chivalry" itself no longer denotes a code of ideal behavior for medieval knights, Martin largely avoids it. General readers are likely to perceive the term as a reference to polite, but outdated and often unwanted, gestures of men towards women. Thus, although the medieval concept of chivalry is a pervasive theme in Martin's novels, when the term "chivalry" does appear, its meaning is most often used to evoke a sense of nostalgia or to convey sarcasm. Even in medieval literature, "chivalry" is a nebulous term. In the twelfth century, Chrétien de Troyes composed what is considered by many to be the first romance, "Erec and Enide." He was aware that he was creating a new kind of literature, a *bele conjointure*, or "beautiful conjoining," by combining the older themes of heroic literature with the emerging theme of chivalry, but he does not specifically use the term "chivalry."

In the first novel of Martin's series, the term "chivalry" makes no appearance, and the term "chivalrous" appears only once, as a reference to hospitality. However, in *A Clash of Kings*, "chivalry" appears seven times, three in reference to songs and stories, another three times as subtle criticism of the showy personage and followers of Renly Baratheon, and finally as a sarcastic description of decidedly unchivalrous behavior. Catelyn Stark uses the term to mock the extravagance and frivolity she finds at Renly's encampment, noting that "Near all the chivalry of the south" (*C of K* 339) has travelled with Renly's army. She is taken aback by the frivolous display of banners, pavilions, jousting, and festivities in the camp considering the imminence of war. Renly, however, prides himself on the "showiness" and lack of substance that Martin seems to equate with the term "chivalry." In battle with his own brother for the Iron Throne, Renly flaunts the extravagance of his troops, boasting that they "carry chivalry" with them (*C of K* 479). Renly's untimely demise, through the subterfuge of his brother, confirms that his brand of "chivalry," showiness without substance, does not lead to success. In its seventh appearance, the term is used sarcastically as Tyrion addresses Ser Boros, who has followed Joffrey's orders in abusing Sansa. He asks Ser Boros whether battering a woman is truly his notion of chivalry (*C of K* 366). Tyrion uses the term to shame Ser Boros, whose boorish acts are obviously antithetical to the notion of chivalry,

In *A Storm of Swords*, the word "chivalry" appears six times and "chivalrous" once. In this novel, the term is often used sarcastically. Lady Olenna questions Sansa about Joffrey, asking her if he is chivalrous; Sansa can only respond "He is comely" (85). She dares not tell Lady Olenna the truth about Joffrey's cruelty, yet she cannot bring herself to use the term "chivalrous" falsely. For Sansa, the term "chivalrous" evokes her idealistic, and naive, fantasies about knights. Readers are told that Sansa and her friends would entertain themselves by "sing[ing] songs of chivalry" (*S of S* 222); the starry-eyed Sansa "loved silk, songs, and chivalry" (*S of S* 269). The knights of Westeros do not live up to her ideals. For example, Osmund Kettleblack, selected to serve the

King's Guard, is described as "a vision of chivalry" in his armor (*S of S* 912), yet he is of questionable virtue. Similarly, Ser Loras Tyrell has a chivalric appearance, but his inner virtues are also questionable (though not by Sansa, who is struck with his beauty). When Jaime assesses Ser Loras, he is reminded of himself as a youth: "all cocksure arrogance and empty chivalry" (*S of S* 923). Martin shows that an impressive appearance cannot guarantee virtue. Even in the songs of Westeros, "chivalry" might convey more of a sense of sarcasm than nostalgia. Consider, for example, the legend of "The Smiling Knight [who] was a madman, cruelty and chivalry all jumbled up together" (*S of S* 916).

The term "chivalry" appears four times in *A Feast for Crows*, as a reference to old songs; as a criticism of Ser Loras Tyrell, who is described as having "simpering chivalry" (394); as a sarcastic reference to sellswords; and, perhaps in a genuine sense, as a reference to Jaime Lannister when Jaime comments that he will keep his word to Edmure Tully. His aunt responds that this act is chivalrous (*F for C* 756). At this point, Jaime is attempting to redeem his reputation and has set out to perform deeds for the good of the kingdom; worthy, selfless deeds that might truly be deemed "chivalrous."

Finally, in *A Dance with Dragons*, the term "chivalry" appears three times and "chivalrous" twice. Its main use in this novel is as a descriptive of Daenerys's attempts to colonize across the Narrow Sea with little success, imposing Westerosi values on other cultures. Daenerys uses the term to tell the Green Grace that her wards are being trained "in the ways of western chivalry" (321). It is used again to denounce the warrior code in Essos, contrasting knights with pit fighters: knights are distinguished by chivalry, which is described as "the code that made a knight more than any pit fighter" (806). Ser Barristan uses the term as he trains the Unsullied. He explains to them, "It is chivalry that makes a true knight, not a sword.… Without honor, a knight is no more than a common killer" (961). Additionally, the widow of the waterfront uses the term mockingly to disparage Ser Jorah's attempts to regain Daenerys's good graces (404). In a rare positive occurrence, the term appears again as a reference to Jaime Lannister, this time for allowing Ser Tytos to yield privately rather than in front of his men (699). This act is, in fact, genuinely chivalrous and provides further evidence for the continued evolution of Jaime Lannister as he tries to overcome his reputation as kingslayer and (attempted) child slayer. If his evolution continues along these lines, Jaime will not only *look* chivalrous, but perhaps, even with the loss of his sword hand, *become* chivalrous. In all, scholars easily recognize that Martin is challenging the notion of chivalry as an ideal through his use of the term. Through his relatively infrequent but meaningful references to the terms "chivalry" and "chivalrous," general readers are guided away from their modern connotations and perhaps better understand the complexities of the rules that govern knightly behavior.

Martin challenges the traditional language of the chivalric code in a number of other ways. For instance, Martin's use of the term "courtesy" does not denote medieval *courtoisie*, the strictly coded behavior at court expected of knights of romance. Medievalists will recognize that Martin's novels do include the same kinds of courtly behavior as in romance through such gestures as homage to the king and through the expectation of respectful and deferential speech to those of high rank. But Martin, like Malory before him, tests the limits of such "courteous" gestures. He largely avoids the term "courtesy" to describe these gestures. Perhaps he does so because of modern perceptions of courtesy as simply "good manners." When he does mention courtesy, it is either in this modern sense of good manners, or it is used pejoratively.

Thus, courtesy in Westeros sometimes refers to particularly flowery or veiled language used to conceal negative news or real emotion. Daenerys is turned down by the Puremen whose support she sought, and she explains to Xaro Xhoan Daxos that they responded to her request with much courtesy. However, their answer was, despite flowery speech, "still no" (*C of K* 576). When Sansa Stark first meets Joffrey Baratheon, she is taken in by his polished manners, which are equated with courtesy. She describes him as "the soul of courtesy" for his rapt attention to her, his apparent wit, and his many compliments about her beauty (*G of T* 299). She soon learns that this smooth veneer of polite behavior thinly conceals Joffrey's cruel and sadistic nature. On her wedding night, Sansa herself is accused of using courtesy to disguise her disgust at her groom, the dwarf Tyrion Lannister. Horrified at the idea of having to consummate her marriage, she does not refuse his advances, but makes clear that she does not desire them, either. Tyrion is infuriated by her polite demeanor, which cannot hide her revulsion for him. He accuses her of hiding behind a veil of courtesy, to which she responds with a saying taught to her by her septa: "Courtesy is a lady's armor" (*S of S* 392). Tyrion himself possesses some degree of genuine courtesy in his decision not to force himself upon his unwilling new bride. Equating courtesy with metaphorical armor becomes, for Sansa, a means to negotiate the prickly and dangerous situation in which she finds herself, at the hands of the Lannisters. Thus, rather than serving as a sign of chivalric worth, the word "courtesy," its meanings stretched and manipulated by Martin's characters, often becomes a veil for true emotion.

Martin uses other, more subtle, linguistic changes to re-direct general readers away from modern linguistic prejudices that may lead to a misunderstanding of the medieval-based chivalric ethos of Westeros. For example, he uses spelling changes to make familiar names "sound" medieval, such as the transformation of "Edward" to "Eddard" and "southern" to "sothron." Similarly, Martin evokes the Anglo-Saxon ash (æ) in his spelling of "master" as "maester." Martin's world thus "sounds and feels 'medieval' yet stays safely sequestered from Earthly history."[31]

More significant to this discussion of chivalry is the title used for knights: "Ser" instead of "Sir." Bloggers have pondered the reasons for this change, many recognizing the discrepancy between the medieval and modern meanings of the word. In a world in which Elton John and Paul McCartney are knighted, the medieval sense of the title is almost lost entirely. Today, "sir," when not a title for British favorites, might simply be a term of respect for older men. Perhaps Martin seeks to avoid these misinterpretations of the medieval title. Another blogger insightfully comments that Martin's odd spelling helps orient readers to Martin's mythopoeic world: "Tolkien once made the point that an alternate world should still have enough elements that are familiar enough for people to be comfortable with. If the world is too strange they might pay more attention to that than the story."[32] Thus, "Ser" evokes the medieval for the general reader and disrupts modern connotations of the title "Sir." Martin uses the alternate spelling to authenticate Westeros; to enhance his readers' immersion in his (pseudo-)medieval world.

Although Martin incorporates subtle linguistic play with chivalric language, most of the inhabitants of Westeros hold as ideals the same attributes of chivalry depicted in romance. Martin does not bend the code beyond recognition, but rather stretches its limits. The most worthy Westerosi aspire to heroic acts such as avenging the deaths of loved ones, protecting the realm, showing fealty to their king, demonstrating prowess and courtly love, and honoring oaths and vows. They also look to the past as a golden age in which chivalry was a less complicated code. As is common in romance, inhabitants of Westeros hold what Charles H. Hackney calls a "possibly misplaced nostalgia" for knighthood of earlier times; the notion that "Knighthood is not what used to be."[33] Chrétien de Troyes begins "Yvain" lamenting the fact that "Now love is reduced to empty pleasantries" and expressing a desire to "look beyond those who are present among us and speak now of those who were; for to my mind, a courteous man, though dead, is more worthy than a living knave."[34] Likewise, in the opening lines of his version of "The Knight of the Cart," Malory compares the base love of his current society to the fictional past of Arthurian romance: "But the olde love was nat so."[35] The Pearl poet shows a similar nostalgia but focuses instead on the military deeds of the past: "More marvels have happened in this merry land/Than in any other I know, since that olden time,/But of those that here build, of British kings,/King Arthur was counted most courteous of all."[36]

In the present of Martin's novels, the Kingsguard is similarly past its former glory. Ned Stark explains this decline to his young son Bran, acknowledging that, although they were once "a shining lesson to the world" (C of K 332), the members of the Kingsguard no longer serve as exemplars of chivalry.

Similarly, the Night's Watch, formerly composed of knights whose duty was to guard the kingdom, consists primarily of former outlaws and misfits, and the Sworn Swords, religious knights re-armed by Cersei Lannister, are cruel and judgmental.

However, Martin's view of knighthood is not entirely bleak. Even some of his vile characters seem capable of reform, such as Jaime Lannister. In an interview with *The Rolling Stone*, Martin discusses the ambiguity of his characters and notes, in particular, the moral ambiguity of Jaime even from the beginning books when Jaime commits the vile act of throwing young Bran from a window: "Bran has *seen* something that is basically a death sentence for Jaime, for Cersei, and for their three children. So I've asked people who do have children, 'Well, what would you do in Jaime's situation?' They say, 'Well, I'm not a bad guy—I wouldn't kill.' Are you sure? Never? If Bran tells King Robert, he's going to kill you and your sister-lover, and your three children.... These are the difficult situations people make, and they're worth examining."[37]

Jaime's shocking act of violence towards Bran is one of the many unexpected turns in Martin's novels that leave readers wondering how his series might conclude. Tolkien was perhaps, as Philip Zaleski and Carol Zaleski claim, "guilty of the heresy of the Happy Ending"; Martin's readers, on the other hand, have learned to expect the unexpected.[38] Martin draws his readers into an alternate medieval world, then appeals to modern sensibilities by toying with their literary expectations. Malory carries the Arthurian cycle through to the death of Arthur and his knights, but the typical medieval romance does not kill off the chivalric hero, especially not early in the narrative.[39] Modern audiences, also, expect heroes to prevail and villains to be punished. However, Martin does not hesitate to kill off or maim beloved characters (Robb, Bran, and Eddard Stark, for instance), or to reward evil ones. Nor can readers count on dead characters staying that way (Berrick Dondarrion, Catelyn Stark, and, if the forthcoming novels parallel the HBO series, Jon Snow).

Martin has been accused of "stunning injustice" for the treatment of his characters, yet the very unpredictability of his novels is one of their greatest attractions. In a recent interview, he explains how he defies readers' expectations from the opening scenes of *A Game of Thrones*: Bran Stark, whom, Martin notes, readers see as a "young King Arthur" is thrown from a window and paralyzed.[40] Readers expect that Bran, a precocious child with dreams of knighthood who seems to hold great promise, will emerge as a hero, not a cripple. Even more controversial, Martin appears, at the end of the fifth book, to have killed off a major character, Jon Snow, who is one of Martin's most popular heroes (perhaps *the* hero of the series).[41] Martin's portrayal of him has built up readers' expectations that he might emerge as a Galahad-like figure, his royal Targaryen blood revealed and allowing him to cure the warring wasteland of Westeros.[42] Although Snow is revived in the HBO series and his Targaryen birthright confirmed, Martin may yet choose to cut him down again or forge a different path for him in the novels, dashing his readers' confidence in who (if anyone) might emerge as a hero for Westeros.

Martin's willingness to kill off favorite characters is, indeed, unusual. Readers either praise or condemn him for challenging their literary expectations in ways that are shocking and perceived as "new." They are alternately shocked, delighted, angered, and even offended, by the unexpected fates of his chivalric characters. Such unpredictability is not merely for shock value, to appease the sensibilities of today's audiences, although he does accomplish this remarkably well. Rather, Westeros is an unpredictable place because the medieval chivalric ethos that undergirds it is an ambiguous and fluid concept, an impossible ideal.

Martin creates an alternate medieval world that conflates various literary portrayals of the demands and constraints on chivalry. He gives scholars of medievalism and medievalists an interesting perspective from which they might re-consider the complexities of chivalry in works such as Malory's *Le Morte Darthur*, and he illustrates the effects of social change on the chivalric code. Through careful linguistic choices and rich character portrayals, Martin shows that the constraints of the chivalric code may make it impossible for perfect knights to exist. However, he does leave some hope that, in response to Sansa's frequent question, "Are there no true knights," there may, in fact, be some who do their best to adhere to chivalric code. In Martin's neo-medieval re-creation of the chivalric code, true knights, whether nobly born or not, are those who do their best to uphold the demands of the chivalric code regardless of its ambiguities.

Two

Chivalry in Oral Tradition

*"How the Long Night came to an end is a matter of legend,
as all such matters of the distant past have become."*
—Martin et al., *The World of Ice and Fire*, 12

The Rich Oral History of Westeros

Hailed "the American Tolkien," George R.R. Martin is frequently compared to the great writer of *The Lord of the Ring* series.[1] Both writers draw heavily from medieval lore and literature, and both have deeply influenced popular culture. In an interview with *Rolling Stone*, Martin notes a key difference between his novels and those of his famous predecessor: "Tolkien can say that Aragorn became king and reigned for a hundred years, and he was wise and good. But Tolkien doesn't ask the question: What was Aragorn's tax policy? Did he maintain a standing army? What did he do in times of flood and famine? And what about all these orcs?"[2] Martin's medieval world is vaster and more detailed than Tolkien's. Both writers, however, create pseudo-histories that serve to authenticate and lend authority to their fictional worlds. Gwendolyn Morgan explains how Tolkien created "his own *auctoritee*" through the posthumously published *The Silmarillion*, which "provides a medieval history to his medieval world." Although *The Silmarillion* is fiction, Morgan explains that this "in no way diminishes it as an *auctoritee*."[3] Martin's pseudo-history is detailed in *The World of Ice and Fire*, but more so than Tolkien, he also creates pseudo-authority within the pages of *A Song of Ice and Fire* through numerous references to the lore that undergirds Westeros.

Martin's attention to detail has been largely shaped through his knowledge of history and lore. He has commented on the ways historical events shape his novels and his liberal use of them: "I like to use history to flavor my fantasy, to add texture and verisimilitude, but simply rewriting history

25

with the names changed has no appeal for me. I prefer to re-imagine it all, and take it in new and unexpected directions."[4] Martin's interest in and incorporation of history and literature is extensive, already inspiring scholarly work, such as Caroline Larrington's book, *Winter is Coming*. One of the more notable ways that Martin authenticates Westeros is through his detailed reproduction of the dissemination of chivalric literature. The lore of Westeros is drawn from a myriad of sources, not all chivalric, though those will be the focus here.

Literature, both oral and written, functions in Westeros much as it did in medieval England prior to Caxton's introduction of the printing press. As legends gain popularity, numerous versions develop. Narratives are preserved, often by maesters, in genealogies, chronicles, chivalric handbooks, and romances, but their origins are often in songs, tall tales, and old wive's tales, such as those related to the Stark children by Old Nan. Bran Stark recalls Old Nan comparing stories to old friends and advising him "to visit them from time to time" (*S of S* 377). Throughout the pages of *A Song of Ice and Fire*, Martin's characters frequently visit and sometimes recount the oral narratives of Westeros, providing for his readers the sense of a deeply textured tradition of storytelling. This chapter explores the rich oral tradition that serves as authority to Martin's fictional world, especially as this tradition reflects the chivalric and heroic literary traditions of the Middle Ages.

The storytellers of Westeros are, like medieval storytellers, simultaneously preservers of history, purveyors of culture, and crafters of legend. Westerosi storytellers emulate the methodology of the medieval minstrel who shapes his matter creatively through song. This matter could be altered for audience and/or purpose. Minstrels are prominent in both romance and heroic literature. For example, the songs of the storytellers (*scops*) in *Beowulf* variously motivate and commemorate heroes. After Beowulf's defeat of Grendel, new songs are composed to glorify the deed: "Secg eft ongan/sið Beowulfes snyttrum styrian/ond on sped wrecan spel gerade,/wordum wrixlan" (Then began the man to sing with wisdom of Beowulf's exploit, varying his words).[5] The storytellers in *Beowulf* present as good and bad examples the actions of past rulers, queens, and warriors. Sometimes, the songs of medieval minstrels serve simply to entertain the men in the mead hall. Songs may also serve as battle incentive and to aggrandize heroes. Westerosi stories serve these same purposes.

The singers, nobility, and smallfolk of Westeros not only preserve, but also shape, legends and lore to suit their own purposes. The most popular tales are, consequently, multi-versioned. The same is true of medieval lore. Arthurian legend, for instance, is also shaped to suit the teller's purpose and is therefore also multi-versioned. Norris Lacy explains, "Arthurian legend is multifaceted, a literature in itself, built up by romancers and poets during the Middle Ages in Europe.... The legend reflects features of medieval storytelling in its more sophisticated forms. To begin with, it is collective, the work of many authors elaborating a shared body of material."[6] Malory, before offering up his own version of Arthur's mysterious death, acknowledges that a number of narratives offer speculation about whether the great king will be revived. Although he borrows from written texts for his account, he suggests that these narratives are oral in origin by repeating the verb "say": "Yet som men say in many partys of Inglonde that kynge Arthure ys nat dede, but had by the wyll of Oure Lorde Jesu into another place; and men say that he shall com agayne, and he shall wynne the Holy Crosse.... And many men say that there ys wyitten uppon the tumbe thys [vers]: Hic iacet Arthurus, Rex quondam Rexque futurus."[7] Writing in the fifteenth century, Malory had available a large body of written material about King Arthur, but legends of Arthur originated in oral lore, and Malory implies that they continue to do so.

The fictional maester who narrates *The World of Ice and Fire* explains that, like Arthurian legend, the Stark family history originated in oral lore: "their legends came before the First Men had letters." He compares the Starks to the Arryns, who "fostered learning amongst the septries and septs, and their good deeds were soon chronicled and remarked on in the devotional works of the Faith."[8] Although the Starks lack the rich written chronicles of the Arryns, their many stories have passed down through the generations, and the Starks shape those stories to instill family pride and enhance family memory. In his recollections of Old Nan's tales of the Night's King of the Night's Watch, Bran Stark notes that many versions of this tale exist. Bran points out that, although legends vary as to the Night's King's family origins, he is certain that the legendary figure was, like himself, a Stark (*S of S* 762). Bran, not unlike writers of Arthurian romance, molds a many-versioned legend to his own purpose, in this case, self-identity.

Tyrion Lannister grapples with several differing versions of the legend of the stone men and the possible existence of a Shrouded Lord. As he progresses towards the ominous Bridge of Dreams, the supposed location of the Shrouded Lord, he hears differing versions of this legend from his travelling companions. Yandry, one of Tyrion's companions, claims that the Shrouded Lord has ruled since Garin's day and is Garin, risen from the dead. Another companion, Haldon Halfmaester, argues that the Shrouded Lord is periodically replaced; one dies and another takes his place. But Duck has "another tale I like better." In this alternate, fanciful version, the Shrouded Lord was originally merely a statue until a ghost-like woman emerged from the fog and kissed him with icy lips (*D with D* 256). Both Tyrion and Martin's readers are intrigued by these multiple accounts which have been shaped by these various tellers for effect.

Songs of Courage, Songs of Sorrow

Oral narratives and songs serve as expressions of chivalric values and can provide a mirror to the medieval mindset. These songs and narratives might bolster courage on the battlefield, ensure favor in the eyes of one's lord, or function as expressions of grief. The *Beowulf* poet illustrates all of these functions of oral narrative but places emphasis on how warriors might use boasting to ensure favor. Boasting is an integral part of feudal culture, serving to ensure favor in a lord's eyes. It often takes the form of *flyting*, or exchanging taunts and insults. Beowulf comes to Hrothgar's court making strong claims about his prowess, but his reputation precedes him. Unferth has already heard aggrandized tales about Beowulf and challenges Beowulf about his exploits. After Beowulf boasts before King Hrothgar's court, Unferth accuses the hero of excessive pride in his own abilities and challenges both the tales he has heard beforehand and the boasts that Beowulf makes in person. Beowulf is not only known to have the strength of thirty men in one hand, but he is also reported to be an exceptional swimmer, and he is renowned as the most powerful of warriors. Unferth, serving an important role in Hrothgar's court, puts these boasts to the test through *flyting*, relating and then challenging the tale of Beowulf and his swimming contest against Brecca.[9] The hero, however, counters with his own version of the narrative. He is able to prove the merit of his boasts and validate the tales of his past glories once he defeats Grendel and Grendel's mother. Subsequently, *scops* take on the role of boasting about Beowulf's feat in defeating these monsters. They spread his fame through new songs.

Although they have a more peripheral role in romance than in *Beowulf*, references to court singing and battle boasting are also evident in romance. Arthur's reputation itself originates in oral narratives. His fame spreads not only because of the exploits of the Round Table knights, but also because those exploits are communicated far and wide, through song and narrative. The Pearl poet opens *Sir Gawain and the Green Knight* with a reference to a re-telling of the noble deeds of Arthur, which he "in toun herde" (heard in town).[10] Narratives of Arthur's glory bring the Green Knight to Arthur's court. He claims his purpose is to test the reputation of the Round Table knights, which has been widely circulated and, he thinks, possibly exaggerated. Whether Gawain, as representative of Arthur's court, passes this test is a matter of debate and beyond the scope of this discussion. However, the test itself is to prove or disprove the boasts of and about the knights of the Round Table that have circulated through songs and stories.

Songs may exaggerate and glorify the deeds and actions of heroes, but they may also serve as negative examples. This is the case in *Beowulf* when the *scop* tells of the uncooperative peace weaver Thryth and of the cruel king

Heremod, both serving as negative examples to contrast with the good behaviors of, respectively, Hygd and Sigemund. Similar stories, positive and negative, circulate in Westeros. The exploits of Barristan Selmy glorify his deeds, while tales about mad King Aerys and Jaime Lannister tend to emphasize (and in Jaime's case, exaggerate) their flaws. Differing versions of an individual's deeds and exploits vary according to the bias of the storyteller. Rhaegar Targaryen, for example, is glorified in the tales recounted by Ser Barristan Selmy. Daenerys Targaryen never met her brother Rhaegar, yet she frequently asks Ser Barristan to relate these tales to her. Based upon the tales that she has heard, she admires Rhaegar and sees him as a model for her own future rule. However, Rhaegar is also vilified in the stories told by Robert Baratheon and Eddard Stark because of his apparent kidnapping of Lyanna Stark. Thus, he is variously cast as hero or villain, depending upon the storyteller. Still other stories indicate that, despite his reputation for being skilled at arms, Rhaegar preferred to sing and play his harp. Perhaps he would have been better suited as a minstrel rather than becoming the subject of minstrels' songs.

Martin illustrates the important role of minstrels in glorifying the deeds of heroes. The spearwives who have accompanied Mance Rayder to Winterfell try to entice Theon Greyjoy to aid them in rescuing Ramsay Bolton's bride. They try to appeal to Theon's ego with the possibility of his heroism being preserved in song by their minstrel (even though Theon's taking of Winterfell was not particularly heroic and their so-called minstrel is actually Mance Rayder in disguise).[11] They urge him to recount his taking of Winterfell, assuring him that Abel will spin a song that casts him as hero, a song through which he will be immortalized (*D with D* 592). The notion of achieving immortal glory through song is highly appealing to heroic sensibilities, although Theon, beaten to submission by Ramsay Bolton, is skeptical. Still, the Westerosi follow the belief that one method of attaining immortality and glory, even false glory, is through song.

As with medieval chivalric narratives, the songs of Westeros might set ideals for good behavior or serve as precautions against bad behavior. Like Theon, Sansa Stark becomes increasingly skeptical about the deeds recounted in her favorite songs. Young and idealistic, she finds her harsh situation at odds with the legends and songs she has taken to heart. Still, these songs serve her well in one instance, when she is a captive in King's Landing after Joffrey's murder. In an attempt to be brave in the face of danger, she strives to emulate the brave women she has heard about in songs (*S of S* 837). Her knowledge of songs, while often leading her to unrealistic expectations, serves to strengthen her resolve and becomes a tool for survival in a dire situation.

When Arya Stark commits to joining the House of Black and White, the "kindly man" who is her mentor uses narrative as an educational tool. He tells his young pupil that she must learn about the origins of the Faceless Men in order to become one of them (*F for C* 456). He recounts, as a critical part of Arya's training, the story of the first Faceless Man who freed slaves from mining shafts. This narrative serves as an example of the selflessness expected of the Faceless assassin and is intended to provide for Arya a model for behavior.

Another example of narratives serving to instruct occurs as the Wildlings pass through the Wall. Jon Snow confronts a girl dressed as a boy who hopes to find her way into the Night's Watch rather than crossing the Wall. Jon recalls an old song about a girl in a similar situation who met a bad ending. He remembers that the lyrics and music were beautiful, yet her tale was nonetheless tragic. He also notes that legends of her ghost still circulate among the men at the Wall. Uncertain how to respond to this situation, Jon uses his memory of this song and the legends associated with it to help him in reaching the decision to reject the girl for her own safety (*D with D* 848).

On the other hand, Quentyn Martell's naive use of lore as a model for behavior leads to his demise. Quentyn considers the dangers of trying to steal one of Daenerys's dragons, but, basing his decision on stories he has heard about dragons, he downplays the risk and tells his companions it will be a "grand adventure." When Gerris tells him that grand adventures can prove fatal, Quentyn concedes that he has a point. However, he finds solace in the notion that true heroes, at least according to stories, do survive (*D with D* 974). Believing the chivalric stories about knights conquering dragons to be true and believing himself to be a hero, Quentyn proceeds foolishly and dangerously on a quest for which he is ill prepared and unqualified. Like Sansa whose head is clouded by fantasies that often leave her disillusioned, Quentyn is also led by false beliefs and assumptions. As Quentyn's narrative evidences, using songs for models of behavior does not always lead to a desirable outcome. One must possess discretion and wisdom when modeling behavior based upon the examples of oral narrative. Quentyn lacks both of these qualities. Further, he has refused to heed other songs that permeate Westerosi culture, songs of death and defeat, that might have served him well as tales of caution.

Singing and storytelling may serve as expressions of grief. In the Anglo-Saxon epic poem *Beowulf*, "mournful songs" frame the narrative. In the opening lines of the poem, after a genealogy of the Danes that highlights the death of Scyld Scefing, the audience learns of stories that have spread after Grendel's attacks on Heorot. These stories ultimately find their way to Beowulf and lead him to Hrothgar's hall. One of the final scenes of *Beowulf* depicts a Geatish woman lamenting Beowulf's death through song. These sorrowful songs are critical to the plot but also set an elegiac mood. Various kinds of sorrowful songs also have a place in Martin's novels. The songs beloved by Sansa cause her grief, not simply because they are sorrowful, but also because they leave her with unrealistic expectations about the knights she encounters.

At the Eyrie, the sorrowful songs of the singer Marillion cause Sansa a more direct form of grief. This singer is falsely accused of murder when Littlefinger (Peter Baelish) pushes Lady Lysa out of her moon door to her death, and subsequently, from his prison, he haunts the Eryie with his nighttime songs. Sansa is bothered by the singer's soulful, sweet voice, which is at odds with his sorrowful songs and also with his evil nature. She notes that his songs reverberate throughout the halls of the castle and cannot be escaped (*F for C* 207). Later, Sansa fears for the sanity of Lord Robert, Lysa's sickly son, when the young boy claims to hear Marillion's songs after the singer has reportedly died. The plaintive songs from the condemned singer (and, Robert thinks, from his ghost) heighten both Sansa's and Lord Robert's distress about Lysa Arryn's death. Both are tormented further by these meta-narratives.

Songs and Politics

Martin emphasizes that stories and songs could serve a number of political purposes. Jon Snow, as Lord Commander of the Night's Watch, sends to Westeros a storyteller, Dareon, for the political purpose of recruiting new men. Samwell Tarly, who travels with the singer, initially has great hopes for the success of this endeavor, as Dareon possesses exceptional singing skills: "His task would be to travel the Seven Kingdoms, singing of the valor of the Night's Watch, and from time to time returning to the Wall with new recruits" (*F for C* 308). However, Dareon turns out to be a disappointment. Samwell concedes that the corrupt singer nonetheless makes the long voyage by sea easier with his entertaining songs, songs that were obviously familiar and loved by the oarsmen and that indicate a rich oral tradition among the sailors. Dareon sings as the oarsmen row, relieving them of their burdensome job with a litany of well-loved, familiar songs. Martin creates a feel of authenticity by providing a list of the names of the sailors' favorites, including titles that would have obvious appeal to men at sea, such as "The Mermaid's Lament" and "The Day They Hanged Black Robin" (*F for C* 310).

This journey requires keeping the oarsmen content, but Dareon is not concerned about his duty to the Watch. The situation worsens when they land in Braavos. Instead of using his talent to recruit for the Wall by singing tales of the prowess of the men who serve, Dareon carouses with women and sings love songs to seduce them. When Samwell confronts him, he abandons the Watch. Although Dareon fails to use his gift of song as he has been commanded, to recruit for the Night's Watch, Martin nonetheless refers to the potential of the minstrel to assert political power.

In Martin's series, the power of the minstrel is sometimes feared, for storytellers can shape their narratives as they please in a fashion that can be damaging. When Theon rescues the "false Arya," the reality of his situation hits home. He is especially troubled that Abel (Mance Rayder) has imagined that an escape might be possible. Believing Mance to be a minstrel, Theon has a telling thought about the minstrel's songs. He fears that Abel will lead them to destruction, noting that singers are "half-mad" (*D with D* 474). He is aware of the contrast between songs, in which heroes prevail, and reality, in which there are no guarantees. He compares the lies of singers to the fake identity of Jeyne Poole who is posing as Arya Stark (*D with D* 747). Theon fears the ability of the minstrel to blur the lines between fiction and reality, truth and falsehood.

Tyrion Lannister resents, rather than fears, the power of minstrels to weave false tales. At Joffrey Baratheon's wedding to Margaery Tyrell, Tyrion fumes over a singer's recounting of the Battle of Blackwater Bay, which seems, for political reasons, unlikely to credit him with the victory. Tyrion realizes that, in the doubly fictionalized songs about the battle he helped to win, his own role will be erased and a new, "false," version will emerge in its place. Tyrion is at the mercy of the minstrels who will surely falsely relate his role in the battle to enhance their own reputations as singers; after all, a dwarf is no fitting hero for a song.

In another misuse of storytelling, Tom Sevenstrings makes a song about Edmure Tully's ill-fated attempt to lose his virginity. Edmure drinks too much, the story claims, and cannot perform in bed. Tom sleeps with the lady instead and then writes a song about a "floppy fish," a crude reference to the Tully motto, a fish, and Edmure's manhood (*S of S* 301). The singer thus destroys Edmure's reputation and repeatedly emasculates him through song. Consequently, Edmure is reported to loathe both music and singers.

Similarly, the Elder Brother of the Silent Isle is frustrated with singers. He explains to Brienne the true nature of the Battle of the Trident. He is particularly bothered by the fact that the songs of glory about this battle fail to tell the whole story. According to singers, he explains, the battle is depicted as a duel between Rhaegar and Robert, who battle over their love for Lyanna Stark. In fact, he points out to her, "other men were fighting too, and I was one" (*F for C* 671). While a few select heroes are the focus of songs, thousands of other fighters are ignored. The aggrandized heroes, however, are the powerful men whose stories can advance the singers; the "other men" are less powerful, less interesting, and, despite their sacrifices, unworthy of song.

On the other hand, songs and narratives can be used to make the unworthy appear as if they are heroes. When Jaime Lannister meets Martin Frey's daughter, she recounts some of her father's exaggerated boasts of prowess, which she equates with Jaime's proven feats. She is eager to tell Jaime that her father has told her stories about how he fought alongside Jaime in battle against the Kingswood Brotherhood. Jaime thinks to himself, "*Father used to boast and lie, you mean*" (*F for C* 642). Unlike Beowulf whose prowess is proven in battle, Martin Frey attempts to build a reputation through false boasts that his naive daughter believes.

The lore of Westeros includes rumors, exaggerations, and falsehoods, often the natural result of multiple oral tellings, but sometimes deliberately crafted for political reasons. Maester Qyborn tortures the singer known as the Blue Bard until he falsely admits to infidelity with Margaery Tyrell (*F for C* 825). As he is tortured, the bard's "song" changes to suit Cersei's political purposes: "I prefer this song to the other," Cersei claims about the forced changes in his narrative (*F for C* 830). However, she realizes that, because of the reputation of minstrels as liars, she will need more evidence than the Blue Bard's confession: "Singers lied for a living, after all" (*F for C* 832). Even with their apparent reputation for untruthfulness, minstrels can wield much political power through their songs.

Information frequently spreads among the various kingdoms of Westeros through rumors. The Lannister are especially puzzled about the mysterious death of Renly Baratheon. About the many rumors concerning this death, Lord Varys explains to Cersei that after the death of a king, "fancies sprout like mushrooms in the dark" (*S of S* 528). Engaged in a battle with the Baratheon brothers for the Iron Throne, the Lannisters are eager to find the true cause of Renly's death. In this case, the unusual circumstances of Renly's death inspire rumors and much speculation. In fact, he is killed by a shadow, a spirit conjured by the red priestess Melisandre.

Other times, rumors are spread deliberately. The Freys purposefully spread rumors about the Red Wedding, attributing the deaths of many of the guests to Robb Stark, who was himself the primary targeted victim. The Freys, however, who decapitate Robb and stitch his direwolf's head to his torso, recast the story, claiming that Robb had miraculously transformed into a wolf and ripped out the throat of the mentally disabled Frey son, Jinglebell (*D with D* 269). They also claim (to cover their own guilt) that Robb's men killed Wendel Manderly, lying that all of the northmen, following their leader, transformed to wolves. They rely on legends about wargs which claim that wargs can "birth other wargs with a bite," and they assert that their actions were in self defense (*D with D* 269). This rumor serves to diminish the heinous crime of the Freys, slaughtering guests in their own home. As hospitality is highly valued in chivalric cultures, this crime is especially egregious.

As another example of a deliberate political rumor, Varys convinces Jon Connington that Jon must fake his own death. He allows a rumor to spread indicating that Jon has drunk himself to death. He explains to Jon that songs about heroes are longlasting, while the deaths of cowards and drunks are "soon forgotten" (*D with D* 340). This rumor serves the purpose of keeping Connington from public attention as he assumes the role of raising, and preparing for the throne, young Aegon Targaryen (although Aegon may be an imposter). In this rumor about Connington's death, Martin also illustrates the antithesis of battle boasts: downplaying feats or using deliberate lies for self-preservation. Connington understands the political necessity of this rumor, and he goes along with it. However, he makes clear that he would have preferred the aggrandized tales of the "gallant exile" (*D with D* 340).

As rumors spread and grow, they can generate fear and panic. Narratives about wolves seem to be proliferating in Westeros. While there may be some "truth" to these stories, accounts of the numbers and nature of the wolves seem fueled by rumor. Septon Meribald recounts some of the rumors, most which include tales about a "monstrous she-wolf" who leads the pack and is fierce and powerful (*F for C* 532). Could this pack leader be Nymeria, mirroring, through her aggression, Arya's progression to assassin? Or is this an example of fear-mongering through storytelling as Westeros grows increasingly treacherous in the midst of political struggles? Because they cannot authenticate the truth about the wolves, the Westerosi easily succumb to the outlandish tales.

False stories are not always readily apparent. The citizens of Westeros are challenged in their attempts to discern which elements of their rich heritage are "real"; which elements are, like the transformation of Robb Stark into a wolf, partly true; and which elements are entirely (pseudo-)fictional. While in the precarious position of treating with Mance Rayder in the midst of a Wildling encampment, Jon Snow spies the Horn of Winter which he knows from legend. He has learned that sounding the Horn will cause the Wall to crumble. However, he wonders if the legends might hold true (*S of S* 1009). Similarly, Bran, faced with crossing the Wall, recalls Old Nan's cautionary tales and hopes that his brother Robb was right in discrediting them. According to Old Nan, the horrors beyond the Wall, which include giants, monsters, and walking dead, cannot pass as long as the Wall holds and as long as the men of the Night's Watch are true to their vows (*D with D* 70). As Martin's narrative progresses, many of the Westerosi legends are, in fact, revealed to be "true," yet his characters must continually wrestle with the often-blurred distinctions between reality and legend.

Medieval history is similarly deeply intertwined with legend. For instance, medieval scholars have long struggled with scanty evidence to authenticate the existence of an actual King Arthur. He is briefly referenced in a sixth-century Welsh text and associated with the Battle of Badon Hill by another Welshman, Nennius, in the ninth century. Already the stuff of legend, Nennius's Arthur is credited with single-handedly slaying 940 Saxons at Badon Hill. Thus, from the earliest accounts, Arthur is attributed with larger-than-life heroic qualities. The early Celtic stories about Arthur would have circulated orally. They spread quickly and acquired new meaning with new generations. Arthur's life story is not fully recorded until the twelfth-century by Geoffrey of Monmouth, who invented much of his material.[12] The actual Arthur, if he ever existed, is clouded by the tangle of narratives associated with him, which became popular about 700 years after the "real" Arthur would have lived.[13]

Martin authenticates Westeros by presenting a vast web of narratives that similarly blur "reality" and fiction. Martin, in *The World of Ice and Fire*, presents "historical" accounts that have acquired the status of legend. For example, in an account Ser Artys Arryn, the Falcon Knight, at the Battle of the Seven Stars, the fictional Maester who narrates claims that details about his victory have been "somewhat embroidered in the centuries that followed," yet he insists that King Artys must have been an actual, if unusual, man. He also notes that King Artys has been confused with a figure from legends who lived many years earlier.[14] How very like the legends of Arthur is this account of Artys, about whom "a hundred other tales are told..., most of them just as fanciful."[15]

Martin draws upon a number of other medieval legends and historical events that mirror the political motivations of his characters. In an interview with *Rolling Stone*, Martin discusses his fascination with the War of the Roses and especially the legendary accounts of the fate of the brothers in the tower. The brothers, the sons of Edward IV, were imprisoned and supposedly put to death. Depending upon the version of the legend, the murders were committed by either their uncle, Richard III, the boys' protector who wanted the throne for himself; the Duke of Buckingham, who had turned against Richard III; or Margaret Beaufort, whose son was a rival to the throne. Deeply influenced by historical accounts of this war and the legends surrounding it, Martin re-shapes the material for his own purposes. He explains, "If you know anything about the Wars of the Roses, you know that the princes in the tower aren't going to escape. I wanted to make it more unexpected, bring in some more twists and turns."[16] Martin evokes this legend indirectly, by raising similar issues of legitimacy and inheritance as various characters vie for the Iron Throne.

Martin sometimes includes direct references and allusions to medieval history that have developed the qualities of legend. For example, upon the death of Edward IV, his brother Richard III forced Edward's mistress, Jane Shore, to a public walk of shame as a sign of contrition. Although this account is believed to be true (whereas the murder of Edward's sons has not been proven), it has the ring of legend and certainly spread as such. In *A Song of Ice and Fire*, Cersei recalls a similar story about her grandfather's death and her father's treatment of his mistress. Immediately, her father banished the lowborn woman, taking from her the rich clothing and jewels that Lord Tytos had given her. Further, she is stripped naked and forced to a public walk of shame (*D with D* 934). In one of Martin's most famous passages (which became a much talked about scene in the HBO series), Cersei herself is later forced to a similar walk of shame.

Martin has another reference to historically based legend in his allusion to the offspring of King James II by his second wife. After James was deposed, legends and rumors circulated in England about this son and later his grandson returning as "pretenders." Similarly, Kevan Lannister labels Aegon Targaryen, who claims to be the rightful Targaryen heir, as a pretender to the Targaryen dynasty (*D with D* 10). Aegon's legitimacy as a Targaryen is left up to question at the end of *A Dance with Dragons*, but perhaps it will be resolved in the final novels as he has returned to Westeros to claim the throne. The legitimacy of the pretenders in England was never confirmed, but Martin draws upon such narratives to shape the political legends of Westeros.

Songs and the Inexplicable

Martin's characters often struggle to discern truth from fiction in the songs and narratives that circulate among them. They seem to wrestle most with the hazy divisions between truth and legend when they travel abroad. As Arya approaches Braavos, she sees the impressive statue of the Titan and recalls the legends surrounding it. According to Old Nan, the statue protects Braavos, and when enemies approach, it comes to life to destroy them. Further, she tells Arya, it eats "the juicy pink flesh of little highborn girls" (*F for C* 126). Whereas Sansa would squeal in fright at this story, Arya is more cynical. She notes that Maester Luwin puts no merit in Old Nan's tale of the statue, and Arya herself concludes that, after all, "Old Nan's stories were only stories" (*F for C* 126). Despite Arya's skepticism about the veracity of Old Nan's stories, she is nonetheless awed by, and a bit frightened of, the statue when she sees it. She, and many of the inhabitants of Westeros, base their opinions of the world beyond Westeros largely on these tales. In this case, Old Nan's story about the Titan has some element of truth: the statue is large and intimidating, an effort to thwart, if not smash, potential enemies.

Similarly, on his journey to Oldtown, Samwell's ship passes Skagos, and he recalls its legends, which he knows through both songs and stories. The legends are ominous, describing a barren land filled with savage people who hold strange customs, such as riding upon giant unicorns rather than horses. Further, he has heard that the people of Skagos are cannibals who kill their victims and then devour their hearts. Evidencing the popularity of these legends, Samwell notes that "Dareon knew the songs well" (*F for C* 314). Samwell, prone to cowardice, is fearful that some of these songs may be true. Even the skeptical and well-learned Tyrion Lannister struggles to discern truth from fiction when he crosses the Narrow Sea. As they pass Valyria, Moquorro describes the red sky, asking Tyrion if he knows the legends about the Valyrian past. Tyrion responds with doubt about the veracity of the sailors' tales he has heard, but he does not dispute them. He knows the legend that one can be cursed by even looking at the coast of Valyria (*D with D* 489). Though quick-witted and cynical, Tyrion cannot completely reject these stories about a land unknown to him.

In addition to the various legends that Martin's characters (and readers) must sift through, Martin's method of presenting various points of view presents the reader with an array of perspectives which must then be sorted and conflated to understand fully a single event. An example of this narrative play occurs with Martin's portrayal of the Battle of Blackwater Bay, presented through the perspectives of several characters: Tyrion Lannister as he first observes and then joins the fray; Ser Davos Seaworth as he leads Stannis's ship into Blackwater Bay only to discover that he is trapped; and Sansa Stark, praying with the women in the sept and sitting by Cersei's side as the battle rages outside. Her knowledge of the battle is confined to the noises she hears and the occasional messengers who are sent to Cersei with reports and updates. The reader must combine all of these accounts to form a full picture of the battle.

Chrétien de Troyes also adopts a method of incorporating multiple perspectives in "Yvain: The Knight with the Lion." His characters describe almost identical encounters at a magical fountain, yet their responses to the encounter vary. The romance begins with Calegronant's account of his experience at this magical fountain, an account that he presents first as it was related to him by a *vilein* (a peasant). Calegronant relates both the *vilein's* narrative about the challenger at the fountain and then his own experience. He fails in battle against the challenger he faces at the fountain, inspiring Yvain to give the adventure a try in the name of family honor. Subsequently, the reader witnesses Yvain's experience, and ultimate success, at the same fountain. The events leading to the challenge—water poured on a rock, a terrible storm ensuing, and a fierce challenger— are identical, but the reader can only fully understand their significance by reading each perspective. First presented as entertainment at Arthur's court when Calegronant decides to tell a story of defeat rather than glory, the narrative then shifts to portray Yvain's victory. Just as Martin's readers must tie together various accounts of a single event, Chrétien's readers assimilate various perspectives of the fountain narrative.

Romance writers make claims of veracity about their works even when those works contain magical elements. In her Breton lai, Marie de France often makes such claims about her tales although magic is typical in the genre. Her lais include accounts of werewolves, shapeshifters, and animals capable of speech. For the medieval writer, such claims of veracity are indicative of the writer's belief that some element of truth or wisdom might be gleaned from the narrative, even with the presence of fantastic details. In the fantasy realm of Westeros, sifting truth from oral narratives is particularly difficult, especially since magic was known to exist in the past and is rumored to exist across the Narrow Sea. Still, most of the citizens of Westeros doubt the existence of magic even though numerous stories circulate that contain accounts of fantastical events. As the ever-cynical Tyrion Lannister claims, "Sorcery is the sauce fools spoon over failure to hide the flavor of their own incompetence" (*S of S* 402). Some of these fantastical tales, however, are revealed to be true, or at least partially true, as Martin's characters find in their struggles to make sense of the largely unknown world beyond Westeros.

Those rumors that emerge as "true" are often the least believable. For instance, rumors run rife when Lady Stoneheart emerges as the new leader of Beric Dondarrion's Brotherhood Without Banners. Jaime Lannister hears frightening accounts about her physical appearance, including wild eyes and a face that is "torn and scarred" (*F for C* 644). This description of Lady Stoneheart, though outlandish, turns out to be true. She is, in fact, Catelyn Stark, whose throat has been slit at the Red Wedding. She is found and resuscitated by Thoros of Myr, the Red Priest who travels with the Brotherhood Without Banners. Lady Stoneheart replaces Beric Dondarrion, who has himself been repeatedly resuscitated by Thoros, as leader of the Brotherhood.

Tales also circulate about Dondarrion, mostly based on truth, but subject to exaggeration. With the help of Thoros, Dondarrion is repeatedly killed and then revived, leaving those whom he encounters in dismay (especially those who "kill" him) and paving the way for outlandish tales. In *A Feast for Crows*, tales begin to circulate that Dondarrion has, in fact, finally died. Jaime hears conflicting accounts about whether and how this has occurred. In once account, Gregor Clegan has stabbed Dondarion in the eye. Addam Marbrand counters this narrative with the widespread story that Dondarrion cannot be killed (*F for C* 644). Thoros of Myr himself confirms Dondarrion's death and Lady Stoneheart's revival in a conversation with Brienne of Tarth, dispelling for Brienne many of the wild tales while validating the truth of one.

One of Martin's characters appears to be on the brink of gaining true knowledge. Having crossed the Wall and being tutored by Lord Brynden, Bran Stark is in the process of learning the deepest mysteries of his world and potentially gaining the wisdom to distinguish between fact and fiction. For instance, he learns that once ravens could speak rather than having parchment attached to their legs to deliver messages. This information confirms one of the seemingly outlandish tales he remembers from his younger days at Winterfell. He recalls hearing about this tale from Old Nan and then asking his brother Robb for verification. Robb responds with laughter and asks Bran "if he believed in grumkins too" (*D with D* 494). Perhaps through Bran, readers will be better able to distinguish Westerosi lore from "fact." In the HBO series, Bran, through his visions, has already learned the truth behind one of Martin's greatest secrets: the identity of Jon Snow's mother.

Not all tales are based upon truth. Wild accounts run rampant about The Hound when the vicious criminal Biter takes The Hound's distinctive helmet and commits atrocities. After Gendry kills Biter, Lem takes the helmet, enjoying the terror that it inspires and wrongly enhancing The Hound's reputation as vicious killer. As the helmet passes hands, the stories proliferate. Prior to his encounter with Biter, Septon Meribald tries to deter Brienne of Tarth when she says she seeks The Hound. The septon gives her a run-down of the outlandish crimes The Hound is purported to have committed. He is accused of leaving in his wake "a trail of butchered babes and ravished maids" (*F for C* 528).[17] Even the cynical Jaime Lannister is taken in by some of the more outlandish tales of Westeros. When he hears of the atrocities performed at Harrenhal, he recalls tales from his childhood about an insane woman who took baths in blood and served "feasts of human flesh" (*F for C* 575). In this moment of doubt, Jaime wonders whether there might be some ring of truth to these tales.

Occasionally, readers might discern (pseudo-)fact and fiction better than the characters of Westeros, creating rich dramatic irony. For example, Septon Meribald tries to dispel misperceptions about the broken men, whom the singers portray as outlaws. Meribald explains the difference between outlaws, who are "driven by greed, soured by malice" and broken men, who are "common-born, simple folk" deserving of pity for being forced into war (*F for C* 533–534). Meribald then describes the process whereby the broken man struggles to survive from day to day and ultimately becomes "more beast than man" (*F for C* 535). As Myke Cole explains in his essay "Art Imitates War," Martin is describing Post Traumatic Stress-Disorder in some of the inhabitants of war-ravaged Westeros.[18] The Westerosi perceive the broken men as merely bandits and outlaws. For Brienne of Tarth, however, who hears and understands the implications of Meribald's narrative, the broken men become objects of pity. Although she would not know the concept of Post Traumatic Stress-Disorder, she recognizes the psychological consequences of warfare and has compassion for the men whom Meribald describes.

Some of the legends of Westeros, though outlandish even by Westerosi standards, are nonetheless taken as truth by gullible characters. Young and naive, Podrick Payne is particularly vulnerable to these more outlandish oral tales. He is an easy victim for Nimble Dick, who loves to embellish and exaggerate. On their way to The Whispers, Nimble Dick describes monsters called squishers. His account is humorous in exaggeration, as these squishers have webbed fingers, oversized heads, a fishy smell, and sharp green teeth. Further, he explains, "They come by night and steal bad children, padding along on them webbed feet with a little *squish-squish* sound" (*F for C* 405). Podrick is frightened by this story, while Brienne recognizes its implausibility, acknowledging Nimble Dick's account as simply a "lively tale" (*F for C* 405).

Nimble Dick also tells an outlandish tale of one of his own ancestors, Ser Clarence Crabb, who was married to a woods witch. According to this tale, Ser Clarence would decapitate those he killed and return home with the head, which his wife would revive with a kiss on the lips. Ser Clarence notes that the heads "gave old Crabb good counsel" (*F for C* 305). Although they could only whisper, the talking was incessant because "When you're a head, talking's all you got to pass the day" (*F for C* 305). This tale of whispering heads, Ser Clarence explains, accounts for the name of The Whispers. Podrick, again believing Nimble Dick's tall tales to be true, is thus very apprehensive at The Whispers. Later, Podrick earnestly reports to Septon Meribald that Silent Sisters have no tongues. The Septon dispels the rumor, explaining the "truth" behind the legend and telling Podrick that this is a story mothers often use to control their daughters. He denies any truthfulness to the story, explaining to Podrick that "A vow of silence is an act of contrition..." (*F for C* 657). Lacking the cynicism of most of the other characters, Podrick takes at face value all of the stories he hears. No wonder Martin portrays him as tentative and unsure.

Catastrophic events and unusual phenomenon often breed outlandish stories to explain the otherwise inexplicable. The medieval populace believed in cause and effect, and thus looked for meaning in phenomena that could not be otherwise readily explained. For instance, Martin alludes to Stonehenge which mystified people in the Middle Ages and thus inspired legends to explain it. Martin describes a similar structure, standing stones forming a circle that, according to Illyrio, was created by giants (*D with D* 89). This passage matches the explanation of Stonehenge by medieval writers such as Geoffrey of Monmouth, who claims that Stonehenge was built by giants. In his account, it was moved across the sea from Ireland to commemorate the deaths in battle of Aurelius Ambrosius' men. Ser Davos Seaworth sees an odd structure off Seal Rock, yet he assumes the structure was built by the First Men. He describes an impressively large bedrock with a top "crowned with a circle of weathered stones" (*D with D* 211). He attributes this long-abandoned circle of stones to the First Men. This structure, with its ring of weathered stones, also echoes Stonehenge.

Comets, which puzzled the populations of medieval England, appear in Anglo-Saxon and medieval literature with explanatory stories. Eleven comets appear in *The Anglo-Saxon Chronicle*, in each instance interpreted as an omen or sign. One of these comets appeared early in the year 1066 and was later interpreted as an omen of King Harold's defeat by William of Normandy. The comet of 1066, as it happens, has been determined to be Halley's Comet. A fictional comet appears in Geoffrey of Monmouth's twelfth-century history: "there appeared a star of great magnitude and brilliance, with a single beam shining from it. At the end of this beam was a ball of fire, spread out in the shape of a dragon. From the dragon's mouth stretched forth two rays of light...."[19] This comet, as interpreted by Merlin, is a sign of the death of Aurelius Ambrosius and the coming reigns of Uther and his son, Arthur.

Even with a general skepticism about magic, many of the Westerosi believe in the power of prophecy and see the Red Comet that appears in *A Clash of Kings* as prophetic. Tyrion Lannister, one of the most blatantly skeptical of Martin's characters, does not place much value in such signs and symbols. In a conversation with Ser Jorah, he compares prophecy to a "half-trained mule" which, despite the appearance of being helpful, "kicks you in the head" if you trust it (*D with D* 534). However, his sister Cersei, though she believes herself to be shrewd and cynical, is haunted by the prophecy of Maege, and even the wise young ruler Daenerys Targaryen must contend with Quaithe's prophecies, which she finds difficult to interpret. The Red Comet of Westeros inspires numerous interpretations and prophecies, primarily serving as a tool for the various contenders to the Iron Throne to justify their rights of succession. Jesse Scoble writes,

> most characters see what they want in [the comet]. King Joffrey sees the comet as a blessing of Lannister crimson; Edmure Tully sees Tully red and a sign of victory; Greatjon Umber sees a symbol of vengeance; Brynden Tully, Aeron Greyjoy, and Osha all see it as a portent of war and bloodshed; and to near-blind Old Nan, who claims she can smell it, the red comet means the coming of dragons.[20]

Considering that the comet appears simultaneously with the hatching of Daenerys's dragons, Old Nan, criticized by the older Stark children for her far-fetched stories, seems closest to the mark.

Dragons are often used symbolically, to represent the unknown or the inexplicable. The coming of Vikings to England, recorded in *The Anglo-Saxon Chronicle*, refers to the invaders symbolically as dragons:

> A.D. 793. This year came dreadful fore-warnings over the land of the Northumbrians, terrifying the people woefully: these were immense sheets of light rushing through the air, and whirlwinds, and fiery dragons flying across the firmament. These tremendous tokens were soon followed by a great famine: and not long after, on the sixth day before the ides of January in the same year, and harrowing inroads of heathen men made lamentable havoc in the church of God in Holy-island, by rapine and slaughter.[21]

Likely, these "dragons" are the carved images on the prows of Viking ships that became symbols for the brutal attackers. Their appearance was combined with other misfortunes, such as famine, to portray the threat of Vikings. The dragon of *Beowulf* can also be interpreted symbolically, evocative of a greedy king who serves as foil to the generous Beowulf. In Arthurian legend, Uther, Arthur's father, is given the title "Pendragon," meaning "dragon's head." Arthur's birth and his father's rule are predicted by dragons that appear in the sky, again indicative of the symbolism of medieval dragons.

The existence of dragons is perhaps one of the most debated topics in Westerosi lore. Tales of Daenerys's dragons make their way across the Narrow Sea to Westeros through stories related by sailors. Dragons are highly symbolic in Westeros, as in medieval literature, and function in much the same way. Although dragons really *do* exist across the Narrow Sea (Daenerys's dragons), the Targaryen rulers as "dragons" are symbolically evoked in the sailor's tales that circulate in Westeros. The dragons likely symbolize not only the possible return to rule of the Targaryens, but also the greed and fury of past Targaryen leaders.

Inhabitants of Westeros discuss the plausibility and possible interpretation of the reports of dragons as related in these sailors' stories. Novices at the Citadel are confused by these varying stories. One novice, Armen, comments in dismay that the versions of these stories are wildly divergent. He notes varying accounts of dragons in Assahai, in Qarth, and in Meereen. He is puzzled by various tales of dragon, lamenting that "each telling differs from the last" (*F for C* 6). Arianne Martell hears stories from the sailors coming into Planky Town. She, too, is confused by the many versions she hears and doubts their veracity (*F for C* 426). In his last days, Maester Aemon Targaryen becomes convinced that dragons have, in fact, returned. Samwell Tarly tries to convince him otherwise. He seeks to comfort and reassure Aemon, telling him that the account is fictional, merely a "sailor's story" (*F for C* 543). Despite his skepticism, Samwell honors Aemon's request to seek the help of Archmaester Marwyn at the Citadel, one of the few maesters to believe in magic. However, thus far in the series, Samwell cannot confirm the veracity of the rumors.

Tyrion Lannister has similar doubts about the existence of dragons although he is very knowledgeable about their past history. Much of his information about dragons has been gleaned from old books. He recalls some of the legends he has read about dragons who hoard jewels and are massive in size. He refers to accounts of talking dragons and riddling dragons as "nonsense, all of it" (*D with D* 840). He does not, however, completely dismiss the books with these accounts, adding that one can also find "truths in the old books" (*D with D* 840). Once he crosses the Narrow Sea, his doubts seem to expand. He asks Griff what might happen if, when they find Daenerys, they learn that the stories about dragons are merely "sailor's drunken fancy" (*D with D* 133). He adds that the world is filled with "mad tales" about creatures that don't exist, and he equates dragons with fantastical creatures including "Grumkins and snarks, ghosts and ghouls, mermaids, rock goblins, winged horses, winged pigs ... winged lions" (*D with D* 133).

Stories spread not only about dragons, but also about the metaphoric dragon, Daenerys Targaryen herself. While playing cyvasse with Qavo to get information, Qavo relates to Tyrion a litany of stories about Daenerys. Many of them portray her as monstrous and bloodthirsty. She is accused of being sexually promiscuous, of feeding infants to her dragons, of breaking oaths and vows, and of torturing her enemies. Haldon calls these tales "mere calumnies," and Qavo responds, "The best calumnies are spiced with truth!" (*D with D* 315). Qavo mentions some events that readers would recognize as true to the narrative, such as Daenerys's stopping of the slave trade, which has involved violence. Thus, Martin illustrates the ways truth and rumor can intermingle. Tyrion, however, remains skeptical about both Daenerys's power and her dragons until he arrives in Mereen and can confirm for himself.

Even as these stories about her dragons are circulating, Daenerys is looking to stories for help in controlling them. All Daenerys, and most others, know of dragons is from lore and legend since no living dragons have been around for several hundred years. When Tyrion observes the Yunkai'i making arrangements in case the escaped dragon Drogon reappears, Tyrion, who is well versed in dragon lore and literature, is certain that their efforts will fail. He is well aware of the strength of dragons and recalls a saying from Septon Barth's *Unnatural History*: "Death comes out of the dragon's mouth ... but death does not go in that way" (*D with D* 831). Daenerys, however, has no books on dragons and must rely upon oral history. All she knows about dragons she learned from tales shared by her brother Viserys. She recalls his fascination with dragon lore (*D with D* 173). The stories he tells her are derived from songs and legends rather than books and contain mostly fictional accounts of dragonslayers. The tales do not give Daenerys actual advice on how to control her dragons, but they do lead her to believe that they will be key to helping her claim the Iron Throne. Through Daenerys's dragons, Martin promises to take the magic beyond the Wall and across the Narrow Sea into the cynical borders of Westeros where songs and stories, many deemed implausible, will prove to be true.

THREE

Chivalry in Written Tradition

*"Bring me the book I was reading last night." She wanted to lose
herself in the words, in other times and other places. The fat
leather-bound volume was full of songs and stories from the
Seven Kingdoms.*—Daenerys Targaryen, S of S 991

Literacy in Westeros

In his book *Writing the Oral Tradition*, Mark C. Amodio explains that
"Orality and literacy are parts of a subtle, complex, lengthy process of cultural
change rather than sudden and (largely) unrelated moments of culture evolution."[1] There is no sudden sea change that marks the transition from an
oral culture to a written one. Amodio argues that "medieval English culture
was far from being the oral one it has seemed to be"[2] and had, at an early
date, a vibrant literary tradition. Westeros seems to follow a similar trajectory
with Martin's creation of both extensive oral and written literary traditions.
Although literate characters are sometimes ridiculed for their book learning,
Westeros nonetheless has a rich written tradition. This chapter provides an
exploration of the literary traditions of Westeros, beginning with a brief
overview of the evolution of Westerosi literacy.

Through a description of the Horn of Winter, Martin depicts pre-literacy
in Westeros with a reference to runes. The First Men, who spoke the Old
Tongue, used runes that were "carved into the golden bands" on the Horn of
Winter (*D with D* 147). These runes reveal the legend that Joramun, a king
beyond the Wall, awoke the giants when he blew this horn. Martin's references
to runic inscriptions bring to mind those carved on the Ruthwell Cross in
Scotland (which match some lines of the Old English Poem "The Dream of
the Rood"). Runes are also found in some Anglo-Saxon riddles and in the elegy

known as "The Husband's Message." In the Arthurian "Lay of the Horn," runes (or some kind of archaic writing) make an appearance on a magical drinking horn, and Arthur must summon his wise counselors to interpret them. In Martin's novels, the reference to runes authenticates a similar transmission of written literature from its earliest origins and allows him to craft a credible view of the evolution of a Westerosi literary tradition. In the present-tense of the novels, runes have been replaced by a more sophisticated form of writing imported with the Andals, and literacy appears to be on the rise.

The rise of literacy in Westeros seems to mirror loosely that of the pre-printing press Middle Ages. Initially, literacy in Westeros was limited to the maesters. These are the scholars of the Citadel whose role in preserving literature is akin to that of the medieval monk. The Citadel itself houses a vast library that contains much of the literature of the Westerosi. Like the scribes of the Middle Ages, the maesters also have the duty to copy these texts. Throughout his novels, Martin points to the significant role of the maester and the importance of written literature in Westeros. In doing so, he accurately represents some important aspects of the transmission of written literature and also the value of books in the Middle Ages.

Gradually, literacy in Westeros began to spread to others in the populace, beginning with the nobility, who had the financial means to purchase books and the leisure to learn to read. For this reason, Westerosi nobility are likely to be literate, while lesser nobility and smallfolk are not. Among those Westerosi who value written literature, many do so simply for the fact that, in the pre-printing press world of Westeros, books are costly and therefore a sign of prestige. As valuable commodities, books are largely either the property of the nobility, some who seem to have private libraries, or the Citadel. For the nobility, owning books and having a personal maester at hand to read and write letters is an indication of worth. Lady Dustin explains that having a master is a status symbol. She claims that those who do not have them are "of little consequence" (*D with D* 545). More than simply signs of status, maesters, in their roles of reading and writing letters for their lords, also have much potential power. Lady Dustin points out this power, calling them "grey rats" who often serve illiterate lords. She speculates that, in their duty of letter writing, they often "[twist] the words for their own ends" (*D with D* 545). She warns that the illiterate who place their trust in maesters should realize that maesters might shape their messages for their own purposes.

For the wealthy of Westeros, maesters also serve the important role of preserving family history through writing. Genealogies can lend authority to familial worth and can also give credibility to familial lore. While in Duskendale, Brienne of Tarth questions the resident maester about Ser Dontos Hollard and his background. The Hollard family, once wealthy and prestigious, lost land and title in the Defiance of Duskendale. The maester does not have firsthand knowledge as the Hollard's family fall occurred long ago, so he refers to earlier accounts of the family's fortune as his authority. These accounts were likely written by one of the Hollard family's previous maesters.

In addition to the library at the Citadel and the collections in the libraries of the wealthy, Castle Black has an impressive collection of old books deep in the cellars. These books are crumbling and, until Samwell Tarly begins sorting through them. The men of the Night's Watch clearly have not recognized their value. Although Samwell and Maester Aemon hope to preserve the books by taking them to the Citadel, Xhondo Dhoru, who is transporting them by ship to the Citadel in Oldtown, tells Samwell that these books can help pay for their passage. He assures Samwell that the books will still go to the Citadel, but the men of the Citadel will have to purchase them from him rather than receive them as a gift from the men of the Night's Watch (*F for C* 743). While Xhondo considers books only as a commodity, Samwell and select others recognize the value of their contents.

Rodrik Harlaw of the Iron Islands, known as The Reader, has such esteem for the intrinsic value of literature that it earns him his nickname. His collection of and reverence for written literature makes him an anomaly among the Westerosi, and especially among his own people, the sea roving Ironmen. The Ironmen regard him with bafflement and disdain. He is described as "ordinary" other than his love for books, a trait which the ironborn believe to be "unmanly and perverse" (*F for C* 231). When his niece Asha visits him in his Book Tower, she finds him intently studying one of his many books. He explains to Asha that books can show the cycles of history. He refers to an esteemed Archmaester who wrote that human nature is static, and "history is a wheel" which can repeat itself (*F for C* 234). The Reader so prefers his contemplative life in his library that he refuses to participate in Asha's queensmoot (the ceremony by which the Ironmen choose their ruler). He tells her that he prefers "dead history" which is "writ in ink, the living sort in blood" (*F for C* 236).

After Asha's queensmoot fails, The Reader encourages her to consult his copy of Haereg's *History of the Ironborn*, but he is reluctant to let her take it from his Reading Tower for fear that it will be ruined. He tells Asha that she must stay in the Tower to read the book because it is so delicate (*F for C* 234). He is concerned not because the book has monetary worth, but because of the valuable information within it: it preserves the history of his people. Haereg's text also verifies the unlikelihood of the Ironmen overturning their choice of Asha's uncle Euron as ruler, and The Reader hopes this information will lead Asha to abandon her own bid to rule and flee to safety.

The negative attitude of the Ironmen towards The Reader is not unusual. The inhabitants of the Iron Island adhere to a heroic culture that values action; thus, notwithstanding the value of books and the potential benefits of literacy, book learning is demeaned by many who see scholarly pursuits as a sign of weakness. The warriors and knights of Westeros, in particular, tend to hold little regard for literature. Jaime Lannister is initially uninterested in book learning, placing greater value on his fighting abilities and finding little value in writing. About his lack of knowledge, his twin sister Cersei, who does value learning but only for her own manipulative purposes, compares him to her unlearned husband and adds that "*All his wits were in his sword hand*" (247). Loras Tyrell, one of Westeros's most admired young knights, also disdains book learning. On the other hand, Samwell Tarly is mocked for his bookishness and lack of prowess by both his father and, when he first joins the Night's Watch, his new brothers. He is sent to the Watch because his father finds his bookishness unmanly and deems him unworthy to wield the family sword.

While travelling through Essos, Quentyn Martell instructs Ser Gerris Drinkwater, another knight who sees no value in books, about the triarchs of Volantis. Quentyn chastises Gerris, who is renowned for his prowess, for not reading. Quentyn is bothered about having to explain information that is readily available in a book which was given to Gerris. When Gerris complains that the book has no pictures, Quentyn counters that there are maps, but Gerris is not appeased. He argues that maps are not truly pictures and that he prefers books about exotic animals. He complains that this particular book "looked suspiciously like a history" (*D with D* 101). And at the Wall, Dolorous Edd offers his own take on what he sees as the uselessness of books. He recalls his septon referring to books as "dead men talking" and adds that "no one wants to hear a dead man yabber" (*D with D* 104).

Not all Westerosi dismiss the value of book learning. Even some who are not maesters are able to recognize the ways literacy can be beneficial. For instance, literacy can be valuable as a means of social ascent, and Ser Davos Seaworth is well aware of this potential. Not nobly born, Ser Davos has advanced to knighthood through his dutiful service to Stannis Baratheon. When he is appointed King's Hand to Stannis, Davos fears that his illiteracy makes him unqualified to serve. However, Maester Pylos agrees to teach Davos, reassuring him that "any man can read" (*S of S* 731). Davos dutifully attends lessons, humbled by the fact that his eleven-year-old son is far more advanced than he is. He persists, though, realizing the importance of literacy if he is to ascend to this position and perform his duties effectively.

The more thoughtful among the Westerosi, particularly those who lack prowess for physical reasons, also place a high value on literature. The diminutive and physically weak crannogman Jojen Reed explains to Bran the benefits of reading: "A reader lives a thousand lives before he dies.... The man who never reads lives only one" (*D with D* 495). Tyrion Lannister, a dwarf who cannot attain many of the requisites of chivalry because of his small stature, arms himself with all kinds of knowledge, especially regarding matters that are chivalric and historical. Tyrion is known for his bookishness and sharp wit. He brandishes knowledge as if it were a weapon. When Tyrion, travelling through Essos, first meets Haldon Halfmaester, Haldon begins by quizzing Tyrion on his knowledge of history. Tyrion meets the challenge and even corrects Haldon, who considers himself extremely well informed, on several facts (*D with D* 125). When Haldon and his companion Duck try to frighten Tyrion with the legend of the Shrouded Lord, Tyrion pauses to remind himself that the Shrouded Lord is fictional rather than real. He equates this legend with other fanciful tales, such as a ghost that is said to haunt Casterly Rock (*D with D* 127). His book learning gives him an advantage in discerning which elements of lore are plausible and which are not (although Tyrion's experiences across the Narrow Sea challenge some of his assumptions).

Though not bookish himself and very skilled in arms, Jon Snow also recognizes the significance of books, especially acknowledging their value in preserving lore. For example, as he learns more about the fascinating history of the Wildling named Leathers, he regrets that he has sent Samwell Tarly to Old Town. He laments that Sam is not around to record the amazing stories of the Wildlings such as those related by Leathers (*D with D* 570). Jon recognizes that writing preserves and documents in ways that oral lore cannot. More importantly, as Jon realizes the magnitude of the threat that exists beyond the Wall, he comes to understand that prowess alone will not be sufficient as a means of defense. He needs the information preserved in the books that are decaying in the cellar of Castle Black.

Jon Snow looks to literature for a solution to the threat from the Others, the biggest threat to be faced by the Westerosi. His search for keys to battling this formidable enemy is complicated by the fact that the written literature of Westeros is not always trustworthy. Oral lore tends to become exaggerated with retellings; likewise, the written tales are equally prone to embellishment. For example, Jon explains to Stannis the benefit of using trails that are no larger than goat tracks for a sneak attack on Winterfell (which is held by the Boltons). When Stannis balks, Jon reminds him of the legend of the Young Dragon who used a goat track to bypass the Dornish watchtowers when he conquered Dorne. Stannis counters, claiming that the reality is clouded by the exaggerations of an author. He claims that Daeron amplified the tale in his "vainglorious book" (*D with D* 253), and he attributes the victory of the young dragon to ships rather than misleading goat tracks. Stannis unhesitatingly discredits the viability of the information in Daeron's book, but the Westerosi often struggle with sorting out the veracity of the tales they hear and read.

One cause of such confusion stems from the fact that Westerosi history and legend are often intertwined. This is true of medieval history and legend, as well, as evidenced by Geoffrey of Monmouth's twelfth-century *History of the Kings of England.* Norris Lacy describes how Geoffrey "uses history, exaggerating, inflating, contorting, inverting, but seldom fabricating at any length about nothing at all."[3] Geoffrey's work was very popular in the Middle Ages, yet he had some detractors. He was labeled a liar by his contemporary William of Newburgh for some of his more outlandish claims, such as his portrayal of Arthur in direct conflict with the Roman Empire, an element of the story that, even in the Middle Ages, pushed his account beyond the point of credibility for some readers.

Robert Stein sees Geoffrey's creative slant on history as a natural evolution that shows "the invention of a dream world containing infinite realms in which to locate events that can be narrated and analyzed for their significance *as if one* were writing history—but without history's constraints."[4] He explains that "It is no accident the great twelfth-century text for the legend of Arthur and for vernacular romance in general, Geoffrey of Monmouth's *History of the Kings of England,* is a work that invents Latin prose fiction by modeling it so directly on contemporary historiography that the two cannot be told apart using purely narrative criteria."[5] Geoffrey so cleverly melded together fiction and history that his work remained extremely popular until the sixteenth century, when it was debunked by another historian, Polydore Vergil.

The pseudo-history and legends of Westeros are similarly melded together. As Ser Davos embarks on a quest for literacy, Edric Storm encourages him by telling of his preferred literary genre as history because "It's full of tales" (*S of S* 860). Edric confirms that Westerosi "history" also contains elements of the fantastic, or at least elements that are highly entertaining. Some of the stories of Westeros date back so far into the past that only cloudy legend, which may be freely mixed with fantasy, remains. The literate are sometimes consulted to make sense of conflicting and hazy accounts. For example, Jaime Lannister (literate, but initially indifferent to literature) questions his young hostage, Brynden Blackwood, about the origins of the longstanding feud between the Blackwoods and the Brackens. Brynden responds that the feud has been recorded by various maesters of both families and that these accounts were written well after the original feud began. He notes that the dates are "hazy and confused, and the clarity of history becomes the fog of legend" (*D with D* 705). Even the bookish Brynden cannot sort out the origins of the longstanding feud, now muddled by time and various tellers.

The tendency to change, exaggerate, and emend is equally true of chivalric literature, particularly Arthurian, which is many-versioned. Any connection between the Arthur of legend and the real Arthur is, as with the Westerosi legends from the Age of Heroes, lost in a "fog." From the earliest references to Artorius in the works of Nennius, real historical events are already "hazy and confused." It is this very haziness, however, that makes the Arthurian literary tradition, and the Westerosi, so richly textured. Although a written text preserves a single version of a narrative, maesters and scribes who record subsequent copies are likely to make changes. The maester or scribe records and copies, but he also has the power to edit and, as such, deliberately alter both legend and historical record.

In the Middle Ages, Chaucer was well aware of the ability of his scribe to alter his writing. His short poem "To Adame, His Scrivener" expresses the poet's frustration at the power of the scribe to emend his poetic creation. Whereas Adam is accused of carelessness, other kinds of scribal emendations are deliberate rather than the result of sloppiness. Even unintentionally, the recordings of scribes may be clouded by the existence of multiple versions of a tale, political happenings, and the natural exaggeration that seems to accompany the creation of legend. Consider, for example, the many faces of the Arthurian character Gawain, who serves as a foil in Chrétien's work, emerges as a hero in some English romances, and becomes the hotheaded instigator of Arthur's final battle in Malory. The hero changes to suit the writer, the time, and the audience.

Medieval writers referred to sources, usually other books or oral tales, both to lend authority to their texts and also to ensure that their works would not be seen as acts of vanity. Where no sources exist, authors might make them up to legitimize and authenticate their work. Invention occurred as the author fashioned the work to suit his or her intent. Thus, Geoffrey of Monmouth refers to a "certain book" given to him by Walter as his source. Although scholars have put forth various theories about his exact source, it has not been identified and may well have been a fabrication. Marie de France relies on the importance of establishing a written tradition to justify her retelling of Breton lais, which she claims to know from oral sources and seeks to preserve in writing. Similarly, the anonymous author of *Sir Gawain and the Green Knight* announces that he is spinning an old story with a new twist by writing it down and using alliteration.

In *The World of Ice and Fire*, the fictional archmaester who narrates refers repeatedly to his sources, a vast assemblage of learning that he is compiling in the fashion of medieval writers. Like medieval writers, he refers to his sources to lend authority to his work. He also questions those sources that don't seem feasible. He notes the untrustworthy nature of storytelling, especially as tales transition from oral to written and, in some cases, to oral again, through song. Those who first wrote the stories down added "details [that] suited them." Subsequently, these narratives were shaped by singers who transformed them "beyond all recognitions" in their attempts to earn a living. "In such a way," the archmaester explains, a First Man can be transformed into a knight "who follows the Seven and guards the Targaryen kings thousands of years before he lived (if he ever did)."[6] His interpretation of the corpus of Westerosi history as multi-versioned and malleable vividly reflects the transmission of medieval written literature.

The Chivalric Function of Literature

The literature of Westeros sometimes functions exactly like chivalric literature: to set ideals for knighthood. Robert Stein writes that medieval romance, often depicted as "the fantasy genre par excellence," also served as a reflection of medieval politics and values.[7] Historian Nigel Saul explores the relationship between literature and chivalric values in fourteenth and fifteenth century England. He explains that "knights ... soaked in the legends of Arthurian romance sought to act out the fictions in their own lives." He adds that "the worlds of reality and the imagination overlapped."[8] In the epilogue to his edition of Ramon Lull's handbook, Caxton reminds medieval readers that chivalric virtues are well illustrated in romance: "And some not well advised used not honesty and good rules again in the order of knighthood, leave this, leave this and read of Tristam, of Percefrost, of Percival, of Gawain, and so many more. There will you see manhood, courtesy, and gentleness."[9] Medieval romance, in other words, is exemplary.

In the Middle Ages, handbooks of chivalry such as those by Lull, Geoffroi de Charny, and Christine de Pizan detailed knightly codes of conduct. In Lull's *Book of Knighthood and Chivalry*, the author explains, "The knowledge of chivalry should be put into books, that the art is known and read in such a manner as other sciences have been read, that the sons of knights learn first the knowledge that pertains to the order of chivalry after they have been squires. They should ride through diverse countries with the knights and there should be no error in the clerks and in the knights under whom they study."[10] Rule books such as this one were thus essential to codify the tenets of chivalry.

The corpus of Westerosi literature includes books that mirror medieval handbooks of chivalry. Martin makes several references to a valuable guidebook for kings of Westeros, *Lives of Four Kings*. The author, Grand Maester Kaeth, intends it more as an instructional manual than a history and appears to shape its contents accordingly. Tyrion Lannister, a self-professed bibliophile, gives his nephew Joffrey this extremely valuable book as a wedding gift. However, Joffrey mocks the gift and subsequently destroys it. Tyrion laments that, if Joffrey would take the time to read this book, he could learn from it and perhaps develop into an effective leader. Tyrion also references another chivalric book that details the law of arms, *The Tree of Battles* (*S of S* 139). Because Tyrion is extremely well read and familiar with chivalric handbooks, he is more knowledgeable about chivalry than most of the knights of Westeros. He sees the value in chivalric books as educational tools.

The White Book of the Kingsguard functions doubly as both history and handbook. Once Jaime Lannister loses his hand and returns to the Kingsguard as Lord Commander, he seriously considers his own responsibility as contributor to this book and his duty to be a role model to future generations through its pages. He describes the White Book as containing a complete history of the Kingsguard with a page reserved for the deeds of each member. He sees preserving this book as "*My duty, now*" (*S of S* 913–914). Jaime puts into practice the lessons of this book when he considers killing Osmund Kettleblack, whom he suspects has slept with his twin sister (and lover) Cersei. He thinks of Kettleblack's brothers and remembers a tale from the White Book which warned that "Brothers can be dangerous" (*F for C* 951). This tale recounts the death of Ser Torrene Toyne who was condemned for sleeping with the wife of Aegon the Unworthy and the attempted vengeance for Toyne's death by his brothers. Jaime verifies this tale by noting that "It's written down in the White Book" (*F for C* 951). He uses this example as a cautionary tale against rash heroic action, a lesson that he would not previously have heeded. The loss of his sword hand certainly explains, to some degree, his newfound caution, yet Jaime's attempts to learn chivalric virtues and to heed the advice in the White Book seem sincere.

Whereas Jaime learns to take the White Book seriously, Ser Loras Tyrell has only disdain for it. He bases his opinion, in part, on the words of Renly Baratheon, whom he admired and loved. According to Lord Renly, books were meant for maesters rather than knights. Jaime attempts to explain the significance of the White Book to Ser Loras, but Ser Loras responds that he likes to look at the images in the book, especially the shields; however, he sees no value in actually reading it (*F for C* 336). Ser Loras, more intent on prowess than learning, holds no regard for this book that contains the history of all the white cloaks. He does, however, know and prefer some shameful tales about some of them which circulated orally. He recalls with amusement, for instance, the tale of Lucamore the Lusty who had numerous wives and children: "They cut his cock off. Shall I sing the song for you, my lord?'" (*F for C* 336). Preferring oral to written lore, Loras explains that the best warriors live on in song. Loras knows only the colorful songs about the knights in the White Book, while Jaime becomes familiar with the written matter. Although the White Book may present a glorified view of the Kingsguard, its function as a book of chivalry is important to Jaime. His renewed interest in literacy, using the White Book as a guide and contemplating his own role in it, helps him move towards attaining chivalric ideals.

Medieval romance served to set ideals for chivalric behavior, yet is equally served as entertainment. The scope and abundance of Arthurian legend testifies to its value as a form of popular entertainment for both men and women. Westerosi romance, on the other hand, seems to be the domain of women and serves primarily as escapism. Certainly, Sansa Stark has read her fill of pseudo-romances, and consequently, she has unrealistic expectations about the knights she meets. Brienne of Tarth is given a collection of romances as part of a cruel joke played on her by Renly Baratheon's men, who have a secret wager as to which might seduce her. Ser Hyle Hunt, pretending to court her, gives her numerous gifts, including a book, "beautifully illuminated and filled with a hundred tales of knightly valor" (*F for C* 299). Like Sansa, Brienne is idealistic about the institution of knighthood and tries hard to hold onto, and live up to, her idealized literary images even in such harsh surroundings. When she learns that the book is given in jest, she is left disgusted and disillusioned by Ser Hunt, yet she clings to her idealistic notions of knighthood. Unlike Sansa who dreams of knightly lovers, Brienne dreams of becoming a knight herself, and she sees tales of chivalry as models for her own behavior as pseudo-knight.

Daenerys Targaryen, wise beyond her years, is not immune to the allure of romance. On her wedding day, Daenerys secretly wishes that her lover Daario would save her from her political marriage to Hizdahr zo Loraq. She imagines that, "*If this were a story*," Daario would challenge her fiancé and then rescue her before she could complete her wedding vows (*D with D* 632). When she dismisses Ser Jorah Mormont from her service and banishes him, Daenerys wants to read as an escape from the heart-breaking task she has just completed, and she chooses a romance. The volume she reads is a gift from Ser Jorah who may have intended the book, which contains accounts of heroes who prevail and villains who meet just ends, to serve as a guide for the young queen and not merely as escapism (*D with D* 632). But instructional literature may equally serve as entertainment. The intellectual Tyrion Lannister also appreciates the escapism offered by literature. While travelling aboard the "Stinky Steward," Tyrion finds three books belonging to the bookish captain, which he reads and rereads (*D with D* 482). Although these books are not referred to as romances, they nevertheless serve as casual reading; much-needed relief for Tyrion on what he considers to be a miserable trip.

When imprisoned by her father after a foiled attempt to kidnap and crown Myrcella Baratheon, Arianne Martell is confined to a prison tower with books that she clearly does not find entertaining. In fact, the subject matter of the books seems deliberately chosen as part of her punishment for defiance. She describes the books—which range from law and geography books to a tedious study of dragons—as "deadly dull," "ponderous" and "dry as dust" (*F for C* 843). She wishes instead for a book about romance, such as "*Ten Thousand Ships* or *The Loves of Queen Nymeria*" which would offer her some comfort and respite from her imprisonment (*F for C* 843). This denial of any form of escapism is a cruel punishment for Arianne. Like Sansa, she longs for the escapism of romance. She shuns the didactic and legal literature her father provides her while she is imprisoned.

Written literature has a number of serious and potentially important functions in Westerosi culture. Martin hints that books may hold the mysteries that will enable the inhabitants of Westeros to fight off the threat of the Others in what may well be a final battle for the Westerosi. Samwell Tarly spends hours in the cellars of Castle Black, scouring through crumbling old tomes for information about the Others which he then reports to Jon. Samwell is so caught up in reading in the dimly lit cellars that Jon must come and fetch him. Jon is taken aback when he finds Samwell, red eyed and exhausted, among piles of old books. Samwell cannot tear himself away from the task at hand, telling himself "*one more book … then I'll stop*" (*F for C* 102). The stacks of books, however, seem endless.

Samwell gives Jon an account of the shape of the books in the cellar, and also an account of the evolution of written history in Westeros. He explains to Jon that the books are falling apart in his hands as he tries to read them and that some of the oldest books have already fallen to pieces or cannot be found (*F for C* 114). These books have been neglected by the men of the Night's Watch, but Samwell and Jon recognize their importance. Jon hopes that they can provide much-needed answers that will save the inhabitants of Westeros from the Others. Samwell tells Jon that he has not yet found much information beyond what they know already. He fears that he is not up to the task of finding the relevant information about the Others and that perhaps he has "just been reading the wrong books" (*F for C* 115). Jon, however, has confidence that Samwell's learning can be beneficial and therefore sends him to the Citadel to hone his intellect and become a maester.

Initially, Samwell objects to Jon's commissioning of him to assume this duty, arguing that he is trying to get better at archery. Jon, however, recognizes Samwell's potential to sort through the books and find answers in the vast library at Castle Black. He reminds Samwell that the Night's Watch has many men who are capable with a bow and arrow, but very few who are literate. He emphasizes to Samwell that he needs someone both intelligent and trustworthy to replace Maester Aemon. Samwell reluctantly admits to the value of a position as maester at Castle Black. Not only could he delve into the books in the cellar to glean valuable knowledge, but he could also use his position to preserve the oral tales that his brothers relate. He concedes that the oral tales recited by Ulmer are fascinating and worth recording (*D with D* 111). Samwell, criticized and mocked for his lack of prowess by his own father and initially by his brothers at the Watch, promises to be an important figure in recording the future history of Westeros and in deciphering the past from the dusty and decaying books in the cellar.

Thus, the written literature of Westeros has, like medieval literature, a myriad of purposes and forms. The corpus of Westerosi literature reflects actual medieval literature, and ranges from chronicles and handbooks to romances and religious works. In a culture torn by strife, action takes precedence over contemplation. Still, literature, in addition to serving to educate, entertain, and preserve history, may hold the key to the ultimate battle against the Others.

Martin's Metafiction

In Tom Shippey's book on Tolkien's mythology, Shippey writes that, with Tolkien, readers get "a sense that the author knew more than he was telling, that behind his immediate story there was a coherent, consistent, deeply fascinating world about which he had no time (then) to speak."[11] The posthumous publication of *The Silmarillion* provides Tolkien's extensive *ur*-narrative, a narrative that reveals the origins and background history of the material in his novels. However, Tolkien's use of background information within *The Lord of the Rings* is less prominent and less extensive than Martin's. Martin devotes ample space in his novels to explore the fascinating heritage that undergirds his primary matter. He adds authority and complexity to an already complex narrative.

One part of the *ur*-narrative of Westeros is the tale of Egg and Dunk, first published as a short story entitled "The Hedge Knight." The events of this narrative serve as prequel to *A Song of Ice and Fire*. In his series, Martin makes occasional references and allusions to this work. Additionally, he refers to numerous other stories behind the immediate story, creating many layers of medievalism within his medievalist text. His characters know these stories well, but most of them do not exist as separate texts that are available to his readers. As characters frequently recall tales from the Westerosi past, Martin's readers can reconstruct much of the backstory. Indeed, Martin's Westeros is so rich in fictionalized history that it has merited its own volume, *The World of Ice and Fire*, which assimilates backstories and legends. Readers can also consult Westeros.org for a wiki that contains a compendium of the back stories of Westeros.

Martin's multi-layered lore mimics, among other genres, medieval romances, which are filled with common tropes and motifs that are re-shaped by individual authors. Carol L. Robinson and Pamela Clements note that "the matter of medievalism, including that of neo-medievalism, includes thousands of collectively owned tropes...." Malory's vision of a medieval past, as Robinson and Clements describe it, is a "bricolage," a compilation of tropes that he assimilates, or cuts and pastes, into a comprehensive (and new, by medieval literary standards) work.[12] Malory had, as Paul Rovang explains, an "extensive body of sources" and "the freedom to choose among his various sources, to shape his *matiere* according to his *sen* and to fill in gaps where they existed."[13] The intricate web of legends in Martin's series are similarly numerous and reworked to suit both the author's purpose and the various needs of fictional storytellers in the realm of Westeros.

For Martin's readers, the rich tradition of Westerosi lore creates verisimilitude which is enhanced by the readers' own familiarity with medieval lore and motifs. Readers well-schooled in medieval literature may recall specific medieval tales as Martin creates rich metafiction that sometimes intersects with medieval literature through specific details and imagery. For instance, Victarion Greyjoy develops superhuman strength in his hand after the Red Priest Moqorro cures it (*D with D* 910). This scene seems directly drawn from *Beowulf* as the titular hero is touted to have the strength of thirty men in one hand. Not only Martin's characters, but also his landscapes, occasionally seem drawn from medieval literature. *A Dance with Dragons* includes a description of a barrow, The Great Barrow of the Barrowlands. The Great Barrow is said to be either the gravesite of the First King or the burial place of the King of the Giants. Other accounts claim that it is simply a hill and not a burial site at all (*D with D* 475). This barrow and its association with the supernatural is reminiscent of the barrows in both *Beowulf* and *Sir Gawain and the Green Knight*. The barrow in *Beowulf* houses the treasures of a dragon who menaces the countryside after a single item is taken from his hoard. In *Sir Gawain and the Green Knight*, when Gawain comes across the Green Chapel where he is to meet his challenger, he, like the Westerosi, wonders if he has found a barrow or an ominous hill best suited for a fiend. Certainly, it is not the kind of chapel he has envisioned for his meeting with the Green Knight.

Martin's characters often evoke medieval, particularly Arthurian, characters even though, as Martin himself has claimed, he does not intend one-to-one correspondences between his characters and those in history or literature. Still, Martin concedes that he wants his readers initially to perceive Bran as a "young King Arthur," but he then dashes their expectations by having him crippled. The struggles of the knights of Westeros, to be detailed in a later chapter, also intersect with those of Arthurian knights. More often, though, Martin's works intersect with romance not through similar characters, but through common allusions and similar kinds of legends.

In Geoffrey of Monmouth's version of the King Arthur story, for instance, the giant Retho is known for making cloaks from the beards of kings. This giant later appears in the *Alliterative Morte Arthure* and shares attributes with King Royns in Malory's work, changing, as legends typically do, with each re-telling. Having one's beard shaved and then displayed by a conqueror was considered disgraceful, for beards were perceived as signs of prowess and honor. Martin echoes and magnifies this motif of an oddly fashioned cloak. Although Ramsay is not a giant, he evokes this king who is infamous for making cloaks from the beards of those he conquers. Ramsay sends a letter to Jon Snow telling Jon that he will not return Mance Rayder to the Wall, but has encaged him. Mance's only warmth against the cold of Winterfell is a cloak made from "*the skins of the six whores who came to Winterfell*" (*D with D* 994). Martin not only borrows, but also magnifies, the cloak motif by having Mance's cloak made, horrifically, of human skin.

Sometimes Martin subtly alludes to specific medieval romances. He seems to be giving a direct nod to Chrétien and Malory in his early reference to Viserys Targaryen as a "cart king." Both medieval writers convey tales in which Lancelot must ride in a cart. In Chrétien's twelfth-century version, Lancelot hesitates two steps, thinking about the shame that will come if he steps into the pillory cart, a cart reserved for criminals. Because his horses have died in his fervent attempts to rescue Guinevere, he has no alternative transportation and so endures the shame. Malory's later fifteenth-century version, filtered through other intermediate versions, does not fully capture the shame that comes with this deed as the cart in his version is used to fetch wood and not a pillory. Still, Lancelot is chastised for this act. Viserys Targaryen, on the other hand, does not understand the tremendous shame associated with riding in a cart and believes the Dothraki, who have taken his horse from him, are trying to make amends with him by offering him the option to ride in the cart rather than walk. The Dothraki, however, who equate manliness with riding upon horseback, are well aware of the disgrace and mock Viserys in their native tongue. Certainly, Viserys Targaryen is no Lancelot, but the shame associated with riding in the cart cannot be lost on readers who are familiar with these medieval narratives.

In another nod to Malory, the longstanding feud between the Blackwood and Bracken families is referred to by Hoster Blackwood as, metaphorically, "the old wound" (*D with D* 705). Readers familiar with Malory will recall this exact phrasing in reference to the literal "old wound" (inflicted by Lancelot) that ultimately kills Gawain. Martin also incorporates the common romance motif of a character using disguise to penetrate a castle. Mance Rayder disguises himself as a minstrel, Abel, in order to infiltrate Winterfell and rescue the unwilling bride of Ramsay Bolton, whom he believes to be Arya Stark (*D with D* 540). In Geoffrey of Monmouth's version of the Arthurian story, Badulf uses this same minstrel guise to rescue his brother Colgrin. In the twelfth-century English romance *King Horn*, Horn also disguises himself as a minstrel to save his love, Rymenhild, from an unwanted marriage. Again, Martin puts an interesting twist on an old motif by casting Mance Rayder in the role of rescuer.

Among the most frequent medieval romance motifs is that of exile and return. In *King Horn*, Horn is exiled when his father is killed, but he returns years later to reclaim his throne. Despite his attempts to reconcile with King Arthur, Malory's Lancelot is exiled from court after the accidental deaths of Gareth and Gaheris, as is Balin upon slaying the Lady of the Lake. Exile also appears frequently in heroic literature and is the worst possible fate for a warrior. This motif is featured in the elegies "The Wanderer" and "The Seafarer,"[14] plaintive poems in which narrators bemoan their separation from lord and kin.

Exile is a prominent theme in Martin's novels. Daenerys Targaryen is similarly exiled, and, like the narrative of Horn, her narrative focuses on her struggle to re-attain her father's crown. Daenerys is joined by other Westerosi exiles, namely Ser Jorah Mormont and Ser Barristan Selmy. Ser Barristan chooses exile when he is deemed too old to serve Joffrey Baratheon, and Ser Jorah Mormont is doubly exiled, first from Westeros for committing a crime and then, when she believes he has betrayed her, from service to Daenerys. Later in the series, Tyrion Lannister becomes another of the exiles across the Narrow Sea after he commits the egregious crime of patricide.

Martin also sprinkles throughout his novels other medieval motifs that are of less thematic importance to his novels. In Malory's "Merlin," Arthur has his first encounter with the Lady of the Lake. While travelling with Merlin after breaking his sword in battle, Arthur glimpses, in the middle of the lake, "an arme clothed in whyght samyte that helde a fayre swerde in that honde."[15] Martin includes a brief allusion to this scene when Tyrion, on the *Shy Maid* of the Rhoyne, sees a Lady of the Lake–type figure emerging from the water. Tyrion sees a hand "rippling below the water and a pale face looking up" (*D with D* 254). Although this lady does not hold a sword, she nonetheless reflects the eerie image of the submerged lady of Arthurian legend.

Astute readers may also notice that Martin creates his own brand of Round Table knights as well as (literally) Round Tables. The Kingsguard, Renly Baratheon's Rainbow Guard, and Daenerys's Unsullied all bring to mind Arthur's Round Table knights. However, Martin reconfigures these knights. For instance, the Kingsguard and the Rainbow Guard seem modeled after the Round Table knights in their primary duties to serve their kings, yet Martin casts most of them as being of questionable morality. The unfaltering loyalty and impressive prowess of the Unsullied also brings to mind Arthur's knights, but, as they are castrated warriors and not technically knights, they present an unconventional model of chivalry. Martin explicitly evokes the physical Round Table in *A Dance with Dragons*. When Hizdahr zo Loraq is imprisoned, his ostentatious throne is removed by Ser Barristan in favor of "a large round table" (*D with D* 1005). He specifies that this table will serve the purpose of allowing Daenerys's advisors to "sit and talk as peers" (*D with D* 1005). Although Arthurian legend includes differing versions of the origins of Arthur's Round Table, it always serves the purpose of having the knights seated together as equals. Ser Barristan's Round Table serves this same function.

Martin's Neo-Medievalisms

Tom Shippey explains that both J.R.R. Tolkien and C.S. Lewis "bring the modern into contact with the medieval" in obvious ways; Shippey gives as example Bilbo Baggins, who is initially "in the identifiably Victorian/ Edwardian world of the Shire…, but who moves steadily into a fairy-tale world."[16] The same is true for the characters in Lewis's *The Chronicles of Narnia* and for J.K. Rowling's Harry Potter, who all leave their familiar worlds to enter fantastic medieval realms. Martin's Westeros, in contrast, is medieval from the opening pages. However, Martin frequently alludes to other medievalist texts, playfully injecting a wry sense of awareness to his narrative that subtly challenges the reader's immersion in his world.[17] In this respect, Martin might be labeled a writer of neo-medievalism. As defined by Robinson and Clements, neomedievalism differs from other sorts of medievalism in that "neo-medievalist works reflect, or pass through, earlier medievalist works, rather than looking directly at the Middle Ages."[18]

Martin also references some stories that are deeply ingrained in Westerosi lore but appear to be entirely his own creations. The popular Westerosi song "The Rains of Castamere" is a vivid example. In another, Pate, a novice at the citadel, is mocked for his name, which he sadly shares with a trickster pig who is the hero in "a thousand ribald stories" about a foolish man who outwits those of higher rank (*F for C* 10). Such tricksters are common in fables, though typically the cunning animal is not a pig. Nevertheless, this legend and the popular "The Rains of Castamere" are deeply embedded in the lore of Westeros and may create verisimilitude for modern readers. In this way, Martin makes Westeros both familiar and fantastic.

Embedded within Martin's novels are "inside jokes" that could only be appreciated by contemporary audiences well-versed in contemporary works of medievalism. Attentive readers might recognize shades of Tolkien's Samwise Gamgee in the character of Samwell Tarly. Oberyn Martell's obsessive chanting about vengeance when dueling with Gregor Clegane not only evokes the significance of the blood feud in medieval heroic literature, but also parodies the chant of Inigo Montoya from *The Princess Bride*. Martin gives a nod to J.K. Rowling by naming two of Brienne of Tarth's tormentors Harry Sawyer and Robin Potter. In another reference to the Harry Potter series, Martin alludes to Lord Voldemort, He-Who-Must-Not-Be-Named. The Red Priest Moqorro worships two gods, the God of Light and "the Other, whose name must not be said" (*D with D* 906). Readers may think of the popular BBC series *BlackAdder* when the sigil of House Wyl of the Boneway is presented as a black adder. In a Monty Python borrowing, an army of young, untrained eunuchs is compared to the real Unsullied of Astapor, fierce warriors who have been freed by Daenerys. Genuine Unsullied, like those who follow Daenerys, will not "break and run when you fart in their general direction" (*D with D* 356). Fans of Monty Python will immediately recognize this reference to the taunting French knight in *Monty Python and the Holy Grail.* Scattered throughout *A Song of Ice and Fire*, references such as these delight the astute readers who recognize them and also add layers of complexity to Martin's medievalism.

Fiction stacks upon fiction in Martin's novels. A particular humorous example of Martin's use of metafiction is Archmaester Marwyn's *Book of Lost Books* (*F for C* 231), a title that indicates a rich history of lost (pseudo-)literature. Martin creates, sometimes through brief references, numerous other examples of meta-legends, such as when Catelyn Stark says to her son Robb: "We're all just songs in the end" (*S of S* 626). But Catelyn, who of course exists only through Martin's writing, is merely a song from the beginning. In a postmodern moment, fictional Sansa Stark tries to emulate the ladies in the fictional narratives that undergird Westerosi lore. Fleeing King's Landing after Joffrey Baratheon's murder, she tries to be brave by recalling a familiar song that depicts courage. Similarly, the Mummers' shows that appear throughout Martin's novels mirror the doubly fictionalized events in the novels. For example, Tyrion Lannister recalls the Mummer's show at Joffrey's wedding that (doubly) fictionalizes the battle between the Starks and Lannisters: one of the Mummers carries a banner that features the direwolf of House Stark, and the other displays the Baratheon colors (*D with D* 578).

Finally, I should point out that even these disruptive moments in Martin's novels mimic a medieval narrative device. *Beowulf* contains numerous digressions and references to other narratives that disrupt (but also enhance) the main plotline. Within the main narrative are references to well-known characters such as Weland the Smith and the Norse hero Sigemund. Some of the digressions are quite lengthy, such as the Finn episode. Romances can also be digressive and may contain disruptive moments as songs, proverbs, and riddles are commonly sprinkled throughout these narratives. Like Martin's neo-medieval references to other works of medievalism, romances may also allude to contemporary events. Malory, for instance, includes intrusions that comment on the current state of affairs as opposed to the "golden age" of Arthur. Further, Arthurian romance has always been anachronistic in ways that surely shattered the illusions of medieval readers. Medieval readers would have delighted in, for example, the state-of-the-art fourteenth-century armor donned by Sir Gawain in *Sir Gawain and the Green Knight*. At the same time, however, they must have been acutely aware that this armor was "modern" and out of place in a tale that claimed to be about the distant Arthurian "past."

In these ways, Martin creates, for fans and scholars of medievalism, a deeply textured fictional world rich in lore and literature. His novels simultaneously evoke medieval chivalric literature, duplicate the written and oral literary traditions of the Middle Ages, and resonate strongly with contemporary audiences. In addition to evoking medieval literature, Martin's novels also connect with other works of medievalism. These connections complicate Martin's portrayal of chivalry, yet also make his work more accessible to general readers. Martin illustrates how medievalism can be possible within a (pseudo-)medieval text and also how multi-layered medievalisms can exist in a medievalist text. He thereby creates the richest of medievalist texts.

Four

Franchise

"I am the blood of the Dragon,' she told herself again."
—Daenerys Targaryen, G of T 105

Franchise in Medieval Literature

In his study of chivalry in medieval England, Nigel Saul writes that "chivalry and nobility went hand in hand. Chivalry idealized the estate of knighthood, while nobility was a way of describing its social exclusiveness."[1] He explains further the importance of birthright as a gatekeeper to the noble class: "The belief was that a man's worth was inseparable from that of his kin. His very being as honourable had been transmitted to him through the blood of his ancestors, themselves honourable men."[2] Historian Maurice Keen defines this essential attribute of bloodline as *franchise*, or "the free and frank bearing that is testimony to the combination of good birth with virtue."[3] In other words, proper bloodline is manifested in the outstanding physical appearance and impeccable behavior that set the nobility above and apart.

Franchise is integral to the fictional knights who populate chivalric literature of the Middle Ages; they are without exception of noble birth. Chivalric literature was intended for an audience of nobility. William Caxton writes in the epilogue of Ramon Lull's *Book of Knighthood and Chivalry* that Lull's book "is not for every common man to have," and he specifies that knights must be "taken of the natural nobility."[4] He highlights that chivalry as a social system is elitist, and he draws clear-cut distinctions between social classes. He adds that "Neither horse, nor amour, nor elections make a knight worthy. He is part of the three estate system where some work, some pray, and some fight; all to God's will."[5] Here, Lull depicts the traditional schema of medieval social orders, typically portrayed as three main estates of society: peasants, clergy, and nobility. This tripartite representation of society served as an ideal model, designed to keep social boundaries intact and to separate the nobility from the masses.

The medieval chivalric romance similarly serves to reinforce a sense of elitism for the upper class. Inherent to good birth are the other chivalric attributes that serve as distinguishing features of the nobility. These are, according to Keen, prowess, generosity, courtesy, and loyalty.[6] Additionally, wealth and title are essential for status to be maintained. Thus, primary characters in the canonical romance are always nobly born and, with a few exceptions, wealthy. Those who have lost wealth through misfortune generally reclaim it through the course of the narrative. For example, King Horn, the hero of a twelfth-century English romance, must work his way back up the social ladder after his homeland is attacked and he is exiled. The focus of the narrative is upon the re-establishment of land, title, and wealth that is the hero's birthright.

Some romance characters may be initially unaware of their noble birth, such as Malory's Percival whose mother deliberately guards him from chivalry, Tor who is raised by a shepherd without knowledge of his true heritage as a king's son, and Arthur himself who is fostered as a child. In each of these instances, the true heritage of the characters is soon apparent. Percival and Tor are noted for their exceptional good looks, a hint that they are of higher status than their initial circumstances indicate, and Arthur proves his birthright by drawing a sword from a stone (although his competitors for the crown are initially skeptical despite this feat). By hosting a cast of primary characters consisting entirely of nobility, the romance eliminates the intrusion of non-nobles, casting them as peasants, dwarves, or hermits who may appear along the periphery of the noble hero's adventures but are never at the heart of the action. They remain clearly outside the parameters inscribed by the romance genre. Knights, even disenfranchised knights, are clearly distinguished from those ranked beneath them.

In reality, social order was much more fluid than its depiction in romance. As J. Perroy explains, had the aristocracy not been consistently replenished, it would have become extinct.[7] The social realities that threatened the medieval notion of a perfect, tripartite society (nobility, clergy, and peasants) are reflected in law books, in household records, and in a variety of literary genres. However, the tensions between social reality and class consciousness are perhaps most apparent in the medieval fabliau.[8] Whereas the romance seeks to preserve the illusion of fixed social estates, the fabliau makes evident the growing complexity of social orders and the effect this complexity had on chivalric ideals. Fabliaux—short, humorous tales told in verse—were prominent in France in the twelfth-century, although a handful appear in England (a few in English and some in Anglo-Norman). These tales frequently play off of and overturn romance conventions. Fabliau writers often toy with readers' expectations in ways that stretch and question chivalric values. For instance, some of the tales begin with what appears to be a typical romance cast of characters and are written in the high style, yet as the narrative progresses, the characters behave badly and the narrative may be interrupted with bawdy situations and language. Further, as fabliaux frequently indicate, one need not be born into the upper class in order to aspire to chivalry. Likewise, being born into the noble class does not in itself make one chivalrous.

A quick glance at a few fabliau titles indicates the comprehensiveness of their social range: *Romanz de un Chivaler, et de sa Dame, et de un Clerk* (The Knight, and His Wife, and a Clerk); *De la Borgoise d'Orliens* (The Bourgeois Wife of Orleans); *Le Vilain Mire* (The Peasant Doctor), and *Du Prestre qu'on porte* (The Priest who was Carried). Knights, clergy, bourgeois, and peasants share the narrative space of the genre, and all are subject to ridicule for their social aspirations or social failures. Fabliaux reflect changing social estates as rich bourgeois might try to buy their way into the nobility via lands and title, or as knights and nobility squander or otherwise lose their wealth. Fabliau knights may be drunk and destitute, and *vilein*, or peasants, may acquire money and buy titles. Typically, the socially liminal character who most digresses from his or her assigned social role becomes the fabliaux dupe, indicating that writers of the genre disapprove of such social movement, or at least see it as the target of mockery.[9] Even with the fabliau's frequent debasement of socially mobile characters, the genre nonetheless provide a nuanced view of societal estates that counters the elitism of the upper-class as depicted in romance. Martin's novels offer a similar view of the possibilities of social ascent or descent and the ways social mobility can affect the perceptions of chivalry.

The Noble Families of Westeros

Whereas fabliaux show social movement, romances depict a fixed upper class distinguished by bloodline. The concept of *franchise* in Westeros mimics that of chivalric literature in that those in power desire a fixed nobility. As in chivalric literature, blood and birthright are highly valued among the high-ranking Westerosi. To the chagrin of many of the Westerosi nobility, however, social change seems inevitable. In fact, socially liminal characters occupy much of Martin's narrative. In this respect, Martin's novels intersect with fabliaux. He portrays the same kinds of social changes mirrored in the fabliau as some of his characters either ascend or descend the social ladder. Some of these social-climbing (and descending) characters are, as in the fabliau, comical. Others are met with violence, humiliation, and even death as a result of their social transience. When the socially liminal characters of fabliau are met with violence and death, the situations do not detract from the comic intent of the genre. In addition to their comic intent, the fabliaux clearly depict fluid societal divisions. Martin depicts similar kinds of complexities through the social situations of many of his characters.

Martin's notion of *franchise* is complicated, especially as it relates to the other requisites of chivalry. When Maester Aemon asks Jon to explain the significance of the links on the Maester's chain, Jon correctly answers. He notes that the collar represents the kingdom, and the links are made of metals that represent the various levels of society, gold for lords and silver for knights. Jon is quick to add that these gold and silver links alone will not suffice. He explains that other metals are needed, as well, including "iron and lead, tin and copper and bronze" to represent the common people: "A chain needs all sorts of metal, and a land needs all sorts of people" (*G of T* 450). This Westerosi hierarchy, symbolically represented by the maester's chain, loosely mimics the tripartite social structure of medieval England.

Specifically, each kingdom of Westeros is governed by a great house that has beneath it a number of noble houses, followed by knightly houses. This hierarchy has been established through both ancient and recent conquests. Separate are the maesters, or "knights of the mind" (*G of T* 580), and the various priests and priestesses of the competing religions of Westeros. Below all are the smallfolk, most of whom are confined to lives of hardship and poverty, but some who manage to climb the social ladder. Societal divisions serve, in medieval romance as in Westeros, to distinguish the elite from the peasantry and the clergy from the layman, and they discourage crossing of boundaries. However, as illustrated in medieval fabliaux, social mobility was possible even with the importance of bloodline. Martin echoes both of these genres in his richly textured world of Westeros. While bloodline is valued, social divisions are not simplistic, nor are they impenetrable.

Even with the societal fluidity of many of Martin's characters, *franchise* remains a highly valued aspect of the chivalric code of Westeros. All of the great houses cite bloodline and lineage as distinctive features that confirm their merit. House Targaryen, one of the oldest and most respected Westerosi houses, can trace its origins to Valyria and has ruled Westeros for the three hundred years preceding the start of Martin's novels. Members of this royal family traditionally intermarry to preserve their noble bloodline and to set themselves apart from other houses.[10] In romance and in Westeros, romantic relationships between nobility and non-nobility are taboo. Nonetheless, in Martin's novels, where social mobility is possible and frequently depicted, tempting situations sometimes arise. Daenerys Targaryen, the last known remaining heir of her family, is aware that her marriage is critical if she plans to win back the Iron Throne that her father lost. She realizes that her love for Daario Naharis, a lowly sellsword, cannot lead to marriage, and she laments, "*Why couldn't he be better born?*" (*D with D* 629).[11] Daenerys asks her advisor Ser Barristan whether her parents, given the choice, would have chosen to marry each other. His response makes clear the importance of preserving bloodline. He tells her, simply, that as queen, her mother had to hold true to her duties rather than follow her heart (*D with D* 631).

Daenerys heeds Ser Barristan's council that duty takes precedence over love, and she determines to marry the nobly born Mereenese Hizdahr zo Loraq, a political arrangement designed to bring peace to the people of Mereen but little personal happiness to the bride. References to numerous other marital arrangements fill the pages of Martin's novels. These arrangements serve not only to align various kingdoms with one another, but also to keep noble blood-lines pure.[12] Although Daenerys believes that she cannot have children, her importance as the last known surviving Targaryen heir and her struggle to reclaim the Iron Throne make her marriage an extremely important political matter.

Like Daenerys, most of the other main point of view characters in Martin's novels also possess noble blood. Brent Hartinger explains that *franchise*, or "greatness of blood," as he terms it, is a common feature of fantasy literature:

> In fact, you could argue that the whole genre is built on a very specific kind of "outsider": the dispossessed king or exiled prince determined to reclaim his throne. From Odysseus and Rama to modern-day characters like Luke Skywalker, Harry Potter, and Tarzan, they may start the story as outsiders, but they have greatness in their blood, and their rightful "throne" is just waiting for them to rise up and seize it.[13]

The surviving Targaryen children follow this pattern of exiled royalty. Viserys, Daenerys and Young Griff, if indeed he really is Aegon Targaryen, are all disenfranchised, seeking their rightful throne.

The trope of the exiled and disenfranchised nobility is common in medieval romance. Disenfranchised royalty and nobility who recover their heritages include Malory's Tor, Percival, and Gareth, and from earlier English romance, King Havelok and King Horn. In *King Horn* and *King Havelok*, the heroes are stripped of their titles as children, and *franchise* is manifested physically through their exceptional good looks. Horn's family is massacred by enemies. Only Horn and his companions are spared, primarily because of the hero's outstanding physical appearance. Horn, with his fair skin and rosy lips, possesses the conventional good looks distinctive of the hero of romance:

> He was briȝt so þe glas,
> He was whit so þe flur,
> Rose-red was his colur.
> He was fair ilke bold.[14]
> (He was bright as glass;
> he was white as a flower.
> His color was rosy red;
> He was both fair and bold.

Because this young hero possesses *franchise* to such a degree, his enemies cannot bear to kill him, so they exile him instead. He lands in a new kingdom and, determined to keep his true identity hidden, he must work his way up the social ladder. His noble blood is ultimately confirmed physically, not only through his handsome appearance, but also in the form of a halo-like glow that appears after he has fallen in love with a princess who doubts his worth. Subsequently, he marries the princess and regains his rightful throne. Similarly, in *King Havelok*, Havelok's father is killed, and his usurper orders Havelok's death. The fisherman assigned to this task cannot bring himself to kill the beautiful young man, and Havelok escapes death through exile. Havelok's nobility is ultimately confirmed when a gold light issues from his mouth as he sleeps. He, too, marries royalty and reclaims his family's throne.

The special qualities and exceptional good looks of the nobility confirm their status in Westeros, as well. Daenerys Targaryen is frequently described as the most beautiful woman in Martin's fictional world, and Young Griff, also praised for his good looks, not only assumes a pseudonym but also must dye his distinctive silver hair to conceal his (supposed) Targaryen blood. The Targaryens are also marked by their violet eyes. These physical attributes hold them separate from (and above) other houses. Other noble families also present exceptional good looks as evidence of *franchise*. The nobly born Cersei Lannister is a great beauty, and her twin brother Jaime is equally attractive. From Starks to Tyrells to Martells, the noble houses of Westeros are known for their attractive appearance, and those of noble birth who do not possess the necessary physical beauty generally suffer for their lack. Problematically, the distinctive looks of the nobility are equally apparent in the bastard Baratheon children who populate Westeros. Gendry Baratheon is noted for his physique and his shock of dark black hair, a distinguishing feature of all true Baratheon children and ultimately a clue that King Robert's "trueborn" children, who possess the distinctive golden hair and good looks of their Lannister parents, are illegitimate.[15]

Proof of *franchise* is not solely dependent on appearance. Another visible sign of birthright is handed down rather than genetically inherited: the possession of a sword of lineage. In Malory's *Le Morte Darthur*, Galahad's sword, formerly belonging to Balin, is one such example as only Galahad, purest of all knights, can attain it. The sword that Arthur draws from the stone, though not a sword passed down to him, nonetheless confirms his bloodline and his right to the throne. Swords are also significant in Westeros as proof of lineage and/or worth, but they sometimes change hands in unexpected ways. Heartsbane, the ancestral sword of the Tarly family, has been passed down to family members for five hundred years, but it is denied to Samwell Tarly, whose father deems him too cowardly, although he is the rightful heir. Ned Stark's children never get a chance to wield their father's sword, Ice, which is used by the Lannisters to behead him. This sword is then re-forged by Tywin Lannister into two swords. He passes one of these to his son Jaime, and the other to his grandson, Joffrey. Ironically, Jaime gives his sword, which he names Oathkeeper, to Brienne of Tarth, charging her to use it as she rescues Ned

Stark's daughters. In a sense, this sword is coming full circle, back to the Stark family, but in an unexpected way. Perhaps Martin's swords are, like Arthur's sword Excalibur, destined to specific owners.[16]

The best example of the link between swords and bloodline in Martin's work may be evidenced by Arya's connection with her sword, Needle, not a sword that has been passed down through generations, but nonetheless one that is filled with symbolic familial meaning and thus has a close link to bloodline. This sword is a gift from her much-beloved half-brother, Jon Snow. Arya considers the symbolic value of her sword when the kindly man at the House of Black and White asks her to relinquish it. She equates Needle with her family members, with Winterfell itself, and with happy memories of her childhood. Most of all, she cherishes the sword because it is a gift from her beloved half-brother who accepted her without regard to her unconventional ways: "Needle was Jon Snow's smile" (*F for C* 455). Arya is willing to relinquish all of her worldly goods in order to become one of the Faceless Men, but she hides Needle, her last link to her birthright as a Stark.

For Stannis Baratheon, a sword serves as an outward sign that he is not only the rightful heir to the Iron Throne, but also Azor Ahai, the Prince Who Was Promised. The red priestess Melisandre claims that Stannis is Azor Ahai reborn, the promised hero of legend who wields the magical sword Lightbringer. The legend relates that the sword itself is intricately linked to blood. In an effort to forge the perfect blade, Azor Ahai killed his own wife with it, and her blood gives it magical properties. Melisandre uses her trickery to make it appear as if Stannis has this sword of fire (*C of K* 149). In truth, Stannis simply has a "burnt sword" (*C of K* 154), not the actual Lightbringer. As blind Maester Aemon tells Samwell Tarly, Stannis's sword gives off no heat; the appearance of fire is simply an illusion.

Still, Stannis, who is described as harsh and unpopular, uses the sword as proof of *franchise*, a visible symbol that he should rightfully rule Westeros. He lacks the charm and charisma expected of royalty, so Melisandre must equip him with this fake sword to convince others that he is worthy of the Iron Throne. The sword alone, however, cannot endow Stannis with the charisma and good looks typical of the nobility. Further, anyone, even a non-noble, can get hold of a sword that rightfully belongs to nobility. This is evidenced by the fact that Needle passes through many hands before Arya reclaims it. Nonetheless, swords, particularly ancestral swords, are accessories that often symbolize and even confirm bloodline and noble birth.

Franchise in Westeros

Martin's point-of-view characters are almost exclusively of noble birth, yet as Brent Hartinger points out, Martin nevertheless emphasizes characters who are outsiders. Hartinger writes that, "of the series' fourteen major point-of-view characters to date—Tyrion, Arya, Jon, Daenerys, Bran, Samwell, Brienne, Catelyn, Jaime, Cersei, Eddard, Davos, Theon, and Sansa—at least the first seven violate major gender or social norms."[17] Tyrion is physically handicapped; Arya defies social expectations for young women; Jon is a bastard; Daenerys, though a female, fights for the Iron Throne; Bran becomes crippled; Samwell is overweight and cowardly; and Brienne is a female who aspires to knighthood. Each of these characters is blatantly nontraditional. They either lack the good looks and behaviors requisite of the nobility or some other aspect of chivalry. In a major departure from medieval romance, Martin rejects the notion that the hero must be male, handsome, good looking, or wealthy. However, all of the point-of-view characters, with one exception (Ser Davos Seaworth), possess noble blood, so they are not truly outsiders even with nonconformity or physical defect. Since most of these unconventional characters are nobly born, Martin does not completely reject the significance of *franchise*, which remains highly valued by the Westerosi.

Martin puts to test the conventional notion of *franchise* not only by portraying "misfit" noble characters, but also by allowing social transience. His novels most closely resemble fabliaux in this respect. As in the fabliau, it is possible in Westeros to "buy into" the nobility. When this situation occurs in the fabliau, the social climbing character generally becomes the "dupe," the butt of an elaborate trick at his or her expense. In *Du Sot Chevalier* (The Stupid Knight), a bourgeois character has bought the title of knighthood. Subsequently, he is unable to fulfill his chivalric duties, specifically his romantic duties towards his new bride. When he repeats the instructions given to him by his mother-in-law, two male guests misunderstand and beat the knight. Similarly, the knight in *De Bérengier au lonc cul* (The Knight with the Long Ass), also the son of a rich bourgeois who has bought his title, is unable to fulfill the knightly requirement of prowess. He hides in the woods and beats his own armor with a stick, returning at night with lies to his new wife about his fighting abilities. When his wife (who is nobly born) dresses in armor and challenges him, he does not recognize her and begs for mercy to avoid the fight. She agrees, if he will kiss her ass. This cowardly knight does so, not recognizing that the ass belongs to a woman, much less his wife.

The outcomes of these narratives, in which the newly titled knight is beaten or shamed, confirm that the genre is ultimately conservative. They depict the negative situations that can arise when social shifting occurs. The message of these fabliaux is clear: true chivalry is the domain of the nobility. While Martin also depicts social transience, his purpose is to mirror the rich and complex social order of the later Middle Ages rather than to provide any kind of commentary about liminal characters. Certainly, his portrayals are rarely humorous. Regardless, the social transience of his characters closely mirrors the kinds of social changes apparent in fabliaux and illustrates the potential for non-nobles to penetrate the higher classes.

One of the most prominent methods of climbing the social ladder in Westeros is through the attainment of a title, especially the title of knight. Rolly Duckfield explains to Tyrion Lannister that the process of becoming a knight is simple. He describes his own social ascent: "Any knight can make a knight, and Griff made me" (*D with D* 125). Duckfield, or "Duck," has been advanced by Griff because of his loyalty. Griff justifies this appointment, explaining Duck's willingness to sacrifice his own life on Griff's behalf and claiming that such sacrifice is sufficient requirement for his Kingsguard (*D with D* 125). Beric Dondarrion later repeats this same sentiment about the ease of attaining knighthood. He also notes that any knight has the power to bestow knighthood on a non-knight (*S of S* 464).

Writing about the reality of knighthood in medieval France, Marc Bloch explains that, prior to the thirteenth-century, every knight did, in fact, have the right to endow another with knighthood, regardless of ancestral blood. By the middle of the thirteenth-century, however, nobility began to feel threatened by the penetration of the lower class, and the methods for attaining legal noble status were restricted and soon after limited to heredity. By the late thirteenth-century, non-nobles could only attain noble status by special dispensation from the king, and such dispensations were rare.[18] Because of the ease with which knighthood can be attained in Westeros, Martin seems to reflect the thirteenth century in which ancestral blood is not necessarily a requisite.[19] However, those without the requisite blood are not viewed as favorably as the nobly born.

In Westeros, knighthood can be granted as a reward for valor, a favorite method of attaining social prestige. Sansa Stark, while in the custody of Littlefinger, finds herself with Ser Lothor Brune as a protector. She knows that, although he is a knight by title, Ser Lothor lacks money and, Sansa believes, noble blood. Sansa observes him and ponders over the fact that he was knighted shortly after successfully fighting in the Battle of Blackwater Bay. Despite his valor in battle, Sansa sees that he is poorly dressed in patched clothing and dirty shoes. He is, she thinks, "no proper knight" (*S of S* 927). Ser Lothor tries to claim a blood connection to a noble family, the Brunes of Brownhollow, but Sansa is unimpressed. He may have become a knight, but he cannot validate this noble birthright. After his father's death, he goes to the Brunes in an attempt to gain their acceptance and legitimize his social status. This meeting does not go well. Afterwards, he "would not speak of what happened" and claims to have learned about the duties of knighthood "the hard way," through battlefield experiences (*F for C* 875). Ser Lothor tries without success to create a blood tie that is non-existent or tenuous at best. He is, in Sansa's view, an imposter regardless of his acts of valor.

One of the more dramatic accounts of social ascent through prowess in Westeros is the rise of the sellsword Bronn, a ruffian who makes no secret of benefiting financially from his fighting skills. Tyrion promises Bronn wealth when Bronn volunteers to champion him at the Vale, and thus the lowborn sellsword's social ascent begins. Tyrion later discovers that his father has given the title of knighthood to Bronn. Bronn describes his sigil and confirms that Tywin has granted him the title: "By your lord father's command, I'm Ser Bronn of the Blackwater now, Imp. See you don't forget it" (*S of S* 54). Tyrion realizes that his father has double-crossed him in an attempt to win Bronn's service for himself, so he reminds Bronn that he had promised him this title (*S of S* 54). Later, when Cersei hopes to get rid of Bronn, she asks Ser Balman to see to it that Bronn is killed. Ser Balman dismisses Bronn as a threat, claiming that he is not a "true knight" (*F for C* 511) and believing that a duel against Bronn will be an easy victory. In this case, the comment that Bronn is not a "true knight" refers to his lack of an impressive bloodline. Foolishly, Ser Balman challenges Bronn to single combat, and Bronn wins, thus proving that, in Martin's world, prowess is not solely the domain of the trueborn nobility.

Bronn later accepts Cersei's offer to marry into the noble House Stokeworth, agreeing to take as his wife the feeble-minded Lollys. When her mother and sister are handed over to the evil Maester Qyborn, Bronn emerges as Lord of Stokeworth. Thus, he moves from a lowly position into a marriage that makes him part, and eventually head, of a noble family. Tyrion is not pleased when he learns that Bronn has betrayed him and will be married off to Lollys. He sees the irony in Bronn's social ascent. The pregnant Lollys gains a husband of status, and "Ser Bronn of the Blackwater climbs another rung" (*S of S* 897). Tyrion believes his conniving sister to be the mastermind behind this marriage. However, in what is either an act of defiance towards Cersei, or respect for the Lannister dwarf to whom he owes his social ascent, Bronn, having successfully risen to the position of lord through his decidedly unconventional fighting skills, names his first son after the nobly born, but physically defective, Tyrion.

Sometimes neither bloodline nor valor is necessary for advancement; Westerosi titles can be granted simply as rewards for favors. For example, Tyrion Lannister, not himself a knight but a member of the royal household, makes this promise to the captain of the ship that is taking his niece Margaery to her new husband. As long as Margaery is delivered safely, Tyrion assures the captain that he will be guaranteed the title of knighthood (*C of K* 589). Similarly, House Clegane, traditionally kennel owners, was granted land when the Clegane patriarch saved Ser Tytos Lannister from a lion. One of the Clegane sons (the father of Gregor and Sandor) was then allowed to serve as squire. With newfound wealth and connections, the family infiltrated the nobility and rose to positions of great power. Both Ser Gregor Clegane and his younger brother Sandor (who rejects the institution of knighthood) serve on the Kingsguard, the most prestigious position for knights of Westeros.

While there are a number of paths to knighthood, money is critical to acquiring this status. Even those born into the noble class must sustain wealth if they are to become knights. At Sweetsister, when Ser Davos is in danger of being turned over to Lord Triston Sunderland, his host Borrell warns him that Sunderland would betray him to the queen for money. Sunderland has a number of sons intent on becoming knights, and he "needs every dragon" to finance their aspirations (*D with D* 138). Borrell explains that Lord Sunderland's sons cannot become knights without sufficient finances, regardless of their noble birth. The necessary accouterments associated with knighthood are expensive, and Lord Sunderland will be hard pressed to provide them for all seven of his sons.

The successful social climbers of Westeros who have been granted knighthood equip themselves with coats of arms that are newly made rather than passed down through the generations. Their attempts to mimic the clothing, and sometimes the behavior, of the true nobility echo the social climbers of medieval fabliaux. For instance, the wealthy old woman in the fabliau *De Jouglet* (Jouglet) tries to dress properly when she visits a poor knight. She hopes to convince the knight that her son has *franchise* in an effort to arrange a marriage for her son to the knight's daughter. Similarly, in *Du Pesceor du Pont Seur Saine* (The Fisherman of Pont-Sur-Seine), a fisherman aspires to a noble lifestyle and adopts the mannerisms and attire of the nobility: "Comme preudom se maintenant" (He lived as if he were a noble man).[20] Although money can provide the necessary equipment of chivalry, bloodline, of course, cannot be purchased and remains a distinguishing feature of the nobility despite the infiltration of wealthy interlopers. In Martin's novels as in the fabliau, these interlopers are often mocked or at least viewed negatively for their social climbing.

In his prequel to *A Song of Ice and Fire*, Martin features a social interloper who aspires to knighthood without birth or money. Dunk, the primary character of "The Hedge Knight," describes his life in this position: hedge knights spend their time "riding from keep to keep, taking service with this lord and that lord, fighting in their battles and eating in their halls until the war was done, then moving on. There were tourneys from time to time, as well, though less often, and he knew that some hedge knights turned robber during lean winters."[21] Dunk raises himself from this lowly position through his service to Aegon Targaryen (King Aegon V) and advances to the position of Lord Commander of the Kingsguard. At the beginning of this narrative, Dunk isn't even an actual hedge knight but has simply taken the armor of his dead lord, who was one. Martin's account of the bumbling young Dunk, ignorant of the etiquette of knighthood and scrambling to provide himself with arms, is certainly comical. However, Dunk is sincere in his efforts to emulate true knights, and he ultimately succeeds. His remarkable rise is due to this sincerity and to his friendship with Aegon, whose true identity he does not originally know.

In the fabliau, lower class characters can raise their social status in similar fashion. Their attempts are also comical, but rarely sincere and always unsuccessful. The genre's primary concern is with shifting social estates, but the tales are best known for their bawdry. In fact, these two aspects of the fabliau are closely intertwined. For example, sometimes fabliau bawdry results from the social climbers' attempts to adopt the euphemistic language appropriate between upper-class courtly lovers. This confusion of language is vividly revealed in the fabliau *La Damoisele qui ne pooit oïr parler de fotre* (The Lady Who Couldn't Hear the "F" Word). In this tale, a noble woman marries a bourgeois man who doesn't know the strictly coded language of the nobility. This poses a unique problem for the couple, as the wife cannot bear her husband's straightforward requests for sex and faints upon hearing them. The couple must invent their own unique language to express their sexual desire. Lascivious language and themes in the fabliau serve as sexualized metaphors for social climbing. The sexual escapades of lower class characters are often an attempt to "penetrate," literally and figuratively, the nobility.

While Dunk attempts to earn the status of knight through prowess and chivalric ideals, Martin portrays several characters whose approaches to social climbing mimic (albeit without comic effect) the situations of the fabliau in which social classes intermingle through sexual relationships. Tyrion Lannister's first marriage to the peasant girl Tysha shocks his father into inventing a terrible lie. He tells Tyrion that she is a whore who has been paid to sleep with Tyrion. In this case, Tysha sincerely loves Tyrion, but Tywin cannot get past her peasant birth and sees her as an opportunist. Consequently, he sets out to destroy her by lying about her past and casting her as a social climber. Another of Martin's characters, Osney Kettleblack, truly is an opportunist. He attempts to raise his status by sleeping with Cersei Lannister. This endeavor proves disastrous for him. After he beds her and does her bidding as means of advancement, he finds himself at the mercy of the High Septon for falsely confessing, as Cersei has requested, that he has slept with Margaery Tyrell.

Perhaps the most ruthless (and so far, successful) social climber in Westeros is Littlefinger, who also aspires to "penetrate" the nobility, first through his amorous relationships with Catelyn Tully and her sister Lysa when they were young, and years later by marrying Lysa. The grandson of a hedge knight, Littlefinger, whose nickname comes from the humble islands where he was born, was ward to the Great House of Tully when he was a child. He claims to have sincerely loved Catelyn, but was refused because of his low birth.

When he impregnated her younger sister Lysa, the Tully patriarch made the girl drink moon tea to prevent the birth of a bastard of lowly descent. Although his attempts to marry the Tully girls failed, Littlefinger continued on his campaign of self-advancement.

Persistence and determination can pave the road to noble status for those without financial resources, and Littlefinger has both qualities in abundance. He works relentlessly to overcome his humble origins. He explains to Sansa his choice of the mockingbird as a self-designated sigil, which he prefers over his family's sigil. Littlefinger's grandfather was a sellsword who came to Westeros from Braavos and thus took the Titan, a famous statue in Braavos, as his sigil. Littlefinger tells Sansa that he prefers his self-crafted sigil of the mockingbird as his grandfather's sigil is "Rather too fierce, for an amiable fellow like me" (S of S 931). In truth, Littlefinger designs his own sigil to distance himself from the one that identifies the lowly house from which he originates.

Like the resourceful bourgeois who might ascend the social ladder in the Middle Ages, Littlefinger cleverly and deliberately moves into positions of increasing esteem. In this climb to power, he was first named Controller of Customs by Lysa's new husband (one of the positions held by real-life medieval social climber Geoffrey Chaucer), and then advances to Master of Coin. Later, when Tyrion offers him Harrenhal, his ambitions are palpable. Tyrion finds it "interesting to watch his face" as Littlefinger considers his lowly birth and the new esteem that Harrenhall could bring to him (C of K 274). He accepts this offer and then furthers his ambitions by marrying the now-widowed Lysa, and subsequently (in an effort to save and then manipulate Sansa Stark) kills his new bride, naming himself Lord Protector of the Vale and guardian of Lysa's sickly son Robert. In Martin's most recent novel, Littlefinger's machinations revolve around Sansa, who is posing as his illegitimate daughter. He plans to reveal her true identity after arranging an advantageous betrothal to Harrold Hardying, heir presumptive of the late Jon Arryn. This marriage would bring both Winterfell and the Vale under Littlefinger's control. Littlefinger's lowly birthright does not deter his ambitions and may account for his ruthless pursuit of status and power.[22]

Another ruthless social climber, Janos Slynt, rises from the lowly status of butcher's son to an appointment as Commander of the City Watch of King's Landing. Whereas Littlefinger, and even Bronn to some extent, learn to play by the rules of the nobility, or at least pretend to do so, Slynt, in spite of his promotions, remains conspicuously corrupt and uncompromising. Jon Arryn, when serving as Hand to King Robert Baratheon, discovers that Slynt has been taking bribes, yet Slynt manages to keep his position. The sycophantic Slynt is later named Lord of Harrenhal by King Joffrey, but he is stripped of his position and sent to the Night's Watch when Tyrion takes over as King's Hand.

At the Night's Watch, the bitter and resentful Slynt continues to cause trouble, particularly for Jon Snow once Jon advances to Lord Commander. Slynt becomes especially bitter when Jon wins the position of Commander over him. In an effort to keep his enemy at arm's length and perhaps gain his friendship, Jon plans to put Slynt in charge of Castle Greyguard when he reopens it. Jon attempts to justify this decision to his companion Giant, explaining that it would be unlikely that someone of low birth could advance to the positions of gold cloak without some positive attributes. Jon outlines Slynt's history, rising from the position of butcher's son to captain of the Iron Gate and then further advancing to the position of Commander of the Kingsguard by Jon Arryn. Since Arryn entrusted him with the defense of King's Landing, Jon surmises that Slynt must not be "so great a fool as he seems" (*D with D* 118). Unfortunately, the young Lord Commander misjudges Slynt. When Slynt refuses the appointment to Castle Greyguard, Jon has no choice but to put him to death. In this case, the arrogance that can accompany a rapid rise in the social order ends disastrously for the social climber. Social climbers in the fabliaux often have similar fates. Although the genre is intended to provoke humor, social miscreants are often punished in harsh ways. Larry Benson describes "fabliau justice," which includes "cuckoldings, beatings, and elaborate practical jokes that are the main concern of the fabliaux."[23] While Martin's punishments are seldom humorous, they similarly can illuminate the consequences of shifting social estates.

Slynt, Bronn, and Littlefinger are all social climbers, and all are, in the tradition of the fabliau, corrupt, or at least incapable of embodying the requisite aspects of chivalry that are thought to come only with pure bloodline. Such depravity is not the case for all of the lowly born who infiltrate the nobility of Westeros. Two of the (arguably) worthiest characters in Westeros, Ser Davos Seaworth and The Hound, are not nobly born, yet they possess other attributes of chivalry. One of Westeros' worthiest and most loyal characters, Ser Davos, the Onion Knight, is an example of this kind of social ascent at its best. Overcoming his lowly birth in the aptly named Flea Bottom, his past career as a smuggler, and the disdain that some true nobles feel towards him, Davos is raised to knighthood and later appointed Stannis Baratheon's Hand. Davos realizes that this position is a stretch for him. He acknowledges that a proper King's Hand should be nobly born, well educated, and esteemed in battle (*S of S* 731). In spite of his low birth, Ser Davos possesses the attribute of loyalty to a great extent, and it is for this quality that Stannis advances him.

As Stannis Baratheon's most loyal supporter, Ser Davos hopes that his sons will reap the benefits of his success. He has particularly high aspirations for his son Devan who will become a lord, "not merely a knight," a prospect that makes Ser Davos more proud "than in wearing the title himself" (*S of S*

732). He marvels at his own social ascent, amazed that he has risen from Flea Bottom to a position that might enable his sons not only to rub elbows with the nobility, but also to marry them. He envisions his grandchildren living alongside the nobility and perhaps even marrying them (*C of K* 147). When he is held captive by the Manderlys and fears they will kill him, Ser Davos writes letters to his surviving sons so that his sons will remember him and the sacrifices he has made on their behalf. He thinks to himself, "I did not do so ill" by escaping a childhood of poverty, becoming literate, and advancing to the position of King's Hand (D with D 424).

Ser Davos never forgets his humble beginnings as a smuggler or his label as Onion Knight: even after many years of knighthood, "deep down inside" he still sees himself as a lowly smuggler who has "bought his knighthood with a hold of onions and salt fish" (*D with D* 136). Such a character could not exist in medieval romance, unless a noble bloodline was later established (as is the case with Malory's Gareth who arrives at Arthur's court serving as kitchen boy, but is later revealed to be Gawain's brother). Likewise, such a character could not exist in the fabliau, unless the character were made a dupe. Although birthright is highly valued in Westeros, Ser Davos illustrates that one can succeed without it. He possesses loyalty, generosity, and courtesy despite his poor bloodline.

Sandor Clegane (The Hound) is a more controversial character, yet I would argue that he represents the social climbers of Westeros more positively than most, in spite of his gruff exterior. The Hound is a curious example of social climbing in that he outwardly repudiates chivalry, the institution that has helped his family advance. House Clegane, formerly kennel masters, were rewarded lands and title for their service to Tytos Lannister. Thus, The Hound's family has been rewarded the necessary title, and his outward rejection of chivalry is strictly a matter of principle. Martin explains that The Hound has refused to take knightly vows because of his hatred for his brother, a knight renowned for savagery (*C of K* 43). Certainly, The Hound has a jaded view of the institution of knighthood, accusing Dondarrion's band of outlaw knights of murder and lies, then telling them that they "might be … knights after all" (S of S 465). He excuses his own vile reputation, explaining to them that he is no different than they are except that he doesn't lie about his role as killer. The Hound recognizes the role of knights as protectors of the realm, and he is forthcoming about the necessity of killing as part of this duty. He takes affront to the more flowery aspects of chivalry that downplay the brutalities of warfare, insulting the outlaw knights who accuse him of savagery by telling them, "bugger your ribbons, and shove your swords up your arses" (S of S 465–466).

Trying to disabuse Sansa Stark of her naïve idealism in the institution of knighthood, The Hound cuts to the chase. He emphasizes the knight's role as killer and attempts to persuade Sansa that her notions of knightly virtue are, in his opinion, incorrect. Sansa counters, "True knights protect the weak." The Hound echoes her own earlier sentiment, "There are no true knights..." (C of K 757). Although he does not respect the institution of knighthood, The Hound does respect his duties and follows through with the orders of his prince, the evil Joffrey Baratheon, even agreeing to kill a young peasant boy who has offended Joffrey. He later attempts to explain to Arya Stark that this killing was simply one of his responsibilities. He has done so at the command of his prince, as a gesture of loyalty. He tries to explain to Arya how an awareness of his own social position and a sense of duty led him to commit this act: "It's not my place to question princes" (S of S 466).

Although he repudiates chivalry and believes that knights are simply killers, The Hound finds himself adhering to the more honorable tenets of chivalry. By offering first to save Sansa and later attempting to deliver her sister home, he protects the weak. Although he claims he only wants to profit from bringing Arya to her family, his treatment of her, though certainly rough around the edges, indicates a sort of fatherly affection, and his relationship with Sansa borders on romantic. Also in tournament, The Hound embodies the better aspects of the code he claims to hate. When pitted against his unhelmeted and greatly despised brother in a duel, The Hound chivalrously refuses to strike a blow at his brother's defenseless face. Ned Stark observes Ser Gregor striking "savage blows" at his brother's head, yet The Hound refuses to strike (G of T 316). Martin strongly hints in A Feast for Crows that The Hound, deserted by Arya, ends up a penitent on the Silent Isle. He appears to have turned away from the corruption of Westeros altogether, perhaps choosing a life of quiet virtue.[24]

Although The Hound has emerged (at least so far) as one of Martin's more virtuous characters, his appointment to the Kingsguard certainly breaks a longstanding tradition requiring sufficient heritage, birthright, and renown. The infiltration of non-nobility into the knightly class cannot in itself explain the complexities of chivalry in Westeros. Social climbers can be either worthy or ruthless, and, similarly, birthright is no guarantor of success. In the romance, the assumption is that all of the requisites for chivalry are inherent in the nobility by virtue of bloodline. The primary cast of characters, notwithstanding slight imperfections such as Gawain's hotheadedness, is virtuous and true. Villainous characters who are nobly born yet treacherous may appear, but if so, their function is to challenge Arthur and his court.

In the fabliaux, however, nobility are blatantly flawed. For example, Le Roi d'Angleterre et le jongleur d'Ely (The King of England the Minstrel of Ely) is a fabliau about a flawed English king in an unintentionally humorous debate with a lowly jongleur. The obstinate jongleur refuses to engage in obsequious language and disrespectfully plays word games with the indignant and outwitted ruler. *Le Male Honte* (The Bad Shame) concerns an Anglo-Norman king who has a misunderstanding with a peasant that similarly causes the king to appear foolish. Both of these tales comment upon the fact that at the height of fabliau popularity, royalty in England spoke French. These tales also reveal the miscommunications that would naturally occur when society mingles, for the representative social groups would be separated by the fact that they do not speak in the same manner, even if they share a common language. Further, they reveal the cultural divide that exists between the nobility and commoners that populate the genre. In Martin's novels, class divisions are sometimes blurred by characters who successfully bridge the societal gap between the social classes. *Franchise* does not guarantee worthiness, and social climbers are not always exempt from virtue.

Social Climbers, Pseudo-Knights, and Failed Knights

The fabliaux *Le Chevalier qui fist sa fame confesse* (The Knight Who Heard His Wife Confess), *De Gauteron et de Marion* (Walter and Marion), *Romanz de un Chivaler et de sa Dame et de un Clerk* (The Knight, and His Wife, and a Clerk), *Le Chevalier a la robe Corbeille* (The Knight of the Fancy Robe) and *De Guillaume au Faucon* (William of the Falcon) all concern noble characters who do not live up to social expectations. For fabliau knights, social failures sometimes manifest as lack of prowess. For instance, in the opening passages of *De Guillaume au Faucon*, the audience is cued to expect unchivalrous behavior from a squire who shows no desire to acquire arms and fight in tournaments. Rather, he feigns lovesickness in order to have his way with his lord's wife. Lack of prowess is also featured in the previously mentioned fabliau *Le De Bérengier au lonc cul* when the titular knight refuses to fight his own wife, whom he believes to be an actual knight as she is disguised in armor. These fabliaux emphasize that prowess is an important aspect of chivalry, and those not willing, or not able, to fight commit a major breach in the chivalric code. Prowess is closely linked to bloodline, and lack of both of these attributes becomes a source of humor in the fabliau.

The important connection between *franchise* and prowess is also evident in Martin's novels. Samwell Tarly, heir of an esteemed noble lord, is disowned by his father for lacking prowess. Lord Tarly fears that his son's cowardice (and proneness to obesity) will tarnish the family's reputation. He fails to see his son's other virtues, including generosity, courtesy, and loyalty. His father refuses to pass down to him the family's sword, telling him that that Heartsbane must be passed down to a man who possesses prowess and that Samwell is unworthy even "to touch her hilt" (*G of T* 268). As the oldest son, Samwell should inherit his father's land and this sword, yet he clearly lacks, in spite of his bloodline, the one aspect of chivalry that his father obviously values above others: "Whatever pride his father might have felt at Samwell's birth vanished as the boy grew up plump, soft, and awkward" (*G of T* 268). Without prowess, Samwell is deemed useless by his father and given the choice of dying in a "hunting accident" or joining the men of the Night's Watch.[25] The family inheritance is reserved for his younger brother, so Samwell preserves his own life by fleeing to the Wall.

Tyrion Lannister and Brienne of Tarth lack a different quality of chivalry: the good looks associated with *franchise*. Tyrion, clearly the most intelligent of the highly born Lannister children, is rejected by his father. When Tyrion's brother Jaime is held captive, Lord Tywin, the Lannister patriarch, must rely on his loathed son. Tyrion fumes to himself that his father does not deem him worthy of inheriting Casterly Rock yet is always eager to call on him when he sees the need (*S of S* 426). Lord Tywin resents Tyrion, not only because his wife died giving birth to him, but also because Tyrion lacks the good looks and physical abilities that should accompany the nobly born. Tyrion, unattractive with mismatched eyes and a beetled brow, and also a dwarf, fails to meet Tywin's expectations for his children and is considered a disgrace.[26] Similarly, Brienne of Tarth fails to meet the standards of knighthood because of her gender although she excels as one of Martin's worthiest and most virtuous pseudo-knights. She also fails to meet the typical standards of beauty expected of noble women. Manly and unattractive, Brienne feels that her unconventional looks are an embarrassment to her family. Certainly, they have prevented her father from arranging a suitable marriage for her.

Quentyn Martell, though not hideous, also lacks the exceptional good looks that are critical to establishing *franchise*. When he crosses the Narrow Sea from Dorne on a mission to marry Daenerys Targaryen, she is unimpressed with his physical appearance. She assesses him with a critical eye and muses over his nickname, Frog. She recalls fairy tales about frogs who are transformed with a kiss into princes, and she jokingly asks Quenyn if perhaps he is under some sort of enchantment (*D with D* 626). Lacking the good looks to win Daenerys, Quentyn hopes that his distant blood connection to the Targaryens will at least help him to tame one of her dragons. He assures his companions that he can trace his bloodline back to her family. His companion Gerris is unimpressed: "Fuck your lineage.... The dragons won't care about your dragon blood, except maybe how it tastes" (*D with D* 870). Quentyn, who clearly has not inherited the blood of the dragon even with his link to the Targaryens, is fatally burned in his failed attempt to bring one of Daenerys's dragons to submission. He possesses neither bloodline nor prowess sufficient to warrant a claim to the Iron Throne.

Just as good looks and prowess are not guaranteed traits for the nobly born, birthright does not necessarily correlate with wealth. For example, the fabliau *Du Chevalier qui fist les cons parler* (The Knight Who Made Vaginas Talk) begins with an account of a poor knight who is trying to regain his lost status. Similarly, another fabliau, *D'Estormi* is about "un preudhomme, qui devint/ Povres entre lui et sa fame" (a knight who, along with his wife, became poor). In some tales, the characters attempt to re-establish wealth by marrying their children to rich bourgeois who have bought land and title. This is the case in *Du Jouglet* (The Minstrel) in which a poor knight marries his daughter to the son of a rich peasant woman. The bridegroom, eager to please his nobly born bride, falls victim to the trickery of a clever jongleur. Such marital arrangements threaten to dilute the noble bloodline and, in the fabliau, lead to disastrous, albeit comical, results.

In Martin's novels, Jon Connington is one of Martin's poor knights; though from a well-esteemed noble family, he has lost both wealth and title. After the death of the Mad King and the subsequent Baratheon usurpation of the throne, Connington, the former Hand of the Mad King and companion to Aerys Targaryen, is forced into exile and poverty. While in exile, he agrees to assume the role of Griff in order to protect the identity of Aerys's son, Prince Aegon Targaryen, who is himself *incognitio* as Young Griff. He also agrees to accept the false rumor that he has died through drunkenness. In *A Dance with Dragons*, Connington tries to regain his status through his support of Prince Aegon and, if he were not stricken with grayscale, possibly through marriage. Still, he regrets the mistakes of his past that led to his downfall. He sees himself as guilty of overreaching: "*I rose too high, loved too hard, dared too much ... and fell*" (*D with D* 879).

Whereas Connington has some good qualities, another knight who loses status, Ser Dontos Hollard, has few redeeming traits. He is the last surviving member of a noble family that fell in status. When his family participated in the Duskendale Rebellion and were stripped of wealth and title and subsequently extinguished, only Ser Dontos was spared. He was sent to King's Landing to serve as squire. His personal descent mirrors the lost status of his family: Ser Dontos is a drunk. When Sansa convinces King Joffrey to spare his life, Dontos is demoted to court fool. Soon after, Sansa receives an anonymous message promising to help her escape from King's Landing, and she dreams that "a true knight" has composed it (*C of K* 280). Instead, she learns that the drunken, disenfranchised Ser Dontos, whose life she saved, is her rescuer. He swears "upon his honor as a knight" that he will protect her (*C of K* 284). He reminds her, "I was a knight once," and she consoles herself, remembering that he has sworn an oath to the gods that cannot be broken (*C of K* 285). With no other resources, she reluctantly agrees to let him help her, but during the rescue, he is killed by Littlefinger, the real mastermind behind the escape.

Dontos' social descent results from his family's fall in fortune and his own degeneracy. However, in Martin's novels, even some of the highest ranking and wealthiest families, including the Lannisters and the Tyrells, are depraved. These families are responsible for many of the brutalities in Westeros, which are performed either by their hands or at their command. The Targaryens have a reputation for cruel acts and insanity, the latter likely resulting from intermarriage in their attempts to preserve their bloodline. When King Aerys Targaryen, the Mad King, threatens both the kingdom and the Lannister family, Jaime Lannister slays him even though Jaime serves as a member of the Kingsguard and as Aerys's sworn protector. Jaime is reviled for this act although he has good reason to rid the kingdom of a dangerous ruler.

Jaime is also initially reviled by Martin's readers who see him hurling Bran Stark out a window in the opening chapters of *A Game of Thrones*. He has a reputation for cruelty and ruthlessness. Although Jaime seems on the road to redemption in the novels, his early behavior and attitude call to question the assumption that birthright and virtue go hand in hand. Aegon Targaryen (Young Griff) cites Jaime as an example when justifying his advancement of the lowly Duck. Griff argues that Jaime is a well-respected warrior and from one of the wealthiest and most noble families in Westeros, yet he does not possess virtue (*D with D* 889). Similarly, Jaime's twin sister Cersei, whose beauty is frequently touted, is depicted as one of Martin's cruelest and most manipulative characters. Thus, Martin shows that it is possible to be both corrupt and noble, although corruption is not compatible with the idealized notion of *franchise* as depicted in romance.

The knights of fabliau share a similar lack of virtue with these Westerosi nobles. In the fabliau, their corruption typically manifests in drunkenness (like Ser Dontos) or a lascivious nature. Frequently, the bad behavior of the fabliau knight leads to his social fall. For example, the poorly behaved knight in *Du Chevalier qui fist les cons parler* (The Knight Who Made Vaginas Talk) has squandered his money and lost his reputation. Unlike Marie de France's Lanval who loses his wealth by placing too much emphasis on the courtly virtue of generosity, this fabliau knight is simply a drunk, and the narrative implies that he has lost his money through wastefulness and sloth. The crude escapades in which he finds himself (acquiring and then taking advantage of the ability to make female genitalia speak) are indicative of his fallen status.

Although the fabliau depict nobility who "deserve" their social descent, Westerosi nobility might lose wealth and title for reasons other than corruption or bad behavior. Loss of wealth does not necessarily correlate with loss of virtue. This is the situation with the demotion of Ser Barristan Selmy. The epitome of chivalry, he is renowned for his service to the royalty (both Targaryen and Baratheon). He is an esteemed member of the Kingsguard and a famous war hero. Possibly more than any of Martin's characters, he upholds the aspects of chivalry that are portrayed in medieval romance: loyalty, courage, honor, mercy. Nonetheless, Ser Barristan is asked to step down from his position as Kingsguard, a move intended to allow King Joffrey to advance Sandor Clegane, The Hound, in his place. King Joffrey cites old age as the reason for the replacement. Ser Barristan is advanced in age, but certainly still capable. He escapes from King's Landing and chooses self-exile, crossing the Narrow Sea to support and eventually become the primary advisor of Daenerys Targaryen.

Just as the Kingsguard is in decline, so, too, is the Night's Watch, traditionally composed of nobly born knights. Over time, the threat beyond the Wall diminished (or so the Westerosi believe) to the point that Martin's characters frequently deny the existence of any threat at all. Thus, most of the Westerosi no longer consider this duty to be honorable, and so the Night's Watch must recruit criminals, bastards, and other social misfits. Those in the current Night's Watch, whether of noble blood or lowly smallfolk, are all to become equal through their vows. Still, despite their vows and despite the fact that they serve the kingdom at large and take no parts in the wars of Westeros, the men of the Night's Watch are not exempt from valuing noble blood. A hierarchy is present at the Watch, and bloodline is a major factor. For instance, when Samwell Tarly tries to negotiate with Cotter Pyke and Ser Denys about their opposition against each other to run for Lord Commander, Ser Denys explains that he is more worthy of the position because of his birthright (*S of S* 1084). Ser Denys later agrees to support Jon Snow, primarily because Jon, although a bastard, has noble Stark blood. From his first moment at the Watch, Jon is set apart by his heritage. Even though he serves no king and is not technically a knight, Jon is clearly a chivalric hero, arguably *the* chivalric hero, of Martin's works. In the HBO series, Martin has made clear that Jon has a noble birthright as the son of Rhaegar Targaryen. Like Percival, he has no idea of this heritage, but the HBO series strongly hints that he will discover it and claim it.

For the Wildlings who live beyond the Wall, *franchise* is an alien concept. When Stannis Baratheon occupies the Wall, he brings to it many of the assumptions and traditions of Westeros concerning *franchise*, and he wrongly believes that these Westerosi values will apply to the Wildlings. Thus, Mance Rayder, the so-called "King-Beyond-the-Wall," is treated as if he truly were of noble birth. Stannis's wife, Queen Selyse, naively believes the same of Mance's self-proclaimed successor, Gerrick of House Redbeard. Once he is donned in the attire of the Westerosi, Gerrick undeniably possesses the good looks associated with *franchise*. Jon sees him and marvels that, cleaned up and clothed in finery, the handsome Gerrick looks "every inch a southron lord" who could easily assimilate with the nobility at King's Landing (*D with D* 986).

While Jon admires Gerrick's noble appearance, he is skeptical about whether the Wildlings will follow Gerrick. He cannot explain to Queen Selyse that *franchise* is meaningless to most Wildlings. Gerrick's ancestry matters to them "as much as being descended from Raymun Redbeard's horse" (*D with D* 987). Jon recalls Mance's advice about the loyalty of Wildlings, which is entirely independent of *franchise*. He tries to warn Stannis that the Wild-lings will be unimpressed by money, position, or family inheritance: "They follow strength. They follow the man" (*D with D* 301). Nevertheless, Stannis, his queen, and his priestess do not heed Jon's warning and persist in their beliefs that bloodline is important to the leadership of the Wildlings.

Insisting upon the importance of *franchise*, Queen Selyse makes an effort to establish Gerrick's bloodline, declaring him the king of the Wildlings and arguing for his legitimacy through "an unbroken line" that can be traced back to the esteemed king Raymun Redbeard (*D with D* 987). Mance Rayder, on the other hand, is cast as a usurper whose mother was of common blood and whose father was a man of the Watch (*D with D* 987). Queen Selyse tries to arrange a marriage between one of Gerrick's daughters and Ser Axell. Gerrick himself fosters this idea of having descended from Wildling nobility. He claims, when he offers his daughters to Jon Snow, that they can offer their new husbands "sons of royal blood," and he boasts of their descendancy from Raymun Redbeard (D with D 850). Another proposed marriage between Westerosi nobility and Wildlings is Jon's arrangement for Alys Karstark to marry the near-barbaric Magnar of Thenn. Although the Thenns do have laws and a social hierarchy, the discrepancy is obvious between the highborn Kar-stark and her Wildling husband, the newly stylized Lord of Thenn and pos-sibly future Lord of Karstark. If Magnar (and other Wildlings who intermarry with Westerosi) does become a lord, social divisions and bloodline will surely be further problematized beyond the Wall.

True Knights and Tainted Blood in Westeros

Social mobility complicates the social divisions of Westeros. However, bloodline remains a key attribute of chivalry. Some Westerosi, including Bran in the early novels, still cling to the possibility of knightly perfection. In the first novel, when Robb hosts the lords of the North, Bran questions Maester Luwin about how many knights will attend. Maester Luwin is bothered that Bran holds knights in such esteem. He tries to explain that, even though the men of the North are not technically knights, they can possess chivalric attrib-utes. He describes to Bran the process by which one becomes a knight, such as holding vigil in a sept and being anointed with oils to sanctify knightly oaths. Since most of the men of the North do not worship the Seven, they cannot take part in this ceremony. However, they are still capable of chivalry; the Maester insists that they "are no less fierce or loyal or honorable" than actual knights and that this ceremony does not necessarily indicate a man's worth. Bran nonetheless clings to his idealistic notions of "true knights" and once again asks the Maester, "How many knights?" (*G of T* 570).

When Catelyn warns the young knights of Renly's court that "winter is coming" and war is imminent, Brienne of Tarth adheres to her own idealized view of chivalry. She insists that, for those who hold true to chivalric ideals, winter "will never come" (*C of K* 350). Even if she were to die in battle, she will live on through songs, in which "all knights are gallant" (*C of K* 350). Brienne herself aspires to live up to chivalric ideals even though, as a woman, she is a most unconventional knight. Regardless of Brienne's determination to maintain personal honor and in spite of her visions of glorified visions of chivalry, the institution of knighthood in Westeros, including the once highly regarded Kingsguard, is in decline. Ser Barristan Selmy's self-exile seems symbolic of this decline as does the appointment of non-nobles such as The Hound, who is not even a knight. The Lannisters stack the Kingsguard with those believed to be loyal rather than those possessing *franchise*, a move that leads the Kingsguard to further decline.

The decline of the Kingsguard seems to be increasingly rapid in Martin's later novels, even though Jaime Lannister recommits himself in earnest after losing his sword hand.[27] When Jaime leaves King's Landing to restore peace elsewhere in Westeros, his twin sister begins to control the composition of the Kingsguard. In Jaime's absence, Cersei fills vacant positions with those she finds easily controlled rather than with those who are most worthy and of the best lineage, as was the tradition of old. Her brother Tyrion approves of the addition of Ser Balon Swann, who is from a noble family and is renowned for both courtesy and skill at arms. Tyrion believes that he will "serve with honor and courage" (*C of K* 714). However, he has doubts about the addition of Ser Osmund Kettleblack, who "looked formidable enough," but was "lowborn, no more than a hedge knight" (*C of K* 714). Tyrion believes that Cersei made this appointment simply so Ser Osmund would be indebted to her and do her bidding.

When Jaime returns, Jaime, too, has his doubts about this addition. He questions Ser Osmund about his worthiness for the position. He accuses him of being a sellsword and asks him who knighted him. When Ser Robert attributes his knighthood to a certain Ser Robert Stone, Jaime points out that this surname indicates a bastard birth or, worse yet, a complete fabrication. He asks himself, "*What was Cersei thinking when she gave this one a white cloak?*" (*S of S* 920)

The Kettleblack family have bought into the knightly class and do not rank high enough to justify an appointment to the esteemed Kingsguard, but they serve, at least temporarily, as Cersei's pawns.

Cersei's motives are themselves desperate as she knows her illegitimate children have no right to the Iron Throne. Bloodline is key for royalty, and she goes to great lengths to prove that her children are the offspring of King Robert and possess the proper bloodline to inherit the throne. Nonetheless, rumors of incest have spread across the kingdom. Joffrey's questionable lineage threatens all of Westeros and causes a frantic battle for who should rightfully sit on the Iron Throne. Even if Joffrey were a Baratheon, his right to the Iron Throne would be questionable as Robert himself usurped the throne from the Targaryens.

The youngest Baratheon brother, Renly, questions his oldest brother's right to the crown and has serious doubts about whether his second oldest brother, Stannis, would succeed as king. Renly explains to Catelyn that Stannis would make a terrible king not only because of his personality flaws, but also because the Baratheons do not truly possess the bloodline requisite for the Iron Throne (*C of K* 352). Neither Renly nor Stannis is the true heir to the throne because Robert, the oldest brother, took the throne by force. Martin seems to imply that, as far as who rules Westeros, conquest is ultimately more important than lineage. Even the Targaryen family gained the throne through conquest. Still, it is critical that those in power establish their bloodline. The Targaryens traditionally intermarried, a move that secured the Iron Throne through bloodline, and yet also likely led to madness. After three hundred years of rule, the remaining members of the Targaryen dynasty firmly believe their bloodline entitles them to the crown. Daenerys repeatedly makes this claim as she gathers forces in Essos to take back the Iron Throne.

In *A Dance with Dragons*, Martin introduces another Targaryen claimant to the throne, Aegon Targaryen. Aegon's ascendency, if, in fact, "Young Griff" is the real Aegon and not an imposter, may have been predicted by prophecy. His father Rhaegar believed his son to be "the prince who was promised." However, prophecy alone will not guarantee his acceptance. Valerie Estelle Frankel questions his legitimacy. She notes the "emphasis on his upbringing rather than his birthright" which "suggests Aegon has been trained for kingship, not simply bred for it."[28] The Westerosi are unlikely to believe that Aegon, who was reportedly killed as an infant, is legitimate. This training may serve him well towards gaining acceptance even if he is proven to be legitimate. Not unlike the young King Arthur whose own birthright, in many versions, is initially questioned, Aegon will have to verify his birthright before the people of Westeros accept him. Even with his Targaryen-like features, he will have to prove himself.

For regional rulers within Westeros, keeping a noble bloodline is critical and is a factor in marital alliances. Robb Stark, King of the North, not only breaks a vital marital pact with the Freys, but also chooses as his bride Jeyne Westerling, who is from a family of questionable blood. When the Lannisters learn of this marriage, they are dismayed. Ser Kevan Lannister comments,

"But with such doubtful blood..." (*S of S* 271). Tyrion is less judgmental having formerly been married to a peasant. He argues that the Westerlings are of sufficient bloodline, yet concedes that they have "more pride than power" (*S of S* 271). The Westerling lineage is not of sufficient worth to merit an alliance with Robb Stark, particularly in a political climate that necessitates a Stark alliance with the Freys.

The most "doubtful blood" in Westeros, however, belongs to bastards, particularly when one of the parents is low born. Catelyn Stark tells Roose Bolton that Roose's son Ramsay, a bastard begotten on a peasant girl, has tainted blood. Bolton agrees that his son's bastard blood is tainted (*S of S* 683). Nevertheless, when he needs an heir, Roose has Ramsay legitimized by the crown, another way that non-nobles and half-nobles might infiltrate the noble class. Ramsay thus becomes a Bolton (bastards are not allowed to take their father's names unless they are legitimized). However, Ramsay's behavior worries his father. Roose has appealed to King Joffrey to legitimize Ramsay as a Bolton and urges his son to "Try and act like one" (*D with D* 467). He cautions Ramsay against the rumors that are spreading about his heinous acts. When Ramsay responds that he is glad people fear him, his father corrects him. He tries to emphasize the importance of discretion, telling him that he can best succeed if he follows his father's footsteps by fostering "a peaceful land" and "a quiet people" (*D with D* 467). One of the more despicable characters of Westeros, Ramsay seems incapable of learning his father's lessons.

Initially, Ramsay seems desperate to prove his worth to his father and to the Lannisters. His desperation leads him to commit atrocities that shock even his father, the cold-hearted patriarch of a house that flaunts as its sigil the image of a flayed man. Justifiably or not, the assumption among Ramsay's detractors is that his bastard blood is a contributor to his egregious behavior. In an attempt to secure Winterfell, the Boltons seek to convince the North that Ramsay has married Arya Stark. An alliance between the Starks and Boltons would enhance the Bolton bloodline and ensure the loyalty of the North. The Boltons are so desperate for this alliance that, when Arya Stark cannot be located, they bring in an imposter bride to pose as Arya. The unfortunate Jeyne Poole is forced to pretend she is the younger Stark daughter so that the Boltons can bolster their claim to Winterfell.[29]

True, Ramsay is vile, but Catelyn Stark is wrong to assume that all bastards are so because their blood is tainted. Catelyn has personal reasons for her strong feelings against bastards. Soon after her marriage to Ned Stark, her husband brought home, and expected her to raise, Jon Snow, his supposed bastard son. Blind to Jon's many virtues, Catelyn resents him and insists that his blood is tainted. When they believe the other male Stark children are dead, Robb tries to convince Catelyn that Jon should be his heir, reminding her that his father has given birth to four male children. Robb's reasoning falls on deaf ears; Catelyn won't entertain the possibility of Jon becoming heir of Winterfell. She responds, "A Snow is not a Stark" (*S of S* 628). Before Robb leaves for the wedding, however, he has his men witness and fix their seals to a document naming Jon as his successor (*S of S* 636).

Jon is painfully aware of his status as a bastard. At Castle Black, he contemplates how this status, along with his stint with the Wildlings, will affect his reputation. He has lived with the stigma of being a bastard, believed to be born "from lust and lies" and to have "treacherous natures" (*S of S* 1011). He has tried hard to overcome this stigma and prove himself a worthy son to his father, but now, he fears that he will be remembered as "a turncloak, an oathbreaker, and a murderer" if he is remembered at all (*S of S* 1011). Jon recalls his childhood dream of becoming Lord of Winterfell and the realization that his uncertain birth will prevent this dream from materializing. He remembers a role-playing game in which Robb dashed his hopes by reminding him that, as a bastard, he can never inherit Winterfell (*S of S* 1088).

When Stannis offers to marry Jon to Val (Mance Rayder's widow) and make his childhood dream a reality, Jon is tempted by this chance at legitimacy. Ultimately, he decides that the price to assume this position is too great. In order to become Lord of Winterfell, Jon would have to forsake his vows to the Night's Watch and disavow the Old Gods his father worshipped and "feed ... the red woman's hungry fire god" (*S of S* 1089). He feels that this betrayal to his family, his home, and the old gods is too great. Jon's loyalty to his family and his adherence to his vows are qualities that indicate his worthiness in spite of his illegitimacy.

One popular theory of fans confirmed by the HBO series is that Jon is half Targaryen. If Martin's novels hold true to the television series, the novels, too, will reveal that Jon's mother is Lyanna Stark and his father, Rhaegar Targaryen. If so, Jon remains a bastard, but one of royal birth. Additionally, some fans predict that Jon will emerge not only as Lord of Winterfell and King of the North, but possibly as Azor Ahai, the legendary "prince who was promised." This hero, as the legend goes, saved Westeros from a period of great darkness. In the tradition of Arthur, "once and future king," some Westerosi believe a prophecy that Azor Ahai will rise again, this time to fight the Others.

Melisandre, the red priestess, originally believes that Stannis Baratheon is Azor Ahai. Stannis, under her guidance, understands that *franchise* is the key to the Iron Throne and might help establish his identity as Azor Ahai. For him, blood becomes a sort of Grail, as Melisandre convinces him that she needs king's blood to perform her magic and lead him to power. She holds Edric Storm, bastard of King Robert Baratheon, as hostage for this reason, though Ser Davos helps him escape before he can be sacrificed. Later, when Melisandre is at the Wall, Jon realizes that Maester Aemon, a Targaryen, and Mance Rayder's newborn son might also be at risk because of their blood-lines (or supposed bloodlines, in the case of Rayder's infant). Jon is frightened for them and wonders if Melisandre will need their blood for her sacrifices (*F for C* 116). Thus, Jon rescues Mance Rayder's son from Melisandre's fires by switching him with the Wildling Gilly's baby. He then arranges for the old Maester and the infant to leave Castle Black (*D with D* 105).

Later, Asha Greyjoy is in similar danger when Stannis captures her. One of Stannis's men, Suggs, predicts Asha's fate at the hands of Melisandre. As the daughter of Lord Balon Greyjoy who rules the Iron Islands, Asha's royal blood may be deemed valuable to Melisandre and doom Asha to death by fire (*D with D* 896).[30] Melisandre is misguided in her attempt to conjure a crown for Stannis through king's blood. She hints at her realization of this error when she claims that repeatedly she sees Jon Snow, not Stannis, in her magical fires. Again, if the novels follow the HBO series, which is ahead on this storyline, she will realize her errors and revive Jon from death at the hand of his own men. Perhaps, as some fans predict, she will even see Jon emerge as the prince who was promised. Jon's bloodline certainly seems to be an essential key to Martin's novels and evidences the significance of blood to the battle for the Iron Throne.

In conclusion, *franchise* is highly valued in Westeros but not generally necessary for some degree of social advancement. Thus, characters such as Ser Davos, Bronn, and Littlefinger all are elevated socially, yet their advance-ment is clearly depicted as atypical. Martin vividly depicts the complexities of *franchise* as these characters struggle to validate their newly attained posi-tions and prove their worth despite illegitimacy, exile, or low birth. Westerosi *franchise* is equally problematic for the noble born. In fact, much of the nar-rative tension stems from noble characters' attempts to validate their blood-line. Young King Arthur proves his legitimacy by pulling a sword from a stone and must later solicit further confirmation from his mother as final assurance of his right. Likewise, all of those competing for the Iron Throne must validate their ancestry and legitimacy. The crown is repeatedly threatened by issues involving bloodline: the illegitimacy of the Barathion children; the exile of the surviving Targaryens; the lack of charisma despite bloodline for Stannis Baratheon; and the unknown heritage of Jon Snow, whom many fans believe may ultimately inherit the throne. Thus, the complex brand of chivalry in Martin's novels, and the ultimate outcome of the series, largely hinges upon *franchise*.

Five

Loyalty

"All that Brienne wanted was to die for him."—S of S 925

Loyalty in Chivalric Literature

In both heroic and chivalric literature, statements of loyalty are affirmed through oaths and vows.[1] The medieval feudal system depended on loyalty to lord and kingdom, and vows and oaths were assurances of that loyalty. The system worked reciprocally: thanes would serve their lords in return for honor and land. Nigel Saul explains "the validity of a promise given on oath" by describing oath-making as "a contract." He adds that, "if a knight broke a promise made on oath, his name would be dishonoured, and his honour was the quality which he cherished most in the world."[2] Thus, the reputations of knights were dependent on holding true to their oaths. Martin has a long legacy of literary portrayals of loyalty which his novels parallel. While prevalent in chivalric literature, the concept of loyalty to one's lord precedes the chivalric code and is also essential to the heroic code (and certainly other warrior codes which are beyond the scope of this discussion). For example, Beowulf's loyalty to his lord Hygelac and, while in Hrothgar's court, to Hrothgar are important aspects of understanding Beowulf's brand of heroism. Though Hrothgar's retainer Unferth accuses Beowulf of *ofermod* (excessive boasting), Beowulf's vow to avenge Hrothgar's court after Grendel's heinous acts is foremost an act of loyalty. He does so in homage to his father (familial loyalty), for whom Hrothgar has done a favor, and also in homage to Hygelac, on whom he bestows many of the treasures that are rewards for his successful slaying of Grendel and Grendel's mother.

This theme of loyalty continues as Beowulf himself becomes king. In his old age, he faces a dragon alone with only one loyal thane, Wiglaf, who is willing to assist him. Beowulf has vowed to fight the dragon single-handedly.

Nevertheless, his men, who have sworn service to him, have a duty to assist him when the fight turns sour. With no consideration of their vows of loyalty to Beowulf, they do not render aid to him in this battle, and Beowulf, although he manages to kill the dragon with Wiglaf's help, is himself killed. The cowardice of these men is a serious offense, but more so is the breaking of their vows to serve Beowulf. Wiglaf strongly chastises them: "Wergendra to lyt/ þrong ymbe þeoden, þa hyne sio þrag becwom" (Not enough men rallied around him when he needed them most).[3] Wiglaf's indictment of their cowardice makes clear that the Geats will not long survive without an effective lord and loyal followers.

The Anglo-Saxon elegy "The Wanderer" emphasizes the significance of the close bonds between a warrior, his companions, and his lord. Exiled at sea after the death of his lord, the narrator mourns his loss of companionship: "Wat se þe cunnað/hu sliþen bið sorg to geferan/þam þe him lyft hafað leofra geholena" (He who has experience knows how sorrow is a cruel companion to one who has few beloved friends).[4] These bonds of loyalty are critical to the narrator's sense of well-being. Another Anglo-Saxon poem, the heroic poem "The Battle of Maldon," comments on the dire consequences of breaches in loyalty. Some warriors flee after Byrtnoth, their leader, is killed rather than continuing to fight for the cause and on behalf of their lord's memory. The fact that these deserters use Byrtnoth's own horse to leave the battle scene makes their act of cowardice even more egregious: many men in the field wrongly believe that Byrtnoth himself has fled, and so they follow suit. Those who remain and fight in the face of the death of their lord show loyalty not only to Byrtnoth, but also to England as a whole, extending the concept of oaths and vows beyond duty to an individual king or lord to a duty towards the kingdom itself.

Loyalty evolves into an important element of the chivalric code, evidenced in the romances of Chrétien de Troyes. It remains generally unchanged from the earlier heroic works, with the added, and often contradictory, requirement of loyalty to lady. In Chrétien's first romance, "Erec and Enide," the titular hero is torn between love for his new wife and his duties on the battlefield. Erec spends excessive amounts of time with his bride, and she chastises him for his subsequent loss of reputation. Thus, he sets out to reestablish his worth on the battlefield. His loyalty to his lady has occupied too much of Erec's attention, so he must reaffirm his commitment to serve the kingdom by engaging in battle. In "Yvain," the hero finds himself in the opposite situation: caught up in adventures, he fails to return to his lady at a designated time and thus must reestablish his loyalty to her. And in "The Knight of the Cart," the hero has a momentary struggle between the courtly requirement of demonstrating unquestioning loyalty to his lady (Guinevere) and a brief thought about his own honor. He hesitates for two steps before accepting a ride in a cart, a humiliating prospect but his only method of transportation. Lancelot is later chastised for this moment of hesitation, having broken the dictate of courtly love that "every act of a lover ends in the thought of his beloved."[5]

The unknown 14th century author of *Sir Gawain and the Green Knight*, frequently referred to as the Pearl poet, emphasizes the impossibility of living up to the chivalric ideal because of conflicting loyalties. In this work, Gawain struggles to balance loyalty to his king and to his host, courtesy to women, and godliness; all requisite to the courtly code yet impossible for the hero to reconcile. As he travels to his appointment with the Green Knight who has challenged Arthur's court, Gawain is offered lodging. He agrees to play a game with his host, yet this game is not merely play. Each evening before the game, Gawain makes a vow that he will honor the wishes of his host and adhere to the rules of the game, which entail an exchange of winnings. The host goes out hunting while Gawain stays at the castle, and at the end of the day, the two exchange what they have won. Gawain is aghast when the lady of the castle enters his bedroom and attempts to seduce him. If he were to succumb to her, he not only would find himself in an awkward situation when the lord of the castle asks for the exchange, but he would also have betrayed his host and committed a sin.

On the first two days in which the lady enters his room, Gawain chooses his words carefully to frame a defense that will not offend her. However, on the third day that the lady of the castle tempts him, he finds himself at an impasse. The Pearl Poet spells out his dilemma:

> For þat prynces of pris depresed hym so þikke
> Nurned hym so neʒe þe þred þat nede hym bihoued
> oþer lach þer hir luf oþer lodly refuse
> He cared for his cortaysye lest craþayn he were
> & more for his meschef ʒif he schulde make synne
> he traytor to þat tolke þat þat telde aʒt

> (For that worthy princess pressed him so hard,
> urged him so near his limitations, that he must necessarily
> either take her love or blatantly refuse.
> He was concerned about courtesy lest he appear brash
> and more so for misfortune if he should sin
> and become traitor to the lord that owned the house.)[6]

He cannot simultaneously obey the lady's wishes, honor his vows to his host, and be dutiful to God. He successfully resists the temptation of the lady but accepts her offer of a gift: a girdle that supposedly has magical protective qualities. By accepting her girdle and not relinquishing it to his host, he breaks his vow to exchange all winnings and commits a breach in loyalty. Consequently, Gawain returns to Arthur's court deeming himself a failure at chivalry, and he wears the girdle as a baldric of shame. That Arthur and the rest of the court do not acknowledge Gawain's failure shows, according to Nigel Saul, "the ambivalence at the heart of chivalry itself." Saul explains that "The issue raised is the eternal one of conflict between an idealized code and the limitations of the humans who live by it."[7] In other words, Gawain finds himself in a situation that makes true loyalty (to God, lord, host, and lady) an impossibility.

Loyalty in Malory's *Le Morte Darthur* even more closely resembles Martin's portrayal of loyalty. Like Malory, Martin explores the difficulties of upholding the chivalric code when conflicts in loyalty arise. Written in the fifteenth century, *Le Morte Darthur* has long been recognized as portraying the complications of the chivalric code as it existed in the later Middle Ages. Malory's work can, in its entirety, be seen as a commentary on the ambiguities of the chivalric code as characters including Balin, Gawain, Lancelot, and even Arthur himself, struggle to uphold the chivalric ideal of loyalty.

Chivalry becomes complicated in Malory's work as knights try to balance often conflicting loyalties to kingdom, king, God, lady, and family. The problems of balancing loyalties are hinted at early in Malory's work with the adventures of the unfortunate Balin. Although Balin meets his initial challenge of drawing a sword and successfully proving his worth, his subsequent adventures result in tragedy. As with other Arthurian knights who win swords, including Arthur himself, Balin chooses to keep the sword that he alone has been able to draw, but in doing so, he displeases the damsel from whom he has won it. Soon after, Balin must choose between settling a blood feud with the Lady of the Lake and honoring Arthur's safe conduct laws. He chooses to settle the blood feud by beheading the Lady, but in the process, he displeases Arthur. Balin is thus torn between loyalty to his family member, whom he feels he must avenge, and loyalty to his king, Arthur.[8] Though not articulated in the Round Table Oath, personal and familial honor are both important aspects of chivalry, and both are at stake for Balin in these initial challenges. These are important elements of chivalry that motivate Balin in his actions. He later tries to make amends with Arthur, and successfully does so, by defeating King Roins. Nonetheless, Balin can not, in the moment he decides to slay the Lady of the Lake, simultaneously show loyalty to both king and kin.

Balin's difficulty with chivalry seems to foreshadow those of Malory's other knights. Lancelot's struggle is the most notable, as he attempts to juggle loyalty to God, king, and lady. He finds that maintaining these loyalties is impossible, however, as his lady is his king's wife, and adultery is an offense to both king and God. Malory's Gawain also struggles with loyalty. In this case, familial loyalty and loyalty to his Round Table companion Lancelot are in direct competition. When Lancelot is accused of adultery with the queen, Gawain initially defends him, even justifying his killing of two of Gawain's brothers and his son. When Gawain refuses to escort Guinevere to the fire for her crimes, Arthur commands Gawain's favorite brothers, Gareth and Gaheris, to do this duty. These knights are young and cannot refuse this command, but they refuse to wear armor in protest.

Lancelot accidentally kills Gareth and Gaheris while trying to rescue Guinevere. This incident sets Gawain on a course of vengeance. He puts his family's honor over this relationship with Lancelot, and over the welfare of the kingdom as a whole, causing it to be divided. Arthur urges Gawain to make amends with Lancelot, but his efforts are to no avail. Arthur himself must struggle with loyalty to his kingdom and to his queen. Thus, he initially turns a blind eye to Guinevere's adultery, though he long suspects it. He does so for the good of the kingdom. Once the affair is exposed, however, he chooses loyalty to the kingdom, noting that queens can easily be replaced, but the Round Table cannot. By choosing the Round Table knights over his queen, Arthur demonstrates that his primary loyalty is to the kingdom, not to his lady.

The Round Table knights of Malory's work take an annual Pentecostal Oath that ensures their loyalty to king and kingdom. Prefacing the Oath is a statement of political intent: "the kynge stablysshed all the knyghtes and gaff them rychesse and londys."[9] In exchange for lands, Arthur requires loyalty, and he expects the knights who serve him to uphold a code of conduct that will enhance his own reputation as ruler. Although the entire code of chivalry is scattered throughout Malory's work, this Oath spells out many of the more important aspects of chivalry and clearly links them to duty and loyalty. Robert L. Kelly argues that the Pentecostal Oath emphasizes the establishment of Arthur as king and ensures the loyalty of his knights: "Malory replaces the ties of brotherhood emphasized both in the *Suite* and in the statutes of the Garter with a bond modeled upon the actual life of the royal court, namely the bond between the king as patron and his chief nobles as clients."[10] Kelly sees the Oath as "an instrument of rule, through which a kingly patron recruits noble retainers to serve the specific, chiefly military, needs of his reign."[11] The annual renewal of the Pentecostal Oath serves as a kind of contract, a reminder of the knights' commitment to Arthur and his kingdom. The renewal of this contract is necessary because of the numerous challenges to loyalty that confront Arthur's knights, such as the challenge that ensues after the deaths of Gareth and Gaheris. Gawain's refusal to make amends with Lancelot after these deaths severs the bonds of brotherhood upon which Arthur depends.

Conflicts of Loyalty

The medieval texts discussed above all highlight the significance of loyalty and the challenges of maintaining it. Martin's novels offer equally interesting wrinkles in the difficulties of balancing conflicting loyalties and holding true to oaths and vows. For both Martin and Malory, the entirety of the chivalric code is revealed in the actions and struggles of their characters. For both, much of the narrative tension stems from characters' attempts to adhere to, or defy, chivalric values. Like medieval writers, Martin uses his characters "as vehicle[s] for the exploration of the conflicts and dilemmas inherent in the knightly ideal itself."[12] Martin emphasizes the significance of oaths by beginning *A Game of Thrones* with an encounter that leads a man of the Night's Watch to break his oath and abandon his duty. The oath breaker, though fleeing for his life from white walkers, is beheaded for his breach of loyalty. This theme of maintaining loyalty against great odds continues throughout the series. Among Martin's characters who face serious dilemmas of loyalty are Jaime Lannister, Jon Snow, Brienne of Tarth, Ser Davos Seaworth, and Ser Jorah Mormont. Each of these characters offers insight into the difficulties of holding true to vows and balancing loyalties.

Martin's Kingsguard is in many ways a reflection of Malory's Round Table knights, and they face similar kinds of conflicts. Like the Round Table knights, the white swords of the Kingsguard swear oaths of loyalty to king and country. For the men of the Kingsguard, loyalty to king takes precedence over all other aspects of chivalry. The Kingsguard are "the royal bodyguards of the Iron Throne" who are "sworn to protect their king and the royal family with their own lives, to obey his commands, and to keep his secrets." A longstanding tradition in Westeros, the Kingsguard was "Historically composed of seven knights sworn to a lifetime of service."[13] Originally, they consisted of the finest knights in Westeros, and they are expected to uphold the ideals of chivalry and to demonstrate unfailing loyalty to king. In the present tense of Martin's novels, however, the Kingsguard is composed of some knights of questionable morality and lineage who are selected simply because the Lannisters find them loyal.

In *The World of Ice and Fire*, Martin describes the origins of the Kingsguard. He traces its inception to Visenya who determined that the Kingsguard would be comprised of seven champions to represent each of the Seven Kingdoms. She also determined that their vows would be based upon those of the Night's Watch, requiring that they forgo marriage and inheritance so that they can dutifully serve.[14] The deeds of the original members of the Kingsguard are recorded in a chronicle called the White Book which serves as a model of chivalry for subsequent generations in the order. Ser Barristan Selmy, before he is banished from King's Landing, recalls the White Book and its original intention. According to his account, the men of the Kingsguard varied greatly according to bravery, integrity, and strength. Some were exceptional for their skills and virtues, but others succumbed to human frailties such as greed and lust. The best of them died while holding true to their duties. The worst, he maintains, were *"those who played the game of thrones"* (*D with D* 804). Selmy notes that the White Book is not merely a collection of glorified tales. Rather, it provides a compendium of both successes and failures that serve as models for the present Kingsguard.

Martin's characters look to the Westerosi past through literary works such as The White Book and through oral history for idealized models of chivalry. The Westerosi frequently acknowledge the imperfections of knighthood in the present as contrasted to this glorified past. In this respect, Martin mirrors some Arthurian romances that refer to a Golden Age in contrast to the corrupt and inglorious present. In Caxton's preface to Malory's *Le Morte Darthur*, Caxton expresses his intent for his readers to use Malory's text as an example and to strive to emulate the Arthurian past. He asks that his readers "take the good and honest actes in their remembraunce, and to folowe the same."[15] Like Malory himself, Caxton implies that contemporary knighthood is in decline. Similarly, Westerosi characters tend to be nostalgic about the past. For instance, Eddard Stark recalls the glorified past when his son Bran asks him if the knights of the Kingsguard are "truly the finest." His father responds, "No longer … but once they were a marvel, a shining lesson to the world" (*C of K* 332).

Members of the Kingsguard may not embody knightly ideals, but they are expected to aspire to them. Few, however, succeed. Varys praises Ser Mandon, a member of the Kingsguard, for possessing the perfect attributes of the Order. Loyalty is foremost among them. He explains that the white swords should be selfless, living only to serve their king. He holds up Ser Mandon as an exemplary white knight who died in defense of the royal family. But Tyrion Lannister knows the truth about Ser Mandon, who tried to kill him in the Battle of Blackwater Bay. He recalls to himself Ser Mandon's actions. Rather than defending the royal family, Ser Mandon was intent on destroying someone of royal blood, Tyrion himself (*S of S* 164). Ser Mandon's duplicity is not exceptional; the men of the Kingsguard are often not what they seem.

The deterioration of the Kingsguard is evidenced by King Joffrey Baratheon's appointment of The Hound, Sandor Clegane, who is not a knight at all. Nonetheless, The Hound replaces the esteemed, but aging, Ser Barristan Selmy simply because Joffrey believes that The Hound will show unwavering loyalty regardless of the despicable acts Joffrey asks him to perform. From the beginning, though, The Hound does not participate in the king's commands to beat Sansa Stark. The Hound is not the only member of the Kingsguard who is conflicted about King Joffrey's unchivalrous commands. Another member of the Kingsguard, Ser Arys Oakheart, also struggles with his duty to obey the rash, cruel young king. When ordered to beat Sansa, Ser Arys reluctantly complies but hits her as lightly as possible, hoping to appease the king without harming an innocent young lady. He later feels pity for Sansa and remorse for his vile actions (*F for C* 275). Ser Arys has other struggles, as well. Like numerous knights in the history of the Kingsguard, Ser Arys also struggles with his vow of chastity.

Knights of the Kingsguard are expected to be chaste, but they are often deficient in this respect. Many have fathered bastards. Ser Arys, though an earnest member of the Kingsguard, falls under the spell of the Dornish princess Arianne Martell. He feels guilt about sleeping with her and recognizes his duty even when not in armor. He chastises himself for his weakness and disloyalty, and he recalls stories of King Baelor the Blessed "who would fast to the point of fainting to tame the lusts that shamed him" (*F for C* 265). He wonders if fasting might cure him of his lust for Arianna. He denies her coy accusation that he must love another woman, claiming that his only other love is duty (*F for C* 271). He refuses to acknowledge that many of the Sworn Brothers break their oaths of chastity without consequence. He thinks instead of the legendary Ser Terence Toyne, whose story is strongly evocative of Lancelot's affair with Guinevere. Ser Terence was caught in an adulterous affair with the king's mistress, a crime which sentenced both to death, destroyed his family's reputation, and led to "the death of the noblest knight who ever lived" (*F for C* 274). Thus, Arys is aware of the possible negative consequences of breaking the requirement of chastity. However, he cannot resist Arianna's charms, and he breaks his oath of unwavering loyalty to king and kingdom. Ser Arys is painfully aware of his own failures regarding his duty to the Kingsguard, yet he seems helpless to amend them. He simply cannot live up to the ideals that accompany his position, and consequently commits several breaches of loyalty that ultimately lead to his death. His guilt likely spurs him to charge foolishly at the powerfully built Dornish guard Area Hotah, who kills him.

The primary reason for the diminished reputation of the Kingsguard is not the longstanding tradition of promiscuity, but the relatively more recent slaying of King Aerys Targaryen II by Jaime Lannister. Jaime begins his career gloriously as the youngest member ever to be appointed to the Kingsguard and as King Aerys's sworn protector. However, he quickly falls from glory when he kills the king whom he has sworn to protect. Slaying one's king, particularly if one is appointed sworn protector, is one of the most egregious crimes in Westeros and one of the greatest imaginable breaches of loyalty. Consequently, Jaime is reviled throughout Westeros and earns the ignominious nickname "kingslayer." In *The World of Ice and Fire*, Martin explains the effects of Jaime's actions as the primary cause for the failing reputation of the Kingsguard: "The Kingsguard swore their lives and honor to defend the king, and Jaime betrayed that in an utterly unequivocal fashion."[16] Martin notes that, as events in the novels progress, readers learn the backstory about Jaime's motives in slaying King Aerys and change their view of him. Sworn to serve both the king and the kingdom, Jaime found himself in a difficult position. Mad King Aerys intended to kill Jaime's father and to destroy the kingdom with wildfire. Jaime is keenly aware of the conflicts of loyalty to his king, his kingdom, and his kin. As he realizes, loyalty to one's king, though a desirable trait of chivalry, is problematic for a knight when the king is insane and irrationally commands the deaths of both kinsmen and countrymen.

Jaime becomes, for Martin, a study on the impossibility of maintaining loyalty in certain situations. No wonder Jaime finds himself caught in contradictions. Even the Lannister motto is ambiguous: "A Lannister always pays his debts." This motto is used, variously, as a threat of revenge or as a promise to return a favor. It enables the Lannisters to be either friend or foe and to leave others unsure of whether to expect loyalty. Like this Lannister motto, chivalry itself is ambiguous. Jaime best verbalizes the contradictions of chivalry when he complains to Catelyn Stark that there are simply too many vows: "they make you swear and swear. Defend the king. Obey the king. Keep his secrets. Do his bidding. Your life for his. But obey your father. Love your sister. Protect the innocent. Defend the weak. Respect the Gods. Obey the laws. It's too much. No matter what you do, you're forsaking one vow or the other" (*C of K* 796). With so many demands upon the knight, any attempt to keep a vow might entail breaking other vows.

Certainly, Jaime has a terrible reputation to overcome. Many of his rash actions in the early novels may be in reaction to his undeserved infamy as kingslayer. Robb Stark says of the Lannisters that breaking oaths is "in their blood" (*S of S* 481). However, once readers get a sense of the difficulties of oath keeping, Jaime becomes more sympathetic. Martin's readers soon find out that initial impressions can be misleading. We first see Jaime committing a reprehensible act: when Bran Stark sees Jaime and his twin sister Cersei having sex, Jaime pushes the child out a window. He puts love for his sister over compassion, exclaiming, as the child plummets to the ground, "What I do for love!" (*G of T* 85). Clearly, Jaime distorts the chivalric sense of familial love and loyalty, though his willingness to kill Bran evidences the lengths he will go to in order to protect his family.

Although Martin initially presents him as the worst kind of villain, Jaime's reputation improves as the series progresses. After losing his sword hand, Jaime takes his vows to the Kingsguard much more seriously and begins a campaign of actions to restore peace in Westeros.

Jaime cites his duty as impetus for staying in the position of Lord Commander despite the loss of his hand (*S of S* 855). He defies Cersei, refusing to serve as King's Hand in favor of resuming, with sincere fervor, this position on the Kingsguard. She complains of his lack of loyalty to her since she has begged him to assist her by accepting the position. When Jaime counters by appealing to his vows, Cersei confronts him with the fact that slaying King

Aerys involved breaking a vow. She sees his refusal as a personal rejection: "You could have had me, but you chose a cloak instead" (*F for C* 335). Jaime's choice of "a cloak," as Cersei describes it, evidences his transformation. His misguided loyalty to his sister is replaced by earnest service to the Kingsguard. He renames his sword Oathkeeper and his horses Honor and Glory in commemoration of this commitment (*F for C* 560).

Still, Jaime is repeatedly challenged. When Cersei orders him to take Riverrun, he is conflicted by his loyalty to his family and his vow of loyalty to Catelyn Stark. He has vowed that he will not engage in combat against either the Stark or Tully families (*F for C* 558). Ultimately, in the novels, Jaime is able to keep this oath, handling the situation with skillful negotiation rather than bloodshed. In a number of other circumstances, Jaime shows restraint and loyalty. Talking to (or at) Ser Ilyn (who is mute), Jaime contemplates killing Osmund Kettleblack, whom he suspects is unworthy and disloyal. However, because of the newfound loyalty he feels to the Kingsguard, he decides against it. He refuses to slay a fellow brother of the Kingsguard and decides instead to "geld him and send him to the wall" (*F for C* 951). Jaime begins to appreciate the vows of chastity required of the Kingsguard, so he resists the courtesan Pia, reminding himself of his vows and assuring himself that the courtesan is better suited for his brother Tyrion than for himself (*F for C* 640). Thus, Jaime resolves for himself the conflicts that previously plagued him, and he embarks on a path towards redemption

Jaime's actions also show an improved attitude about the significance of justice and loyalty to kingdom. Trying to end the feud between the Bracken and Blackwood families and gain the loyalties of both, he negotiates with Lord Bracken. When Jaime questions Bracken about his devotion to Robb Stark, Bracken's response shows a lack of sincere loyalty but nonetheless seems reasonable to Jaime. His reasons show practicality; he claims that he "saw no sense in dying for the dead" or "shedding Bracken blood for a lost cause" (*D with D* 698). He explains to Jaime that he kept faith with Robb Stark and will, as long as Jaime is just, maintain faith to him. Thus, Jaime helps Lord Blackenwood preserve his dignity when he changes alliances by not forcing him to kneel in front of his own men. Giving the excuse of a muddy yard and inclement weather, he allows Bracken to kneel inside, privately, once they have ironed out the details of their agreement (*D with D* 699). Earlier, Jaime hangs some outlaws on the boundary between King's Landing and Riverrun. One of them wears the crimson cloak indicating a Lannister affiliation, yet Jaime, with a newfound sense of justice, hangs him, also. Blackwood remarks on the change in Jaime's behavior and jokingly warns him that he may earn a new nickname, "Goldenhand the Just," if he continues this course of fair-mindedness (*F for C* 57).

Deeply concerned about the legacy he will leave in the pages of the White

Book, Jaime certainly appears to have newfound regard for his oaths of loyalty to the kingdom. In the HBO series, Jaime's road to redemption is not so clear cut. His retaking of Riverrun results in the death of the Blackfish. Also, his lust for Cersei seems for the most part unabated although he does cast her a doubtful look when he returns to see the devastation she has caused at King's Landing in his absence. His possible realization of his sister's power-hungry actions may well cause the HBO version of Jaime even more struggles with loyalty.

Another of Martin's characters who struggles with conflicting loyalties is Jon Snow, whose commitment to the Night's Watch presents numerous challenges. Although the men of the Night's Watch serve no king and are not necessarily knights, they nonetheless take one of the strictest oaths. This oath comes at a steep price: those who swear it must forsake many of the commonly valued aspects of chivalry, such as familial loyalty, loyalty to ladies, and personal glory, in order to focus solely on loyalty to and protection of the kingdom. The men swear, "*I shall take no wife, hold no lands, father no children. I shall wear no crowns and win no glory. I shall live and die at my post. I am the sword in the darkness. I am the watcher on the walls*" (*G of T* 522). As their oath dictates, their sole responsibility is protection of the kingdom from the terrors beyond the Wall.

Jon is not himself a knight but was trained in chivalry from his youth and taught to value chivalric ideals. He enters the Night's Watch as an idealistic young man denied lands and title because of his bastard birth, but he is eager for the opportunity to serve and protect his realm. His beloved Uncle Benjen is already a member of the Watch, and Jon wrongly assumes that the brotherhood he will be joining will consist of similarly chivalrous men. However, neither birthright nor virtue is requisite for the men of the Night's Watch. They come from all walks of life and are socially leveled by their shared oath; rapists, nobly born sons, exiled knights, and common criminals all live and serve together. The men of the Watch take vows of loyalty to the kingdom at large, but the Watch is largely dependent on loyalty among the brothers. Regardless of their disparate backgrounds, they must work together to fulfill their duties.

Jon, from the distinguished Stark family, is initially disillusioned by his new brothers at the Wall, who seem decidedly unchivalrous, and he treats them with disdain. His first experiences at the Watch are unpleasant because of his unwillingness to accept them. At jousting, Jon mercilessly defeats his opponents until the armorer Donal Noye chastises him, making him aware that he has had more opportunities than they have had and that he is humiliating them. At this point, Jon begins helping them train. Once Jon has accepted his fellows, he begins to excel in service to the brotherhood and develops true loyalty to the Watch and to his companions. For instance, Jon protects Samwell Tarly from the other brothers of the Watch when Samwell, who is fat and cowardly, first arrives. He reassures Samwell that the relationship between brothers of the Watch transcends the typical bonds of friendship (*G of T* 271). Jon no longer sees himself as separate from, and above, his companions.

When he himself becomes leader of the Watch, Jon is advised not to take new recruits, some with criminal backgrounds, into the forest to swear their oath of loyalty. He reminds his men of the origins of the Night's Watch and the purpose of the oath: to bind together "highborn and low, young and old, base and noble" (*D with D* 507–8). The sense of brotherhood in the Night's Watch is longstanding and tantamount to their duty. Jon stands firm in his trust that the new recruits will hold true to their vows despite their past crimes. He insists that the words and the rituals are important parts of binding the men together in service (*D with D* 507–8). However, despite his firm belief in the importance of the oath, Jon never forgets his family in Winterfell.

Part of Jon's willingness to join the Watch and take such a difficult vow stems from his status as bastard. Early in his tenure at the Watch, the Lord Commander Mormont reminds Jon that his half-brother Robb will inherit Winterfell, marry well, and rule while Jon must be resigned to the austere and chaste life of the Night's Watch. He asks Jon what he will do, and Jon admits that he will be deeply bothered by his misfortune but will nonetheless hold true to his vows (*C of K* 106). Jon makes this confident declaration, yet from the beginning of his service, he is faced with a number of difficult decisions and conflicting loyalties. He nearly abandons the Night's Watch when he learns that his father has been killed and his brother is going to war. Jon is reminded of his oath by his brothers in the Night's Watch who keep him from deserting. They tell him that the words are binding, and he cannot leave once he has uttered them. Further, Grenn tells him that the men of the Watch are now his brothers, more so than the blood brothers he left behind (*G of T* 779). This reminder of his commitment to this brotherhood convinces Jon to return to the Watch rather than defect. However, he continues to struggle with conflicting loyalties.

In *A Storm of Swords*, Jon finds himself in a true test of loyalty. He must fake betrayal to his brothers in the Night's Watch in order to serve them. Jon must first kill one of his own brothers, Qhorin Halfhand (who has commanded him to do so), and then live amongst the Wildlings to convince them that he has deserted his post. He finds this situation increasingly difficult. The Wildlings will believe he has broken his vows when he is actually holding true to them by performing the extremely difficult task Qhorin has put before him (*S of S* 93). One of his biggest tests of loyalty occurs in the aftermath of a battle between the Wildlings and the men of the Watch. He observes the enemy wearing the gear of his brothers: "Ygritte wore the cloak of Qhorin Halfhand … one of the bowmen his boots" (*S of S* 92). Whereas the chivalric code typically demands vengeance, Jon must demonstrate loyalty to the Watch by keeping quiet and feigning loyalty to the enemy, even as they are flaunting their victory over his sworn brothers.

Jon's relationship with the Wildling Ygritte is necessary for him to convince the Wildlings that he has joined them, but his developing love for the Wildling woman complicates matters further and leads Jon to forsake his vow of chastity. He then becomes torn between his loyalty to the Night's Watch and his loyalty to Ygritte, whom he sincerely loves. When he first succumbs to Ygritte, Jon, filled with regret, promises himself that that he will resist in the future. However, Martin writes, "it happened twice more that night, and again in the morning" (*S of S* 339). Repeatedly, although he resolves to resist her, Jon succumbs to Ygritte. Like Malory's Lancelot who is torn between romantic love for Guinevere and his duty to Arthur, Jon is torn between love for a woman and duty to his kingdom, two aspects of chivalry that, in these cases, are not easily reconciled.

Finally, Jon is able to leave Ygritte, but because he cannot completely abandon familial loyalty, his struggles to devote himself entirely to the Watch persist. As Lord Commander, Jon is repeatedly tempted by Stannis Baratheon, a contender for the Iron Throne, to desert the Watch. Stannis tries to draw Jon into his service, offering him Winterfell as a reward. Jon contemplates Stannis's offer of the Wildling princess Val as his bride and the promise that he might become heir of Winterfell. These offers are especially appealing when he believes that his nemesis Janos Slynt may become commander of the Night's Watch. Whereas he had to pretend to break his vows while with the Wildlings, he realizes that "this time it would not be a ruse" (*S of S* 1059). He is tempted by the thought of what such a position might entail but has little difficulty refusing Stannis. However, when he believes that his younger sister may be married off to the vicious Ramsay Bolton, Jon feels the bonds of familial loyalty and is again tempted to leave the Watch. Ultimately, he recalls that his vows require him to forsake his family commitments. Further, as Lord Commander, he would remind any of his men of the magnitude of their vows, if they were in a similar situation (*D with D* 416). Nevertheless, Jon struggles with his commitment. Repeatedly, familial loyalty and honor tug at his conscience.

In *A Dance with Dragons*, Jon makes a difficult decision for the good of the realm: he realizes that the men of the Night's Watch must align themselves with the Wildlings, their long-time enemies, in order to protect those beyond the Wall. Bowen Marsh is deeply troubled by Jon's decisions to let the Wildlings pass into Westeros and to place trust in two of the Wildlings, Leathers and the Magnar. When Jon claims he trusts them because they have made vows to him, Marsh responds with a reminder that Wildlings cannot be trusted to keep oaths. After all, their leader, Mance Rayder, a former member of the Night's Watch, broke his vows. Marsh reminds Jon that Mance "turned his cloak" and proceeded to lead a rebellion (*D with D* 782). Jon tries to assuage Marsh's concerns by explaining that he has taken hostages from the Wildling's families to ensure their allegiance. Jon and Marsh then bitterly argue over the true meaning of loyalty. Marsh feels that Jon is committing treason by letting the Wildlings pass, but Jon reminds him that the oath taken by the men of the Watch requires them to guard the realms of all men, including Wildlings; their vow of loyalty extends to the welfare of all men and supersedes the long-standing enmity between the Wildlings and the Night's Watch.

When he receives a threatening letter from Ramsay Bolton, Jon decides that he must go to war against him, a move that will require him to break his oath to the Night's Watch. Before he has a chance, Marsh leads a revolt against him. In an act that he justifies as loyalty to the Night's Watch, Marsh and some of the other brothers stab Jon, citing "For the Watch" as they do so. At the conclusion of *A Dance with Dragons*, Martin leaves both Jon's fate, and the issue of loyalty, unsettled. In the HBO series, Jon is killed at the instigation of Marsh for his decision to involve men of the Watch in his fight against Ramsay Bolton rather than for his decision to let the Wildlings pass. Jon is subsequently revived by Melisandre, and most fans believe the novels will follow suit. He returns to Winterfell under the council of Ser Davos and his sister Sansa. He abandons his role as Lord Commander, defeats Ramsay Bolton, and is declared Lord of the North.

Many readers see Jon as a Galahad-like figure who may cure the warring wasteland of Westeros once his true heritage (as half Targaryen, according to the HBO series) is revealed. Regardless of how the HBO series and novels may ultimately differ, Martin has set up Jon Snow as an unconventional model of chivalry, yet one who is virtuous and has promise to become a key player in restoring peace to Westeros and defeating the white walkers. His many struggles with loyalty clearly illustrate the conflicting demands inherent in the chivalric code and also show how well-intentioned men strive to balance these demands.

Unconventional models of chivalry fill the pages of Martin's novels, including the pseudo-knightly orders that require oaths of loyalty. Among them are a band of outlaw knights known as Brotherhood Without Banners and a band of mercenaries known as the Golden Company. The Golden Company consists of sellswords who fight for pay, yet they have won some renown by their reputation for holding true to all contracts. Thus, despite their ill repute as mercenaries, they are known for a certain kind of loyalty towards those with whom they have contracted their services. The Brotherhood Without Banners, on the other hand, more closely resembles a traditional order of knights. Even with their outlaw status, the members of the Brotherhood, led by the Lightning Lord Beric Dondarrion, have a bond that unites them in a common quest to defeat the Lannisters in the name of Robert Baratheon. Lord Beric labels himself and his men "king's men" even after Robert has been slain. Once Robert has fallen, their loyalty is directed to defense of his realm (*S of S* 463). Their loyalty to a dead king is reminiscent of the Anglo-Saxon warriors in "The Battle of Maldon" who continue to fight after their lord is struck down. For both bands of warriors, loyalty to kingdom gives them incentive to continue the fight even after the deaths of their lords.

The members of the Brotherhood Without Banners are loyal not only to the Baratheon cause and to the realm, but also to one another. The Red Priest Thoros of Myr explains, "We are brothers here.... Holy brothers, sworn to the realm, to our god, and to each other" (*S of S* 464). Arya Stark's companion Gendry admires this bond when he encounters the Brotherhood. He chooses to join this band of renegades primarily because of their strong sense of loyalty to one another. When Gendry joins the Brotherhood, he expresses admiration for their honorable behavior and pledges them loyalty. He is impressed by their loyalty to the dead king Robert and to one another, and he admires the fact that they gave The Hound a trial rather than sentencing him immediately to death. For these reasons, he tells them that he desires to serve the Brotherhood as their smith (*S of S* 539). Gendry, bastard son of Robert Baratheon, is neither a knight nor a warrior. However, his eagerness to swear loyalty to these brothers and his skill as a smith will be boons to the Brotherhood.

At the furthest end of Martin's spectrum of pseudo-orders lie the Brave Companions, also known as the Bloody Mummers. Led by Vargo Hoat, this renegade band of sellswords come from all across Martin's world. Martin makes no mention of vows or bonds of brotherhood other than a shared love of violence and cruelty. They are infamous for chopping off the hands and feet of those they capture. They serve as a parody of knightly orders in their utter disregard for chivalry and complete lack of loyalty.

Oaths and Vows

For the knights of medieval romance, vows to God are a significant part of chivalry. Martin's knights and pseudo-knights, with a few notable exceptions, are not particularly religious. Perhaps for this reason, Martin does not devote much attention to the actual ritual involved in knight-making, which requires an oath to the seven gods. In a rare reference to dubbing, Jaime Lannister remembers his own dubbing ceremony at the age of fifteen and mentions the role of the Warrior, one of the seven gods. He recalls certain aspects of the ritual, such as placing his sword on the lap of the Warrior, laying his armor at the base of the statue, and kneeling before the altar. He remembers the ritual as transformational: "A boy knelt; a knight rose. *The young Lion, not the Kingslayer*" (*F for C* 176–7). Martin draws out a more complete description of dubbing and the oath of knighthood in his prequel to *A Song of Ice and Fire*, "The Hedge Knight." Here, the ritual involves moving the sword across the shoulders of the soon-to-be knight as these words are spoken:

> In the name of the warrior I charge you to be brave. In the name of the Father I charge you to be just. In the name of the Mother I charge you to defend the young and the innocent. In the name of the Maiden I charge you to protect all women."[17]

The ceremony in this particular situation is a spur-of-the-moment occurrence immediately before a trial by combat. A squire is made into a knight by another knight to ensure equal numbers in what Martin terms a "trial by seven." As Martin repeats throughout his novels, "any knight can make a knight," and in desperate situations such as the one referenced here, such decisions might be made hastily. Nevertheless, readers here get some sense of the role of the gods in the dubbing ceremony. The Brotherhood without Banners have their own form of a dubbing ceremony. When Gendry decides to join them, he is "dubbed" by the lightning lord. Even this renegade pseudo-order of knights includes a nod to the gods in their vows. Next, a list of duties is cited. The new member of the Brotherhood vows to defend the weak, obey his superiors, demonstrate courage, be true to the king (Robert), and attend to all duties, no matter how mundane. Gendry kneels as he makes this vow and is then officially a member of the brotherhood: "Arise Ser Gendry, knight of the hollow hill, and welcome to our brotherhood" (*S of S* 540).

Dubbing ceremonies such as the ones discussed above are relatively rare in Martin's novels, and the significance of the Seven to the institution of knighthood does not dominate the thoughts or actions of most of the knights of Westeros. For the most part, Martin associates knightly devotion to the seven gods with zealotry. The Faith Militant, the military branch of the Seven, is composed of zealots. As Brienne of Tarth travels with Ser Illifer and Ser Creighton, they come across the Sparrows, a group of septons who carry the bones of holy men. They warn Brienne and her companions about the ravages of war and make an urgent plea that knights should "forsake their worldly masters" and join the Faith Militant in defense of the Holy Faith" (*F for C* 91). The Sparrows urge the knights of Westeros to abandon all loyalties except the Holy Faith. This is not a message of peace, however. The High Septon in charge of the Faith Militant is a dangerous enemy to the throne. A few knights, including Lancel Lannister, heed this plea. After his experiences in the Battle of Blackwater Bay and in Cersei Lannister's bed, Lancel becomes increasingly pious and unhinged, leading him to join the Faith Militant and turn against his family members who control the Iron Throne.

When Cersei foolishly allows the Faith Militant to resume an old tradition of taking up arms, her plan backfires. Cersei is too power-hungry to realize that she will be unable to secure the loyalty of the Faith Militant. They swear their loyalty to the High Septon, not to King Tommen, Cersei's son. The High Septon seeks control of the throne for himself and has no intent of doing Cersie's bidding. Cersei's intent is to use their power for her own ends, initially to bring down Margaery Tyrell, whose influence and popularity Cersei resents. While the Faith Militant do imprison Margaery at Cersei's request, they then use their newfound authority against Cersei herself, imprisoning her also and then exposing her to a "walk of shame" for her sins. In the HBO series, Cersei brings this order to ruin, but again, readers must wait to see if Martin's novels will follow the same path.

In contrast to the Faith Militant, most of the knights of Westeros are not portrayed as devout, yet they frequently make vows to their gods as outward expressions of heartfelt loyalty. One of many examples is the vow made by Brienne of Tarth when she swears fealty to Renly Baratheon and becomes a member of his Rainbow Guard: "I swear it by the gods old and new" (*C of K* 344). As Brienne's vow illustrates, even though Martin's institution of knighthood is sworn to the new gods (the Seven), his knights and pseudo-knights, recognizing the two main religions of Westeros, frequently invoke both sets of gods. By honoring both the religion associated with Westerosi chivalry and the older religion of Westeros, Brienne and other knights who make their vows to various gods strengthen their resolution and embrace a broader view of Westerosi chivalry than that limited by worship of the Seven.

Even the Crannogmen, looked down upon by the rest of the Northmen, are capable of loyalty and value the solemn vow. Their vows reflect their earnestness as well as their system of belief. The crannogmen Jojen Reed and his sister Meera make a solemn vow when they commit to the cause of the Northmen. They swear by "earth and water ... bronze and iron ... ice and fire" (*C of K* 329). In *A Storm of Swords*, Meera reiterates this vow to Bran Stark as assurance of her commitment to him (132). Beyond the Wall, some of the Wildlings, although they insist that they are free and serve no man, come to understand the importance of oaths to the Westerosi. When Gilly learns that Mance Rayder's child is in danger from the red priestess, her first response to Jon Snow reveals her understanding that oath breaking is a serious offense punishable by death. She tells Jon that the baby is innocent. An infant cannot break an oath, and she begs him not to allow Melisandre to burn him (*D with D* 105). Thus, in Martin's novels, oaths and vows are measures of loyalty that transcend the institution of knighthood and that often transcend or downplay religious intent.

So far, we have looked primarily at the oaths and vows of orders and pseudo-orders of knights and warriors. Vows made by knights to individuals are much more common in Martin's novels. Just as commitment to a brotherhood can lead to challenges of loyalty, knights and warriors also sometimes struggle to maintain loyalty to a single individual. Brienne of Tarth provides a vivid example of this type of loyalty and the struggles that can ensue. Brienne adopts the typically masculine aspects of the chivalric code, assuming the male role of warrior and for all intents and purposes becoming a female knight. Caroline Spector confirms Brienne's success at doing so, writing that "[Brienne] remains a shining example of honor and dedication in a world where those things are more spoken of than practiced."[18] In her earnestness to succeed at chivalry, Brienne dedicates herself to serving her lord or lady. Brienne's allegiances are bestowed on those who treat her kindly, and she is conflicted when put in situations that threaten those allegiances.

Readers first see Brienne showing unwavering loyalty to (and unrequited love for) Renly Baratheon. She defeats the flower of chivalry, Ser Loras Tyrell, in a joust, and as a reward asks to join Renly's order of knights, the Rainbow Guard. Although as a woman she is neither dubbed a knight nor given the title "Ser," Brienne's inclusion qualifies her as pseudo-knight. She is awarded a place in Renly's Rainbow Guard and serves as his standard-bearer. However, her loyalty is not to her fellow knights in the Guard (who are cruel to her), but to Renly himself, whom she loves. After Renly's death, Brienne makes another vow, this time one of vengeance against Stannis for Renly's death. Although she has not yet achieved this vow in the novels, she succeeds in exacting this vengeance in the HBO series. Ironically, at the time she first makes this vow, Renly's surviving men do not appreciate the intensity of her loyalty to him and accuse her of killing her beloved lord.

Following Renly's death, Brienne swears loyalty first to Catelyn Stark and then to Jaime Lannister, promising both that she will find and return the Stark daughters. When she swears her loyalty to Catelyn, her vow reveals her struggle with gender identity but also evidences her loyalty: "Then I am yours, my lady. Your liege man, or … whatever you would have me be" (*C of K* 562). She promises to defend Catelyn and die on her behalf, if necessary. She takes seriously the task Catelyn gives her of delivering Jaime home to the Lannisters in exchange for the Stark girls. This duty is a demonstration of Brienne's vow of loyalty to Catelyn.

With Jaime as her hostage, Brienne sets off to King's Landing. Jaime is bitter, resentful, and relentlessly cruel to Brienne in the early stages of this journey. Eventually, however, as the two survive the horrors of being held captive at Harrenhal, he comes to respect Brienne's loyalty to those she serves. Jaime later convinces Ser Loras Tyrell that Brienne has not slain Renly, encouraging Ser Loras to talk to her himself. He tells Loras that Brienne is "loyal past the point of sense" (*S of S* 924). He cites as evidence her faithfulness to Catelyn Stark in returning him to King's Landing, and he expresses utter confidence that she would never have harmed Renly. He then asks Loras to "judge her fairly, on your honor as a knight" (*S of S* 925). Ser Loras does so and is soon convinced of Brienne's loyalty. He comes to understand that Renly kept Brienne close because, while others wanted rewards, Brienne simply wanted to love and serve him. When Jaime gives her his sword Oathkeeper and asks her to find Sansa Stark, Brienne realizes the enormity of the responsibility Jaime has given her: his honor depends on her success. At this point, she makes a vow of loyalty to Jaime. She assures him that she will track down Sansa and safeguard her, "For her lady mother's sake, and for yours." Brienne recognizes the difficulties in upholding the various vows she has made. She admits, though only to herself, that it is easy to speak "noble words"; putting those words into actions is a different matter, because "deeds were hard" (*F for C* 81).

Brienne soon realizes just how hard deeds can be. In *A Feast for Crows*, Lady Stoneheart (formally Catelyn Stark) gives Brienne the choice of betraying Jaime or having her companions and herself put to death. Among her companions is Podrick Payne, who has himself served Brienne loyally and with whom she has formed a close bond. In the novels, Podrick first begins following Brienne in an attempt to locate Tyrion, whom he has served loyally.[19] As the two travel together, Brienne begins training him at arms, and they develop a friendship. Lady Stoneheart leaves Brienne no good alternative as she must betray either Podrick (and be killed herself) or Jaime, both who have placed their trust in her and both to whom she feels a strong sense of loyalty. She has sworn loyalty to Jaime in her vow to find the Stark girls, yet Podrick has proved a loyal companion. Brienne reappears briefly in *A Dance with Dragons* reunited with Jaime, leaving readers to speculate if, in perhaps yet another of Martin's unexpected twists, she has made the difficult choice to betray Podrick, or whether she is leading Jaime back to Lady Stoneheart. In either scenario, she may have been forced to break an allegiance and to become herself an oathbreaker.[20]

Similar to Brienne's intense sense of devotion, Ser Davos Seaworth also shows unwavering loyalty to an individual. Ser Davos is closely bound to Stannis Baratheon, contender to the Iron Throne, even though he disapproves of Stannis's principal advisor, the red priestess Melisandre. Ser Davos, initially a smuggler from Flea Bottom, owes his social ascent to Stannis. During Robert's Rebellion, Davos smuggled food, including onions, to Stannis and his men during a siege. As punishment for the crime of smuggling, Stannis has the ends of Davos's fingers chopped off, yet he spares the smuggler's life for his good service in providing him with food. For this act, Davos feels both gratitude and loyalty; he knows that Stannis could have had him put to death for his past crimes. Davos's loyalty is further rewarded; he is given land, raised to knighthood, and eventually appointed as Stannis's Hand. Davos clearly takes to heart his vows to Stannis and answers affirmatively when Stannis,

upon promoting him to Hand, requires loyal service, unquestioning obedience, and a willingness to fight any of Stannis's enemies (*S of S* 499). Davos
reluctantly accepts this appointment (he believes that he is unqualified for
such a position) but then works diligently and earnestly to maintain his loyalty to the stern and often misguided Stannis.

　　Davos becomes increasingly challenged by this loyalty as Stannis becomes
increasingly influenced by Melisandre, whom Davis knows to be a murderer.
Thus, he is torn between loyalty to Stannis and his own conscience. He is
intensely loyal to Stannis, yet he also feels a sense of duty to protect those
whom Melisandre threatens, especially Edric Storm, bastard son of Robert
Baratheon. Because Edric is a king's son, Melisandre believes that his blood
is holy and will help her in her quest to seat Stannis on the Iron Throne.
Thus, Davos helps Edric escape. When Stannis confronts Davos about doing
so, Davos replies with an explanation of his loyalty. He recounts his vows to
Stannis, particularly his promise to protect his people: "Is not Edric Storm
one of your people? One of those I swore to protect? I kept my oath" (*S of S*
866). Although he knows the risks he takes by speaking truthfully to Stannis,
whose view is increasingly clouded by the opinion of Melisandre, Ser Davos
remains staunchly devoted and continues to speak his mind to assist his lord
in rightful actions. He is even imprisoned after the Battle of Blackwater Bay
in spite of his valor when his plot to kill Melisandre is revealed, but he is
spared, again, because of his loyalty to Stannis. Although Melisandre does
not approve of Davos's actions and although he has plotted to kill her, even
she appreciates the strength of his loyalty. Although she disagrees with many
of his actions, she cannot deny that his loyalty is unquestionable (*D with D*
449). For this reason, she keeps his son Devan safely with her rather than
having him travel with Stannis to conquer the northlands.

　　Although Stannis relies increasingly on Melisandre, Davos continues to
offer him advice, as well. He attempts to dissuade Stannis from a futile attack
on Claw Isle. Lord Celtigar of Claw Isle swore fealty to King Joffrey, so Stannis,
advised by Ser Axell, wants to attack him and his remaining men. Davos tries
to convince Stannis not to kill the men who knelt along with their lord,
explaining to him the nature of loyalty. They have sworn a vow of loyalty to
their lord and thus have followed his decisions. Stannis, however, sees them
as traitors since Joffrey is not rightfully king and their lord follows Joffrey.
Stannis believes they should have been true to him, the true king, "even if
the lord [they serve] proves false" (*S of S* 495). Stannis is unwavering in his
opinions and apparently unable to comprehend the nature of true loyalty.
Davos, regardless, remains unwavering in his devotion.

　　Davos campaigns tirelessly for Stannis. He travels across Westeros and
does his best to secure loyalties for Stannis's cause. He takes on the difficult
task of convincing Wyman Manderly to agree to an alliance. Manderly is

reluctant to commit because the Lannisters hold his son Wendel. With Davos's encouragement, he does align, but not overtly. Repeatedly, Davos is successful at exemplifying loyalty to his lord in trying circumstances, and even with the challenge of Stannis's unpopularity, he manages to secure some important alliances for him. In the HBO series, following Stannis's death, Davos aligns himself with Jon Snow and serves to guide him through his battle against Ramsay Bolton. Thus, in both the novels and the televised series, Ser Davos remains one of Martin's most loyal characters.

A final example of loyalty to an individual is evidenced in the relationships between Daenerys Targaryen and her followers, most notably Ser Jorah Mormont and Ser Barristan Selmy. Initially sent to spy on her and report his findings back to King's Landing, Ser Jorah shifts his loyalty to Daenerys. Ser Jorah crosses the boundaries of loyal thane, however, when he falls in love with her. She does not reciprocate his feelings and finds his advances inappropriate. Ser Barristan, on the other hand, flees from King's Landing after Joffrey Baratheon removes him from the Kingsguard. He travels across the Narrow Sea to support Daenerys, whom he believes to be the rightful heir to the throne. Both men become her friends and most trusted advisors.

Daenerys is therefore devastated when she learns that both Ser Barristan and Ser Jorah have betrayed her, Barristan by failing to reveal his true identity and Jorah by spying on her on behalf of the usurper. She wonders if all Westerosi knights are untrue, and she laments, "Was there no one she could trust, no one to keep her safe?" (*S of S* 791). Although she pardons Ser Barristan, she banishes Ser Jorah, whose breach of loyalty she deems unforgivable. Nevertheless, his loyalty to Daenerys continues even after she has exiled him. In Martin's most recent novel, Ser Jorah finds himself enslaved on Slaver's Bay, feverishly working for a way to re-gain Daenerys's good graces. In a declaration of loyalty, he explains to the widow of the waterfront why he seeks Daenerys, "To serve her. Defend her. Die for her, if need be" (*D with D* 404).

Daenerys replaces Ser Jorah with the sellsword Daario, whom she loves. Dario swears loyalty to Daenerys with a flamboyant gesture that leaves Martin's readers, and her advisors, questioning his sincerity. He bows so low that his face nears her feet, and he makes a vow that is eloquent yet exaggerated: "My sword is yours. My life is yours. My love is yours. My blood, my body, my songs, you own them all. I live and die at your command, fair queen" (*S of S* 583). Daenerys remains conflicted about whether Daario's familiarity with her might interfere with his sense of duty, and she herself wonders if he is truly trustworthy. Having been warned that she will be betrayed three times, once for blood and once for gold and once for love, Daenerys is cautious in determining who among her followers is capable of true loyalty.

Although Daenerys depends increasingly on Daario, Ser Barristan remains her protector, as well. When Daenerys marries Hizdahr zo Loraq for political reasons, Ser Barristan refuses to show him loyalty. He recognizes that Daenerys's marriage to Hizdahr is strictly political. After Daenerys flies away on her dragon, Hizdahr dismisses Ser Barristan from his duties. Ser Barristan, however, has no desire to serve Hizdahr. Whereas he was humiliated upon his dismissal from service to the Kingsguard in Westeros, he sees no shame in Hizdahr's dismissal since he knows he could never follow Hizdahr (*D with D* 799). For Ser Barristan, trust and respect are essential to loyalty, and he feels neither for Hizdahr. After consulting with two of Daenery's other advisors, Grey Worm and the Shavepate, Ser Barristan determines that Hizdahr would be best kept in prison until they can determine his true motives. They remove Hizdahr from power, and Ser Barristan holds the throne, not as an assertion of power for himself, but as an act of loyalty: he is confident that Daenerys will return and continue to rule.

Regardless of the fact that she has numerous enemies and her second husband may have tried to murder her, Daenerys Targaryen inspires the loyalty of many of those she encounters in Essos. Readers first see Daenerys offered in marriage to Khal Drogo, who is a Dothraki leader. The Dothraki, a nomadic warrior culture, value strength and seem, upon her first impressions of them, barbaric. However, Daenerys soon recognizes some similarities between the Dothraki "brotherhood" and the Kingsguard. Both make vows of loyalty to their lords, but she notes a clear distinction. This loyalty, for the Dothraki, "went further than that … they were the khal's brothers, his shadows, his fiercest friends. 'Blood of my blood,' Drogo called them" (*G of T* 391). Daenerys appreciates the strong bonds of brotherhood among the Dothraki that seem to her to transcend the Westerosi bonds of knighthood and that serve for her as a model on her journey to seek loyal followers.

Ser Jorah points out to Daenerys some important differences between the Dothraki and the Westerosi codes of loyalty. He wants her to understand that, upon her husband's death, the Dothraki will be unlikely to show loyalty to her son. They follow Khal Drogo's strength rather than his family line and will not feel loyalty to his infant son (*G of T* 707). Still, after the deaths of her husband and infant, upon the birth of her dragons, Daenerys manages to gain the support of a small band of Dothraki. She gains the loyalty of others she encounters, as well, including the Unsullied who have been trained to serve without question or emotion. These eunuch warriors are subdued by cruel masters and have never before experienced the freedom or respect that Daenerys grants them. Repeatedly, Daenerys promises freedom and justice in exchange for loyalty.

Another, and perhaps more common, method by which leaders might inspire loyalty is through reward. The reward of land is critical to the feudal system. Upon first gaining the throne, one of King Arthur's earliest gestures is to distribute lands and title to ensure loyalty. Likewise, Tywin Lannister, acting on behalf of his family, distributes lands to gain loyalty to the Lannisters. He tries to meet the demands of those who appeal to him: "this castle and that village, tracts of lands, a small river, a forest, the wardship of certain minors left fatherless by the battle" (*S of S* 262). He is able to appease the lords who serve him by taking land from those who had supported Stannis, exacting a system of reward and punishment. All those who have betrayed the Lannisters have land and power stripped away from them and redistributed to those deemed loyal (*S of S* 262). The kind of loyalty offered by the Lannister patriarch, however, is clearly political, and those who serve him do so for gain rather than for love or respect.

Tywin's son Tyrion, even with his physical challenges, inspires more genuine loyalty than his father. The rag tag band of retainers that he assembles develop a battle cry, "Half man!" indicating their loyalty (*G of T* 686). Tyrion has also made these men promises of financial reward, yet those who serve him seem to develop respect for him and loyalty to him. This is likely because, in marked contrast to his humorless, power-hungry father, the dwarf Tyrion is clever, often kind, and self aware. Throughout the series of novels, one of Martin's favorite catch phrases is "words are wind." Vows and oaths are merely words, and Tyrion's men never utter them. Their actions in battle demonstrate their loyalty to Tyrion.

Misguided and Feigned Loyalty

The actions of Theon Greyjoy illustrate how loyalties can sometimes be misguided. Theon desperately wants to demonstrate familial loyalty to the Greyjoy family, but in doing so, he betrays the family to whom he was fostered in a peace agreement. As a child, Theon was sent to Winterfell after his father's failed rebellion against King Robert Baratheon. He was raised alongside the Stark children and treated kindly. When Theon is a young man, Robb Stark sends him back to the Iron Islands as emissary. Theon believes his father will receive him warmly and will agree to an alliance with the Starks. To his surprise, he returns to the Iron Islands and finds that he has been replaced as his father's heir and that his father no longer sees him as worthy. To gain his father's approval, Theon betrays the Starks, taking Winterfell by force after Robb's death and feigning the deaths of the two youngest Stark children. Theon's misguided loyalty, to his cruel father rather than to the family who raised him, proves disastrous for him when he falls victim to Ramsay Bolton. Ramsay commands his own twisted brand of loyalty, torturing Theon into submission and forcing him to assume the role of his personal servant Reek.

The more mercenary characters of Westeros show no loyalty to anyone but themselves. They feign loyalty for their own gain. Foremost among these characters is the newly titled knight and former sellsword Ser Bronn. Bronn's social ascent begins when Tyrion Lannister promises him wealth in return for championing him at the Vale. Tyrion certainly has no illusions about Bronn's sense of loyalty: "Duty, honor, friendship, what's that to you?" (*G of T* 454). Bronn's response, having been offered gold by Tyrion for his service, clearly expresses his refusal to conform to the usual dictates of chivalry that govern fealty. He agrees to serve Tyrion but makes clear that he will not be a conventional liege. He states that he will not "bend the knee and m'lord you every time you take a shit" and is "no man's toady" (*G of T* 455). Tyrion later discovers that his father, Tywin Lannister, has given the title of knighthood to Bronn before Tyrion has the chance, thus attempting to steal away Bronn's allegiance. Unlike Ser Davos, who is genuinely loyal to Stannis, Bronn is simply looking for the fastest way to advance, and his skill at fighting paves the way to a title. Bronn values advancement, not loyalty. He is eager to accept Cersei's offer that he marry into the noble house Stokeworth. Bronn names his first son after the nobly born but physically defective Tyrion, perhaps to mock the Lannisters, or perhaps as an indication that he has, after all, felt some sense of loyalty to the man who paved for him the road to success.

Though not knights or warriors, Varys and Littlefinger also merit discussion here, as both are major players in the political happenings of Westeros, and neither shows any clear sense of loyalty to others. Littlefinger is more like Bronn in that he feigns outward loyalty for his own advancement. Unlike Bronn, who makes no attempt to hide his intentions, Littlefinger is a trickster, always keeping close at hand his motivations and deliberately misleading those who dare to trust him. Adopting the romance device of the rash boon, Littlefinger asks Tyrion and Cersei for a favor in exchange for helping align the Lannisters with the Tyrells. When they ask him what he demands, he does not give a direct answer.[21] Instead, he "glanced at Tyrion with a sly smile" and adds, "I shall need to give that some consideration. No doubt, I'll think of something" (*S of S* 535). Littlefinger chooses to assess his options, undoubtedly looking for what will be of most personal benefit. The Lannisters are desperate for this alliance and agree to whatever he will demand. Littlefinger explains his philosophy to Sansa Stark after "rescuing" her and killing Ser Dontos. He describes his strategy of confusing his enemies to ensure that his motives and future actions cannot be guessed. He suggests making "moves that have no purpose, or even seem to work against you" (*S of S* 841). His political machinations always serve his own personal interests and are no more than a game which he designates "The only game. The game of thrones" (*S of S* 841).

Littlefinger is an opportunist whose sole loyalty is to his own advancement. Vaerys, on the other hand, claims that his loyalty is to the kingdom. However, his actions throughout the series leave not only the other characters, but also Martin's readers, wondering about his true intentions. He is a major manipulator behind the scenes, plotting and putting into action a number of plans that affect the leadership of the kingdom. In *A Dance with Dragons*, Varys finally reveals his loyalties, insisting that they are, in fact, for the good of the realm. Before killing Kevan Lannister, Varys states his intent of bringing Aegon Targaryen to the throne. Regardless of certain acts that might indicate his sincerity, Varys has proved such a slippery character that readers may still doubt his true intentions and question where his genuine loyalties might lie, if anywhere at all.

Clearly, loyalty is no easy matter for Martin's knights and pseudo-knights, just as it was no easy matter for the knights of medieval romance. Beverly Kennedy explains the dilemma of Malory's "True knight," who must balance feudal, religious, and courtly obligations: "Not many men could ever keep this ideal of True knighthood, because most would find it too difficult to resolve the conflicts which could arise between service to God and service to one's lady or between service to one's king and country and service to one's lady."[22] Kenneth Hodges writes,

> at the intersection of all the levels of discourse are merely desperate characters such as Launcelot and Arthur, trapped among the competing, contradictory demands of the various chivalries. Read dialogically, *Le Morte Darthur* is not simply a tragedy of characters; it is a tragedy of ideas. Chivalry is not intrinsically evil, nor do the best characters fundamentally fail to live up to some true code; rather, chivalry is noble but fatally flawed, fatally unstable, and so too must be its practitioners.[23]

If one follows the course of the perfect Godly knight and achieves true loyalty to God, as does Galahad, the only choice is rejection of earthly matters such as love of women, and if one follows the course of the perfect earthly knight and exemplifies true loyalty to lord and lady, as does Lancelot, one cannot achieve spiritual perfection. Despite Galahad's resolve to attain perfection in the form of the Grail, his actions, while restoring the Waste Land, do not cure the ills of Arthur's court, a court in which the ambiguities of chivalry ultimately lead to the destruction of the Round Table.

Martin's novels are also filled with various accounts of loyalty: false loyalties that are bought, feigned, or misguided; and true loyalty that inspires service and courage. No wonder Sansa Stark is confused about what constitutes a "true knight." Loyalty provides the cohesion that unites kingdoms. It also inspires the kind of devotion that can determine who ultimately sits upon the Iron Throne. In a tumultuous, complicated kingdom such as Westeros (and Camelot, for that matter), holding true to vows and oaths of loyalty can be the greatest of challenges. Ultimately, the contender who inspires most loyalty may well win the game of thrones.

Six

Prowess

"What do you think a knight is for, girl? You think it's all
taking favors from ladies and looking fine in gold plate?
Knights are for killing."—The Hound, C of K 756

Prowess in Chivalric and Heroic Literature

As Sandor Clegane proclaims, knights are "for killing"; their primary
function is to defend the king and the realm. Prowess is the ability to fight
skillfully; it entails valor on the battlefield, skill with weaponry, and, yes,
killing. Martin's pseudo-medieval world is extremely violent, both as it is
portrayed in the novels and as depicted on HBO. He justifies his propensity
for bloodshed as both accurate to medieval warfare and in many ways prefer-
able to modern warfare:

> There's something very close up about the Middle Ages. You're taking a sharp piece of
> steel and hacking at someone's head, and you're getting spattered with his blood, and
> you're hearing his screams. In some ways maybe it's more brutal that we've insulated
> ourselves from that. We're setting up mechanisms where we can kill human beings with
> drones and missiles where you're sitting at a console and pressing the button. We never
> have to hear their whimpering, or hear them begging for their mother, or dying in hor-
> rible realities around us. I don't know if that's necessarily such a good thing.[1]

Martin's fans are certainly not spared graphic details as he presents a horri-
fying picture of warfare. Much could be said about the technology of warfare
as it is described in the novels and as it is depicted in the intricately shot battle scenes in the HBO series. However, my focus in this chapter is specifically
on Martin's portrayal of battle etiquette and the psychological attributes that
should accompany prowess. Martin's portrayal of warfare is in many ways a
reflection of the etiquette and virtues in medieval chivalric literature.[2] Worthy
knights and warriors should not merely "hack at heads." On the contrary,
they should follow guidelines that monitor their behavior and govern their

114

motives. Prowess must be curbed by other virtues, such as mercy, wisdom, and justice.

At a first glance, Martin's battle scenes and those in medieval literature have some distinctive differences that might make a comparison seem unfruitful. Fighting in romance and heroic literature is bloody, but highly stylized. By presenting snippets of battle, medieval authors omit much of the chaos that would occur on an actual battlefield, the kind of chaos that Martin tends to dwell upon in his novels and that is so graphically depicted on the HBO series. On the other hand, medieval authors tend to gloss over some aspects of battle while presenting others, especially those featuring the hero and his closest companions, in almost slow-motion detail.

The Anglo-Saxon heroic poem "The Battle of Maldon" records the defeat of Earl Byrtnoth and his men after Byrtnoth allows the Vikings to cross the Blackwater River at low tide. The writer recounts the exploits of individual fighters in an orderly fashion that minimizes the effect of what must have become a chaotic and bloody battlefield. A pagan warrior kills one of Byrtnoth's retainers. Another, often a kinsman, retaliates in vengeance. Oaths are sworn, boasts are made, and body parts are neatly hacked off. Chaos ensues when a traitor hops on Byrtnoth's horse and flees the scene, leaving many men to believe that Byrtnoth himself has fled.

Still, in the midst of battle chaos, when all is clearly lost for Byrtnoth's men and the leader has himself been killed, each of the remaining warriors, in order of rank, takes time to make a speech which includes a vow to fight to the end. Readers get a sense of the battle through these individual portrayals of the actions and vows of the warriors. Martin has something akin to this effect by using point-of-view narrators to relate the events of the Battle of Blackwater Bay. Readers must piece together the accounts of Ser Davos, Tyrion, and Sansa to get a full picture of the battle action. Ser Davos views the battle from aboard his ship amidst spreading wildfire; Tyrion views from the shore and participates directly in the fighting; Sansa, secured in the Red Keep, relies on the sounds of battle and the occasional report. From each of these perspectives, the battle is narrated to emphasize violence and chaos.

Both romance and heroic literature contain scenes of graphic violence (Beowulf ripping Grendel's arm from the socket; Ganelon's death by drawing and quartering in *The Song of Roland*; Chrétien's Percival killing the Black Knight with his javelin; Lancelot beheading Meleagant). Graphic details, however, are kept to a minimum when compared to Martin's detailed, lengthy battle scenes. For example, the battle between Arthur and Lucius in Geoffrey of Monmouth's *History of the Kings of England* begins with what Robert Stein calls a "perfect first sentence" which states simply that the battle was long and the two exchanged blows: "Here, however, this perfect first sentence is the last sentence; the chivalric duel goes no further, as both Lucius and Gawain are swallowed up in the general combat, and we hear no more of their meeting."[3] Thus, violence is presented more for effect than realism.

In *The Song of Roland*, Charlemagne's enemies are evenly sliced in two from the scalp down, the mighty sword penetrating through the body of the infidel and into the body of his horse. Modern readers might envision an almost cartoon-like scene in which the body neatly peels in two. Charlemagne's men not only boast before killing, but somehow have time to curse and desecrate the corpses of those they vanquish. After Roland slays the evil pagan Chernuble, he addresses his corpse: "Knave, you should not have set forth,/For from Mahomet you shall have no aid:/No scoundrel such as you will win the day."[4] Such descriptions are a far cry from the kinds of violent details in Martin's novels and from the realities of actual medieval warfare. However, the medieval writer is not particularly interested in accurate depictions of the battlefield. Rather, his interest is in the attributes that accompany prowess: bravery, loyalty, mercy, and honor, to mention a few. A comparison between Martin's portrayal of prowess and that in literature can provide valuable insights: notwithstanding the differences in how battle scenes are depicted, Martin's novels also emphasize and provide important commentary on the chivalric attributes that should accompany prowess.

Both on and off the battlefield, hardship, pain, and, certainly, the likelihood of violent death (all of which Martin vividly depicts) are requisites to the life of a warrior or knight. In his fourteenth-century manual of chivalry, Geoffroi de Charny specifies the necessity of hardship for the effective knight:

> Hence it should be understood that good knights may have to undergo hard trials and adventures, for it can truly be said to them that when they want to sleep, they must keep vigil; when they want to eat, they must fast; when they are thirsty, there is often nothing to drink; and when they would rest, they have to exert themselves all through the night; and when they would be secure from danger, they would be beset by great terrors; and when they would defeat their enemies, sometimes they would be defeated or killed or captured and wounded and struggle to recover; this is not to speak of the perilous adventures they may encounter on their journeys in search of deeds of arms, such as the danger of crossing sea or river, ... of passing over treacherous places or bridges, of encountering riots or robbers. All these dangers must they endure.[5]

As Geoffroi notes, medieval knights face various kinds of danger that are not necessarily on the battlefield. In *Sir Gawain and the Green Knight*, the anonymous author alludes to but does not detail an assortment of challenges the hero undergoes, including fighting giants and enduring harsh weather, as he makes his way to his appointment with the Green Knight. Chrétien's Lancelot undergoes unexpected duels from challengers and a grueling climb over a treacherous sword bridge. He overcomes these obstacles one by one on his quest to rescue Guinevere. Once he succeeds, the challenges are no longer needed to motivate the story. Thus, there is no mention of the Sword Bridge or Underwater Bridge that, as Lancelot and Gawain were earlier told, are the only ways to get to Meleagant's castle. These challenges seem digressive, yet they serve to prove the martial abilities of the hero.

Knights and the warriors who preceded the institution of knighthood are foremost men of action. The heroic epic *Beowulf* vividly illustrates that deeds take precedence over words. When Beowulf is greeted by the coast-guard upon his arrival in Denmark, he boasts that he has come on a mission of action, to avenge King Hrothgar of the monster Grendel's crimes. The coast guard responds to Beowulf's boasts with cautionary words: "Æghwæþres scheal scearp scyld-wiga gescad witan, worda and worca, se þe wel þenceð" (A noble warrior with a keen mind can draw the difference between words and actions."[6] He points out that Beowulf's *flyting*, or battle boasting, is worthless if he cannot bring to successful fruition the deeds that he proposes. Heroic literature denigrates those who are guilty of *ofermod*, an excess of self-confidence that results in brazen and unmerited boasting. As the Westerosi often say, "words are wind."

In fact, Beowulf does possess the necessary skills associated with prowess: bravery, strength, and cunning, and he proves that his boasts have merit. He also possesses other important attributes that prefigure the chivalric code and complement prowess. For example, he humbly gives the glory to God after his victories over Grendel and Grendel's mother. He generously offers to Hygelac the many rewards that Hrothgar distributes to him, both as a sign of his own loyalty and also as assurance of continued peace between the Danes and Geats. Clearly, Beowulf is a loyal and devout thane, unlike his own thanes so many years later who desert him in his time of need. Prowess, however, is his strongest virtue, enabling him, and only him, to defeat the monsters that have plagued Heorot and to restore peace to Hrothgar's hall.

One of the ways romance is distinguished from heroic literature is by a reduced emphasis on prowess, largely due to the genre's focus on softer aspects of chivalry such as proper behavior towards ladies and etiquette at court. However, prowess remains key to the identity of the knight of romance, whether his fighting serves the realm or is to gain individual glory or the affections of a lady. The genre is typically described as a series of adventures through which a knight proves himself, "adventures" denoting obstacles to be overcome, such as fighting in duels and battles. The plot of the romance often involves the knight's attempt to balance prowess with other aspects of chivalry, especially courtly love. In "Erec and Enide" by Chrétien de Troyes, the plot revolves around the titular character's attempts to re-establish his prowess after his reputation has suffered from excessive time spent with his wife. In Chrétien's "Yvain," on the other hand, the titular character becomes so intent on pursuing glory through battle that he neglects, and nearly loses, his lover. Both knights engage in battle to gain personal glory and to reclaim their worth. While Malory's *Le Morte Darthur* includes numerous battle scenes that are similarly fought for personal glory, his Arthurian knights also fight for the security of the kingdom and out of loyalty to Arthur. Both the early battles in *Le Morte Darthur* in which young Arthur is establishing himself as well as Arthur's final battle against Mordred are, like the primary battles in Martin's novels, fought for control of the realm.

Medieval handbooks of chivalry, such as those written by Ramon Lull and Geoffroi de Charney, delineate the rules of chivalry in a straightforward manner. Battlefield etiquette is critical to the narratives of both heroic texts and romances. However, codes of behavior are not always explicitly expressed in these forms of literature. Rather, they must be inferred by the actions and words of characters. Shannon French explains, "A code can be hidden in the lines of epic poems or implied by the descriptions of mythic heroes."[7] Like these medieval writers, Martin seeks to explore the social role of the knight and the function of prowess, but readers must look at the actions of various characters to piece together the rules of etiquette valued (or supposed to be valued) by the Westerosi.

In the epilogue of his edition of Ramon Lull's *Handbook of Chivalry*, Caxton sets up the work as exemplary:

> O ye knights of England, where is the custom and usage of noble chivalry that was used in those days? What do you now, but to go to the banes and to play at dice? And some not well advised used not honesty and good rules again in the order of knighthood. Leave this, leave this and read the noble volumes of Saint Grail of Lancelot, of Galahad, of Tristam, of Percefrost, of Percival, of Gawain, and so many more. There you will see manhood, courtesy, and gentleness.[8]

While Martin's novels include some examples of "manhood, courtesy, and gentleness," readers are more likely to find examples of murder, treachery, and deceit. However, by presenting an often cynical and brutal view of chivalry, Martin offers readers and scholars insight into the complexities of the chivalric code and, perhaps, a new lens to consider the social roles of knights and warriors. Although Martin's knights and warriors do not always behave ethically (on or off the battlefield), the implicit guidelines and expectations that are meant to govern them closely align with those gleaned from heroic literature and romance, and also those delineated in chivalric handbooks. Martin draws out the struggles and ambiguities of these guidelines and expectations as his characters struggle to abide by them or blatantly defy them.

Nigel Saul writes that "In a sense, what chivalry did was ritualize war."[9] It imposed certain rules and restrictions on warfare. Robert L. Kelly argues that Arthur's Round Table knights serve as "an instrument of rule."[10] The order of the Round Table provides "an institution through which a royal patron recruits noble retainers to serve the specific, chiefly military, needs of his reign."[11] In other words, the knights of the Round Table serve the king. They also, however, have a duty to protect the realm. Ramon Lull more specifically describes the role of knight as protector: "The knight must maintain and defend women, and respect and defend those less powerful than he."[12] The Kingsguard and other orders of Westerosi knights are much like the Knights of the Round Table. They were originally formed to serve the king and to protect the realm. Their primary function is defense, yet honor, humility, loyalty, intelligence, and mercy should temper the actions of true knights.

Training for Knighthood

Training to perform military duties effectively can be a lengthy process. Lessons in prowess and the attributes associated with it typically begin in youth. Martin has numerous passages in which young men (and some young women) practice jousting and learn skills of weaponry. In *A Game of Thrones*, the Stark brothers (never to become actual knights) train at jousting and stage mock tournaments, a formative part of their upbringing that is referenced throughout the series. Their father Eddard teaches them other values as well, such as how to administer justice. When Eddard condemns a deserter from the Night's Watch to death, he insists that, since he made the sentence, he must himself administer the penalty. Later his sons Robb and Jon both follow his example when they are in positions of administering sentences.

Battle etiquette and training (or lack thereof) is a key formative factor in the development of knights. While the Stark brothers are naturals at weaponry and learn the etiquette of justice that accompanies prowess, not all the children of nobility fare so well. Samwell Tarly is ultimately disowned by his father for his lack of prowess. Tommen Baratheon similarly holds little promise as a warrior. He is beaten by Bran at Winterfell in a mock tournament and later ridiculed at King's Landing by his cruel older brother Joffrey when he participates in a faux tournament. Training is hardly beneficial to Joffrey, either, as he shows little talent at shooting arrows in practice and as his mother insists that he is kept out of harm's way during the Battle of Blackwater Bay.

Knightly training continues into adulthood. In his *Book of Knighthood and Chivalry*, Ramon Lull explains the importance of training in order for the knight to fulfill his duties as defender of the realm: "Knights ought to take coursers to joust and to go to tourneys, hold an open table, to hunt harts, bears, and other wild beasts, for in doing these things the knights exercise themselves to arms and thus maintain the order of knighthood."[13] Tournaments serve doubly as entertainment and training. They provide knights with a chance to practice the etiquette of warfare and also function as a popular spectator sport. As the battle for the Iron Throne is underway, Martin's knights do not often participate in tournaments. However, tournaments do have an important place in the narrative. The tournament in which Rhaegar Targaryen offers a rose of victory to Lyanna Stark sparks a war, setting off the events that motivate the entire series of novels.

Tournaments are meant to train knights and to serve as entertainment, yet they can be treacherous. In *A Game of Thrones*, Martin describes a later tournament, the Hand's Tourney, from the perspective of Sansa Stark. Sansa has been sheltered from the brutality of warfare. The violence of battle is typically glossed over or entirely omitted from the songs that have shaped her idealistic notions of chivalry. Even after witnessing her first death at this tournament, she is unmoved by a young man who is killed in the mock combat. She acknowledges to herself that "she should be crying…, but the tears would not come" (*G of T* 287). She does not personally know this young knight, and he has not impressed her in the tournament. She decides that he is "nothing to her … some stranger from the Vale of Arryn whose name she had forgotten as soon as she heard it" (*G of* T). Her father, however, realizes that the youth's death is senseless and sad, and Sansa eventually has this realization herself once she becomes disillusioned with knights.

Esteemed Westerosi knight Ser Barristan Selmy, posing as Arstan Whitebeard, explains to Ser Jorah Mormont the often-unpredictable outcomes of tournaments: "A man will win one tourney, and fall quickly in the next. A slick spot in the grass may mean defeat, or what you ate for supper the night before" (*S of S* 111). Tournaments are intended to hone a knight's fighting skills; they showcase and glorify the prowess of knights. They are meant to mimic battle and have strict rules for participation, yet both injury and death are possibilities. This is one reason that actual tournaments in the Middle Ages were monitored and sometimes censored.

The literary tournaments of medieval romance are also treacherous, but typically less graphically depicted than in Martin's novels. In Malory's "The Fair Maid of Astolat," Lancelot fights *in cognito* against the other knights of the Round Table. He is badly injured in a tournament. Not recognizing him, Bors inflicts a serious wound in Lancelot's side, and Lancelot must be nursed back to health by Elaine of Astolat. While Arthur's knights are sometimes injured in tournaments, the ultimate outcome is generally predictable: Arthur's knights typically win. In Chaucer's "The Knight's Tale," the ending is less predictable, but Chaucer's main purpose is to highlight the role of fate that allows Arcite to win the tournament, but Palamon to win the prize, the lovely Amazonian Emilye.

Tournaments are accompanied by much fanfare; medieval writers often relish in describing the details of the arena, the clothing of the ladies in the audience, and the lavish armor of participants. Chaucer's "The Knight's Tale" devotes hundreds of lines to describing the physical structure and ornamentation of the tournament arena. Martin's novels also emphasize the lavishness and expense that accompany tournaments. They are extravagant affairs that make clear the importance of wealth to prowess. Armor and weaponry are costly requisites of knighthood. As illustrated by various versions of the Lanval stories, knights without wealth quickly lose esteem. Lanval, who is renowned for his generosity, squanders too much of his money and suffers the consequences until a fairy lover gives him a bottomless purse. Obviously, money is necessary for advancement. Lords who host tournaments use the occasion to showcase their wealth, and those who can afford to participate showcase both their skills at fighting and their equipment. Thus, tournaments serve not only to hone the skills of knights and to entertain, but also to establish status.

Although possession of arms does not guarantee prowess, the prowess of a knight is measured, in some respects, by the equipment of warfare, especially the worth of his horse and the value of his sword. Ramon Lull notes simply that proper gear is a necessity: "[The knight] must have a good horse and complete harness."[14] Geoffroi de Charney explains more fully the link between prowess and wealth. Deeds at tournaments, he writes, "earn men praise and esteem for they require a great deal of wealth, equipment, and expenditure."[15] In Martin's novels, wealthy knights display expensive adornments and weapons (such as Jaime Lannister's distinctive golden armor). In contrast, the assembly of renegade "knights," The Brotherhood Without Banners led by Beric Dondarrion, piece together loose ends and craft make-shift equipment from battle scraps. In Martin's "The Hedge Knight," Dunk, destitute after the death of the hedge knight he has served, must scrounge for armor and even sells his horse to buy the proper equipment.

Although I will not discuss in detail the kinds of weaponry Martin uses, I do want to emphasize their symbolic significance as they relate to the chivalric virtues that should accompany prowess. Swords are seen as extensions of the knight or warrior himself and, while they are no more costly than some of the other necessities of battle, they have special value and meaning.[16] A worthy sword signifies a worthy knight. Like sigils, swords are handed down through the generations. They may also be won in battle. From Beowulf's Naegling (and Hrunting, generously loaned to him by a chastened Unferth) to Excalibur, swords are a critical part of medieval literature and the primary weapon used in combat. Brienne of Tarth explains the significance of swords in Westeros when she considers the sword that Jaime has given to her. Although she has not inherited this sword, she is aware of its significance: "It was a sword fit for a hero.... Each man bore a famous sword, and surely Oathkeeper belonged in their company, even if she herself did not" (*F for C* 94). In fact, this sword has a deep history, having been forged from Eddard Stark's familial sword, Ice. Appropriately, Brienne intends to use this sword to rescue the Stark girls. Holding a similar regard for her sword, Arya cannot throw her tiny sword Needle into the water, even after she vows to forgo her former identity to join the Faceless Men. It serves as her last link to her former life, and it represents her determination to seek vengeance against those who have struck down her family members. For Arya, Needle is a symbol of determination and resolve to avenge those who have wronged her and those whom she loves.

Swords forged from Valyrian steel are of particular value and may well be the key to fighting the biggest threat to Westeros, the Others. As an illegitimate son, Jon Snow is not given a sword carried by his ancestors. Thus, Jon is honored when Jeor Mormont gives to him the sword meant for Jeor's own son (called a bastard sword for its length, though Jon can't miss the appropriateness of this term).[17] However, Jon also feels that this sword is not rightfully his own. Later, Jon realizes that the Valyrian steel from which the sword has been forged has special properties. When Tormund questions Jon about how he thinks they might fight the white walkers, Jon remembers the information that Sam has gleaned from the ancient books in the cellar of Castle Black. He recalls the magical powers and extreme strength attributed to swords made with Valyrian steel. However, he wonders if the stories about these swords will hold true because "the true test came in battle" (*D with D* 853). The success of the knight and perhaps the fate of Westeros are largely dependent on swords, not just the warrior's ability to wield his weapon in battle, but also, in this case, inherent properties of the sword itself. Just as the sheath of Excalibur has protective properties for Arthur, so, too, the Valyrian swords appear to have magical qualities. In the HBO series, their magical qualities are evidenced during the battle at Hardhome when Jon faces off against the white walkers.

Possession of weapons (even magical swords), skill with arms, and brute strength are necessary for prowess, but they do not guarantee true glory unless accompanied by other virtues and attributes. Charles Hackney explains that "In every society that has had a warrior tradition, there has existed the idea that a warrior of excellence is more than just someone who is good at hurting people, and that the crucial difference is the warrior's moral character."[18] By linking armor and weaponry to the virtues of knighthood, Ramon Lull emphasizes this point to his medieval audience. He explains that, for example, the shield represents "defense of his prince," the gauntlet "keeps him … from touching evil," the horse assures "noblesse of courage," and the reigns indicate that "the knight should be led by chivalry and duty."[19] Lull delineates the virtues of chivalry: Faith, Hope, Charity, Justice, Prudence, Strength, and Chastity. Prowess should be combined with these virtues, even on the battlefield in the throes of battle. Historian Nigel Saul explains that, in actual medieval warfare, chivalry had a critical role:

Chivalry, far from being a romanticized fantasy separate from the knight's everyday experience, was absolutely central to it. There was a continuum between the knight's nurturing of his skills in the tournament lists, where the culture of chivalry was rooted, and his actual practice of arms.[20]

He lists the salient qualities of chivalry, particularly mental ones that accompany prowess on the battlefield:

> Courage, honour and achievement went hand in hand. Honour, the reward for courage, contrasted with shame, engendered by cowardice, an attribute abhorrent to knighthood. A knight who performed brave deeds humbly and without arrogance was a knight who acted chivalrously.[21]

Martin's portrayal of prowess is particularly meaningful when considered in conjunction with these chivalric virtues. As his knights engage in battle, Martin's readers sometimes witness courage, honor and glory.

Often, chivalric virtues in Martin's novels appear in unlikely form, as when the dwarf Tyrion Lannister fights bravely at the Battle of Blackwater Bay. Martin also illustrates how these virtues might be challenged in the thick of battle. Tyrion, in spite of his bravery in battle, falls victim to the trickery of his sister and is nearly killed by one of her cronies. The Hound, known for his courage in battle, flees when confronted by his greatest fear, fire. Repeatedly, Martin's knights and warriors are placed in dire situations that challenge them and call to question the possibility of maintaining virtue amidst the chaos of battle. Other times, he portrays knights who disregard the need for virtue all together. Ser Gregor Clegane, who kills without motive and without any consideration of rules and virtues, is perhaps Martin's most extreme example of such disregard.

Prowess and Chivalric Virtues

Ramon Lull explains that "A knight should be courteous, should speak well, and should have good harness and fair horse. Chivalry is not the horse or arms, in the power, but is rather the knight himself, if he is committed to chivalry."[22] Although courtly etiquette seems at odds with the violence that occurs on the battlefield, knights and warriors were expected to embody equally both martial abilities and courtesy. True knights and warriors follow strictly coded rules that should govern and temper their behavior in combat. Beowulf, for example, follows a strict code of martial behavior even when battling against monsters and a dragon. He insists on a fair fight by refusing armor in his fight against Grendel, and he only reluctantly agrees to wear armor against the dragon. In Chaucer's "The Knight's Tale," sworn enemies Palamon and Arcite temporarily put aside their differences to help each other arm before battle. In Malory's "The Siege of Benwick," Lancelot refuses to engage in battle against his king even when Arthur lays siege upon his castle. Both Arthur's and Mordred's men adhere to the truce described in "The Day of Destiny" until by chance an adder causes one of the knights to draw his sword. In other words, fighting is not a free-for-all. Similar instances in which knights measure prowess with courtesy can be found throughout Martin's novels. Loyalty and duty are combined when one-armed Jaime Lannister returns to Harrenhal to rescue his former enemy, Brienne of Tarth. The Hound demonstrates a respect for the rules of battle when he refuses to attack his much-loathed brother's unhelmeted head. And Barristan Selmy educates his young squires, teaching them how to wield their weapons and defend themselves, and also "chivalry, the code that made a knight more than any pit fighter" (*D with D* 806).

Proper speech as dictated by rules of courtesy is also intricately connected to prowess. Malory's account of Sir Gareth illustrates the connection between these two attributes. Sir Gareth is plagued by the insulting language of both Sir Kay and the lady he escorts, Lyonet, who has called him a "kychyn knave"[23] because he served in the kitchen, by his own request, when he first entered Arthur's court. The court is unaware of Gareth's heritage (he is Gawain's brother). He endures numerous insults but ultimately proves his worth through his own use of courteous speech and through his success in battle. Ruth Lexton explains the importance of combining prowess with courtesy and argues that the marriage of these chivalric virtues is exemplified through Gareth's actions: "Not only does Gareth prove the prowess of his hands, but also his adventures show that true martial service must operate in conjunction with civil speech. For example, when Gareth defeats the Green Knight and receives an offer of service, he requires courteous language from Lyonet to fulfil it."[24] She argues that courtesy, for Malory's readers, is "a form of restraint on violence,"[25] and as such prevents knights from becoming, as The Hound claims, merely killers. Thus, Gareth shows "how martial service may be transformed into domestic service at table,"[26] both by his early service in Arthur's kitchen and his later success on the battlefield.

An essential part of courtesy in romance is proper behavior towards women, which encompasses not only proper speech, but also behavior on the battlefield when the love or honor of a lady is at stake. The very purpose of many romance battles is to win the love of a lady. Repeatedly, Lancelot is placed in situations in which he must use his fighting skills to rescue his queen, Guinevere. He fights on her behalf not solely because of his amorous feelings towards her, but also because his king has approved of this duty. In Malory's "The Poisoned Apple," Arthur himself makes this known to Guenevere when Lancelot is not available to defend her in battle: "What aylith you … that ye can nat kepe sir Launcelot uppon youre syde?"[27] As king, and therefore judge, Arthur cannot fight on his wife's behalf and has need for one of his knights to take on this duty, especially since the queen has a propensity for getting herself into situations requiring rescue. Lancelot obediently assumes the role of Guinevere's protector and champion. However, he stretches the limits of courtesy too far by falling in love with his queen. His relationship with Guinevere crosses the line of duty and complicates his relationship with Arthur as well as the other knights of the Round Table.

In his manual of chivalry, Geoffroi de Charny praises feats of arms performed on the behalf of ladies although he refers to knights who fight solely for this reason as "naive" because they are "unaware of the great honor they could win through deeds of arms." They succeed, nevertheless, because "they put their hearts into winning the love of a lady."[28] While Geoffroi condemns fighting for the sole purpose of winning a lady's love, he nonetheless condones ladies who encourage and inspire knights to perform worthy feats of arms: "Men should love secretly, protect, serve, and honor all those ladies and damsels who inspire knights ... to undertake worthy deeds that bring them honor."[29] Geoffroi takes no issue with knights who are inspired by ladies, but he makes clear that the fight must serve some greater purpose beyond amorous intentions. In Lancelot's case, his repeated defense of Guinevere fulfills his duty to Arthur, yet his love of Guinevere problematizes his service and makes questionable his true intentions.

Knights frequently battle on behalf of ladies and are inspired by them to commit great deeds of arms. Love interests, however, can also serve as impediments to success on the battlefield. For the lovesick knight, love affairs can cause conflicting loyalties that dampen the knight's zest for battles when those battles are not directly concerned with his lady. In the Old French romance "Aucassin and Nicolette," the hero initially refuses to fight for his father's land because his lover has been forbidden to him. When forced onto the battlefield, his first attempts against the enemy are disastrous as he falls into a reverie about Nicolette and is promptly taken captive. His love for Nicolette so consumes him that he has little concern for his family or the threat to his kingdom by enemy forces. After his father promises him that he can kiss Nicolette if he vanquishes their foe, Aucassin fights with zeal, but his motive is his lady, not the welfare of his kingdom.

In Chrétien de Troyes' "The Knight of the of the Cart," Lancelot, en route to rescue Guinevere, is torn between his duty to her and his duty to those he encounters along the way; including several women in distress and an entire village that is being held hostage. Lancelot assists those who request aid, but he is conflicted about his priorities. He has sworn to help those in need, yet as a courtly lover, he is expected to be unwavering in his quest to rescue Guinevere. Like Aucassin, Lancelot is distracted from his other duties by love. Similarly, Chrétien's Erec has such zeal for his new bride that his zeal for battle diminishes. Erec is so overwhelmed with love that he neglects his other knightly duties. As the narrative progresses, he struggles to re-establish his reputation for prowess.

While fighting on behalf of women is a frequent occurrence in romance, chastity is considered a virtue, as it ensures that a knight will not be distracted by thoughts of love. In the midst of a war over the Iron Throne, Martin's knights have little time to fight on behalf of their ladies, yet they are frequently distracted by amorous thoughts and actions. Clearly, the love of ladies is perceived as a longstanding distraction for the high-ranking knights of the Westerosi Kingsguard and also for the men of the Night's Watch. For this reason, they are required to make vows of chastity. These vows are measures to ensure that the men avoid lascivious and potentially distracting behavior that might keep them from devoted service to the king or, in the case of the Night's Watch, to the realm. As Geoffroi de Charny makes clear, knights have a duty to protect the entire realm and not act solely on behalf of their ladies.

Ramon Lull explores the conflicts that can arise when a knight is overcome with lust. He writes that "Lechery and chastity fight against one another, and the arms with which lechery wars on chastity are youth, beauty, heavy drinking, and eating too much meat, bright clothes, bravado, falsehood, treason, injury, and the despising of God and his glory."[30] Most of the knights of the Kingsguard engage in the activities that Lull describes. They seem to hold little value for their vows of chastity. In fact, they tend to display their vices freely. The men of the Night's Watch are as a rule isolated from contact with women other than, occasionally, Wildling women. Females are generally not allowed at Castle Black for their own protection against these lustful young men who are deprived of female contact. This isolation does not deter lustful thoughts, however, and becomes a challenge for their Lord Commander on those rare occasions when women are nearby. The men must be warned, for instance, to keep away from Craster's wives when they lodge at Craster's Keep.

Most of the Westerosi knights and warriors who have taken vows of chastity seem unbothered when they succumb to their lust. A few, however, struggle earnestly to keep their vows. In the present of Martin's novels, Jaime Lannister sleeps with his twin sister Cersei, and Ser Arys Oakheart is seduced by the Dornish princess Arianne Martell. Both are members of the Kingsguard and have sworn vows of chastity. At the Wall, Jon Snow succumbs to the Wildling Ygritte. Martin does not explicitly portray courtly love, yet through these characters, he explores the tensions that can arise when vows of chastity are broken and when knights and warriors are distracted by love of women. Jon and Arys feel guilt even as they engage in their illicit affairs, while Jaime's guilt comes only after the loss of his sword hand. This loss leads him to soul searching about his role in the Kingsguard. Jon, Aerys, and Jaime are rare among Martin's knights and warriors in their conflicted feelings about love and duty. They aspire to uphold chivalric values, and they are aware of their failures and flaws. Martin's portrayal of knightly virtues may seem bleak. However, Arthur's knights, with the exception of the virginal Galahad, are not perfect, either, although their vices are displayed less flamboyantly than those of the men in Martin's novels. Gawain is known as something of a lady's man in the English tradition of Arthurian literature, and Lancelot's adulterous affair with Guinevere knocks him out of contention for the Grail and ultimately causes the downfall of the kingdom.

Knights and warriors of medieval romance usually engage in battle for a purpose larger than personal glory: loyalty to an individual, an institution, or a greater cause. Prowess is thus closely aligned with loyalty and often manifests on the battlefield as a physical demonstration of the bonds between lord and thane or the bonds between family members. True knights and warriors should also demonstrate loyalty to the kingdom, including all of its members, even peasants. Lull writes, "After his knighting, [a knight] ought to ride among the people; the knowledge of his pledge keeps him from evil."[31] He adds that "the office of a knight is to maintain the land."[32] When many nobles deny King Arthur as rightful heir, the assent of the commoners solidifies his right to the throne. At the end of Malory's *Le Morte Darthur*, many of the commoners have grown weary of the warfare under Arthur's rule and support the usurper Mordred. Although peasants collectively have the potential to exert influence, their welfare is not truly a romance concern. The romance was intended for a noble audience and is populated primarily by noble characters. Peasants rarely make an appearance in these works, and when they do appear, they have only minor roles.[33] The lack of concern for commoners in the romance is illustrative of their insignificance in the mindset of the medieval nobility. The actions of the nobility often have a profound effect on those of lower status that is glossed over or ignored in the genre.

Martin's novels give a graphic picture of the effects of warfare on the lower class yet also make clear that the majority of the Westerosi nobility are, like their historical and literary counterparts, not much concerned with the welfare of those beneath them. In times of warfare, particularly, the common folk might suffer most as knights pursue glory through prowess. Historian Nigel Saul gives the real-life example of William the Conqueror who harried parts of England in 1069–70. Saul discusses the devastation that William's actions had upon the peasantry:

> One of the attractions of burning and harrying was that it minimized direct conflict between members of the warrior aristocracy.... However, the price for this apparently civilized policy was paid by ordinary folk—humble peasantry and townsmen. The burden and cost of war were thrust firmly onto their shoulders in the form of loss of livestock, burning of crops and of property.[34]

Martin repeatedly describes a similar devastation of the land as his characters travel across Westeros. Many towns are burned or deserted, and examples of extreme poverty, much which results from warfare, are abundant.

Martin also explores the ethical conflicts that might arise in the rare noble who acknowledges the plight of the lower classes in times of war. For example, Brienne of Tarth is shocked by the actions of Ser Quincy Cox toward the peasants who pay homage to him. Outlaws arrive, and rather than trying to defend the smallfolk according to his sworn duty, Ser Quincy simply bars his gates. While Septon Meribald is sympathetic to Ser Quincy's dilemma, Brienne is critical of his refusal to help the defenseless: "*a true knight is sworn to protect those who are weaker than himself, or die in the attempt*" (*F for C* 665). Brienne is one of the few characters who holds true to this ideal of protecting everyone in the kingdom. Her thoughts indicate that she would not hesitate to put her own life on the line for commoners.

Ironically, those whom knights are meant to protect sometimes end up as victims, and this is especially true when a game of thrones is involved. Fighting in Westeros, as in romance, is rarely about protecting the weak, but rather it is about the most powerful asserting their authority. Ramon Lull writes that "Chivalry and justice accord so strongly, that without justice chivalry may not be."[35] This is a lesson that Jaime Lannister appears to be learning in *A Dance with Dragons* as he travels across Westeros attempting to make truces and right wrongs. Although his concern is not primarily for the commoners, they will surely benefit from his emphasis on negotiation over warfare.

Whereas Jaime, at this point, favors negotiation over battle, combat can be used as a means of administering justice. Ramon Lull explains the duty of the knight to defend "those who are neither powerful nor strong."[36] Trials by combat can be fought on behalf of those who are not physically able to defend themselves. Trials by combat are very frequent in Arthurian literature as Arthur's knights are called upon to champion the women they encounter. Lancelot is repeatedly called upon to defend Guinevere when she is accused of various crimes. In Malory's "The Knight of the Cart," for example, she is accused of sleeping with Arthur's knights while they are all in Mellyagaunce's custody. (She has slept only with Lancelot, though she does not admit to this.) Mellyagaunce is killed in the duel with Lancelot that results from this accusation. In "The Poisoned Apple," she is falsely accused of attempting to poison Gawain and has a difficult time finding a knight who will come to her defense. She has sent Lancelot, her usual champion, away, and her reputation is clearly in decline to the point that none of Arthur's knights is particularly eager to assist her. Although she finds a reluctant champion in Sir Bors, Lancelot returns in the nick of time to defend her.

For Martin, trials by combat are introduced with some interesting wrinkles.

Twice, Tyrion Lannister requires champions. In the first incident, the sellsword Bronn (not yet a knight) steps in on his behalf. While trials by combat in romance are often in defense of ladies, Bronn fights for Tyrion because the dwarf is physically unable to defend himself in one-on-one combat. Tyrion requires a champion when Lysa Arryn wants to have him put to death. He is accused of killing Jon Aryn and of attempting to kill Bran Stark. Bronn comes to Tyrion's defense, surprising the witnesses with his easy victory. Later, Tyrion is accused (again wrongly) of murdering King Joffrey. In this trial by combat, Oberyn Martell offers to be his champion, pitting himself against Ser Gregor Clegane. For Martell, this duel also serves to settle an old feud. Both Oberyn and Ser Gregor die as a result of this battle, yet it is not Ser Gregor's last opportunity to fight. When Cersei Lannister needs a champion, rather than choosing one from among those whose loyalty she has tried to buy, she has the maester Qyburn create a new champion for her, which is likely from Ser Gregor's headless corpse.

Prowess should be curbed by mercy. Arthur's knights are expected to offer mercy to those whom they have defeated as long as the defeated requests it and, if fighting on behalf of a lady, as long as the victorious knight has her approval. When Mellyagaunce asks for mercy in Malory's "The Knight of the Cart," Lancelot is torn between this request and Guinevere's insistence that no mercy be granted. He solves this dilemma by offering Mellyagaunce a second chance at battle, this time fighting with a handicap. Lancelot goes into battle unhelmeted and with his left side unarmored. This leaves him vulnerable to attacks by Mellyagaunce's lance. He wins the battle even with this handicap, and Mellyagaunce is promptly decapitated.

Mercy is also an important, if often neglected, aspect of Westerosi chivalry. When he first arrives at Castle Black, Jon Snow has much to learn about curbing his fighting abilities with mercy. He readily defeats the other recruits in jousting matches. This is mock battle, and his opponents are neither killed nor seriously injured. However, they are shamed in front of their brothers. Jon is ultimately chastened and learns to treat his brothers, who have had not had the advantage of training in their youth, mercifully. He begins teaching them fighting skills rather than humiliating them. Later, as Lord Commander, Jon joins a sparring session of young recruits who are training under Iron Emmett. While sparring with these recruits, he offers to fight three against one to teach them a lesson about battle. When one of the recruits, Jace, notes that this isn't fair, Jon knocks him to the ground and tells him that war itself can be unfair (*D with D* 412). Jon has learned to be merciful, yet he also knows the hardships of battle and seeks to prepare his young recruits.

Daenerys Targaryen is not a warrior or knight, but a ruler. For her, the value of mercy seems innate rather than something she must learn. She instructs the Unsullied, who have been trained as warriors rather than knights, to temper prowess with mercy when conquering Yunkai. She asks Grey Worm to act with both "wisdom as well as valor" and to "spare any slave who runs or throws down his weapon" (*S of S* 573). She uses her authority to hold court and administer justice, always with the intent of treating her subjects fairly and with mercy. For Martin, mercy can appear in unexpected circumstances. An early sign that The Hound, Sandor Clegane, is not the brute he originally seems to be, also involves mercy. When he comes across a man who escaped the Red Wedding and is mortally wounded, he "eased his dagger into the man's chest almost tenderly, the weight of his body driving the point through his surcoat" (*S of S* 887). This is an act of mercy to relieve the man of a lingering death.

Other characters display a blatant lack of mercy. Notable among them is Arya Stark. When The Hound is grievously wounded, he asks Arya to put him out of his misery. Showing her increasing preoccupation with vengeance, she tells him that he is undeserving of mercy, and then she abandons him (*S of S* 1039). Arya is blinded by vengeance. She ultimately becomes one of the faceless men, killing machines with no regard for mercy. While attempting to take Winterfell, Stannis Baratheon also shows little regard for mercy. He refuses to forgive the men who have resorted, in their desperation, to eating the corpses of their fallen comrades. Stannis offers these men instead to the Lord of Light (*D with D* 895). His decision is motivated by his own desire for power and the dire circumstances in which he finds himself at this juncture in the narrative.

Leaders sometimes must make difficult decisions that seem merciless but are necessary. One example is in the opening pages of *A Game of Thrones*. Eddard Stark decides to behead Gared, a man who has deserted the Night's Watch, although Gared has clearly lost his mind after his encounter with the Others. We learn that this is not the first deserter Eddard has put to the sword. Eddard firmly believes in the credo that deserters must die because they have broken their vows. He wants to illustrate this lesson to his sons, who witness the execution. Likewise, Jon Snow, as commander of the Night's Watch, beheads Janos Slynt after Slynt has disobeyed Jon's command. Slynt begs for mercy in the moments before his death, but Jon ignores him. Jon knows that he will lose the respect of his men if he grants mercy to Slynt, and he probably doubts if Slynt is sincere in his pleas for mercy. As King of the North, Robb Stark condemns and puts to death Rickard Karstark. Seeking vengeance on the Lannisters, Karstark kills two of their relatives whom Robb holds captive. Karstark does not explicitly ask for mercy from Robb, but he cites the kinship between Robb and himself in an effort to deter his death (they are distant cousins). Robb does not heed Karstark's warning that this death will amount to kin killing. The deaths of the two young Lannisters, who have been murdered in their sleep, takes precedence over Karstark's flimsy claims of kinship. In these instances, the reasons for the execution override the call for mercy. The chivalric code requires that those in charge make difficult decisions such as these.

In romance, the recipient of a merciful act must himself behave honorably in return, adhering to the requests of the victor. Honor, critical to the reputation of the medieval knight, is illustrated in Malory's romance when defeated captives who have been shown mercy must pledge to report to Arthur's court as captives. The chivalric code makes such pledges unquestionable; true knights will act according to their pledges. Martin's Westerosi code echoes this sentiment. When Robb Stark sends Ser Cleos Frey, a Lannister cousin, as emissary to the Lannisters, he tells Frey that he must make a pledge to deliver the message, return with a response, and then resume his captivity. Frey responds, "I do so vow" (*C of K* 109). Frey tries to be true to his word, although he is subsequently imprisoned again for the attempted escape of some of his men.

Honor can also be illustrated through the concept of safe conduct, which frequently appears in romance. In Chrétien de Troyes' "The Knight of the Cart," Lancelot must offer safe conduct to a damsel who requests it. He escorts her along her travels and must defend her from any challengers. This code of conduct pertains to both women and men. In Malory's "The Knight with the Two Swords," Balin is deeply bothered when Sir Garlon, riding invisibly, kills two knights who are under Balin's escort. He feels compelled to amend this breach of courtesy. In Martin's novels, Brienne is well aware of the concept of safe conduct as she escorts Jaime Lannister back to King's Landing after Catelyn Stark has released him. His safe return, she hopes, might ensure the exchange of Sansa and Arya Stark. Brienne holds dear her pledge to fulfill this mission. In contrast, Theon Greyjoy, under the influence of Ramsay Bolton, offers safe conduct to the Ironmen who have held Winterfell. He promises safe conduct and puts forth a letter written in Lord Bolton's hand (*D with D* 284). Theon has over-reached and cannot protect the Ironmen who have followed him. The Boltons have little regard for chivalric etiquette or honor and do not make good on this promise despite the hand-written letter. Thus, Martin uses both positive and negative examples to illustrate the significance of chivalric virtues.

Wit, Trickery and Excessive Zeal

Prowess should be guided by intellect. As Ramon Lull explains, "Knights must possess wit and discretion."[37] The intellectual aspects of chivalry are more fully drawn out in Martin's novels than in the writings of his medieval predecessors. Especially, Martin likes to explore how those without physical abilities might use their wits in place of prowess. Jaime Lannister, who transitions from being one of Westeros's most glorified knights to being an invalid, is a case in study for how other attributes might substitute for fighting ability. Jaime, as readers initially encounter him, is morally corrupt but brilliant on the battlefield. His sole focus, other than sleeping with his twin sister, is his reputation for prowess. Martin describes his commitment to warfare: "The Warrior had been Jaime's god since he was old enough to hold a sword.... He was a warrior, and that was all he would ever be" (*F for C* 175). Malory's Lancelot makes a similar claim about his role as a knight when a damsel requests his love, telling her that he is devoted to military service: "But for to be a weddyd man, I thynke hit nat, for than I muste couche with hir and leve armys and turnaments, battelys, and adventures."[38] For both Jaime and Lancelot, their reputations for an abundance of prowess cover dark secrets: Jaime's incestuous affair with his own twin sister, and Lancelot's adulterous affair with his queen (which is indicated at a later point in Malory's narrative).

Jaime's success on the battlefield is naturally dependent upon the use of his sword hand. Once he loses his sword hand and with it his ability to fight, Jaime finds it necessary to hone some of the other attributes that should accompany prowess. He contemplates his worth without the ability to wield a sword: "*Was that all I was, a sword hand?*" (*S of S* 415). He attempts to learn jousting one-handed, but his efforts are unsuccessful. Bruised and battered after practice jousting with Ser Ilyn, Jaime tells Lew Piper that his injuries are from a night of raucous lovemaking (*F for C* 569). He would rather the lad believe he has been with a whore than know that he has been injured while desperately attempting to learn to fight one-handed.

Jaime's efforts to learn to fight without his sword hand are futile: he is irreparably damaged as a warrior and must learn to rely on other traits, especially his wits. Ironically, in this process, he gains something he could not attain before when his fighting skills were intact. Particularly, Jaime hones his skills in diplomacy and negotiation. He insists on returning to rescue Brienne of Tarth from Harrenhal, and he subsequently works as a diplomat, restoring peace and making critical negotiations in his travels across Westeros. At least in the novels, he seems to be on a course of redemption similar to Malory's Lancelot, whose repentance begins with his failed quest for the Holy Grail and is complete only when, following Guinevere's example, he removes himself from the court to a life in the church. Jaime shows no inclination to join the septons (as does his cousin Lancel), but, lacking a sword hand, he learns to use his intellect not in addition to, but in place of, prowess.

Lull writes that "many battles have been vanquished more by master, by wit and industry, than by multitudes of horsemen and good armour."[39] Jaime's brother Tyrion Lannister has had to rely on "wit and industry" his entire life. As a dwarf, Tyrion is physically unsuitable to be a knight. He repeatedly uses his wits and sharp verbal skills to get out of situations that seem to necessitate prowess. His ability to escape treacherous situations by means of his wits makes Tyrion one of Martin's most beloved and interesting characters. For example, as Tyrion and Bronn travel to King's Landing, they encounter some men from the mountain clans who greatly outnumber them. Tyrion uses his wits to save himself and Bronn, and even manages to secure the service of the clansmen. Even though he is physically unsuitable for knighthood, Tyrion does manage to fight well when the situation is necessary. When King's Landing is attacked by Ironmen crossing to the shore, Tyrion is assigned by his father to the rearguard. He leads his ragtag men (an assortment of sellswords) in a defense, successfully scattering the enemy and wielding his weapons with some success. He fights valiantly and rallies his men when the battle seems to turn against them. His success on the battlefield and his ability to inspire loyalty are evidenced by the enthusiastic battle cry of his men: "Half Man! Half Man!" His valor is admirable, but the battle is won primarily because of his wits: Tyrion devises a great chain that entraps the enemy's fleet in the Bay.

As Lord Commander of the Night's Watch, Jon Snow also comes to appreciate the value of intellect as a companion to prowess. Physically, Jon is more than capable, but his status as bastard is itself a kind of handicap. It prevents him from having social access to the trappings of knighthood and leads him to settle for a position in the Night's Watch. He excels in this position, not only proving himself at fighting, but also combining his fighting abilities with demonstrations of wisdom. He often seeks advice rather than acting on a whim. For example, when Maester Aemon leaves a book for Jon Snow and marks a specific passage, Jon locates and reads the suggested passage. Aemon hints to Jon that this passage contains important information that should be heeded, and he tells Jon that "Knowledge is a weapon…. Arm yourself well before you ride forth to battle" (*D with D* 115).

As Jon comes to realize what must be done to fight against the Others, he recognizes the necessity of knowledge and how it can, in fact, be a weapon. He sends Samwell Tarly first to the books in the cellars of Castle Black and later to Oldtown to become a maester. He plans for Samwell to return to the Night's Watch and serve as Jon's advisor and maester at Castle Black. Jon also shows much careful thought in his decision to allow the Wildlings through the Wall. He knows this will be an unpopular decision, but Jon understands that the Others, not the Wildlings, are the true threat to Westeros. In *A Dance with Dragons*, however, Jon lets other instincts motivate him. He rashly determines to battle Ramsay Bolton, a decision based on emotion rather than reason. In the HBO series, Jon's emotions serve him well, motivating him to survive and win this battle even against great odds. In most circumstances, though, Jon has measured his actions with contemplation and after considering the opinions of those he trusts.

Intellect as a necessary component of chivalry can be linked to trickery. In Geoffrey of Monmouth's *History of the Kings of Britain*, Merlin uses trickery so that Gorlois can sleep with Ygraine. Gorlois's death in combat is a side-effect of this deception. In Malory's work, Lancelot occasionally uses trickery in a playful manner. He disguises himself in tournaments to engage in battle against the other knights of the Round Table. He knows they will not fight him with their full strength if they recognize him as one of their own.

When heroes resort to trickery, it is often put to good ends. For example, in the English romance *King Horn*, the hero adopts the disguise of a minstrel in order to rescue his love Rimenhild from the clutches of his enemy. Similarly, Jaime Lannister uses lies and trickery for good causes in several instances to rescue Brienne of Tarth. First, he claims that Brienne's homeland is filled with sapphires in order to save her from being brutally raped. In fact, her home, the Sapphire Isles, is so named because of the beautiful color of the surrounding water, but the lie is necessary and effective. He later tells his escort, Steelshanks Walton, that if they don't return to Harrenhal, he will tell his father that Walton has dismembered him (*S of S* 614). In truth, his hand has been taken at the command of Vargo Hoat, but Jaime can think of no other means to persuade his escort to turn back again. His intent is to free Brienne, and again, his efforts are successful.

Nigel Saul explains the role of trickery on the medieval battlefield: "Chivalric war was a tough down-to-earth business, and trickery and subterfuge formed part of it as much as colourful jousts and eve-of-battle *pas de armes*, but contemporaries had no difficulty in accepting its apparent contradictions. If they admired knightly heroism, they were also aware of the careful planning and good provisioning that actually won wars."[40] In romance and heroic literature, feigned retreats and other ruses are common battlefield strategies. The use of trickery is prevalent in Martin's battle scenes, as well. Stannis Baratheon uses the sorcery of the red priestess to kill his brother Renly before the battle begins. More often, though, trickery occurs on the battlefield itself. Tyrion Lannister, as previously mentioned, uses trickery at the Battle of Blackwater Bay, both by creating a chain to block the Bay and then by using wildfire as a weapon. In the same battle, Ser Garlan Tyrell dons the armor of Renly Baratheon, making many believe that Renly's ghost has returned to battle to seek vengeance against Stannis Baratheon. Siege strategies certainly entailed trickery, as well. Martin's use of germ warfare mimics the medieval siege strategy of hurling diseased bodies over castle walls. Ser Barristan realizes that the Yunkai'i are catapulting the corpses of those who died from the Pale Mare into the walls of Meereen (*D with D* 1016). Battlefield tricks such as these are often considered strategic rather than unchivalrous.

In contrast, one-on-one combat requires true knights and warriors to obey certain strictly coded rules and to avoid trickery that might give them an unfair advantage in battle. For this reason, Beowulf insists on fairness in his one-on-one fight against Grendel by refusing to wear armor, since he knows that Grendel will wear none. Those who don't follow the rules, killing senselessly or fighting unfairly, commit serious breaches of the chivalric and heroic code and are thus extremely dangerous enemies. Both Chrétien's and Malory's depictions of Meleagant/Mellyagaunce focus on the villains' breaches of courtesy as they fail to adhere to the rules of fair combat. When Malory's Mellyagaunce slays Lancelot's horse, Lancelot notes that he is in grave danger because of his opponent's unwillingness to fight fairly: "Alas, for shame! ... that ever one knyght shulde betray anothir knyght! But hyt ys an oldeseyde saw: 'A good man ys never in daungere but whan he ys in the daungere of a cowhard.'"[41] To avoid combat, Malory's Mellyagaunce later captures Lancelot by feigning hospitality. He offers Lancelot a tour of his castle only to have Lancelot fall through a trap door. In Chrétien's version, Meleagant rubs poison in Kay's wounds and has Lancelot kidnapped by a dwarf. Although Malory's version of this character is cowardly and tries to avoid combat, Chrétien's Meleagant must be restrained from fighting and refuses, when jousting with Lancelot, to obey the rules. When the combat is halted, he ignominiously continues to rain blows upon Lancelot. He possesses prowess without any sense of abiding by codes of conduct for fair fighting,

Martin's novels contain numerous examples of knights and warriors who fail to abide by the expected rules of combat. Notable among them are the Sons of the Harpy. In *A Dance with Dragons*, the Sons of the Harpy issue attacks by nightfall, leaving Daenerys Targaryen uncertain about how to avenge the deaths of those who serve or how to prevent more murders. She wonders whether knights could stand up against the unconventional tactics of this enemy: "What good would lances do against cowards who killed from the shadows?" (*D with D* 38). Daenerys sees these night attacks as cowardice. She knows that the Sons of the Harpy would not fight fairly in face-to-face combat with true knights and are thus, like Meleagant/Mellyagaunce, extremely dangerous enemies. The Sons of the Harpy, however, are trained in subterfuge rather than chivalry. Ser Barristan's newly trained knights will not be able to defeat them with traditional rules of combat.

Because the primary motivation of most of Martin's knights involves the struggle for control of the Iron Throne, his comprehensive portrayal of chivalry certainly emphasizes prowess over intellect and the other softer elements of chivalry. However, true knights should be brave, fair, and skillful in battle, but not overzealous or unrestrained. Ser Barristan is praised for having many virtues. He values prowess most, yet he understands how to harness his passion for battle. Thus, when he faces off against the pit fighter who is guarding

Hizdahr zo Loraq, he thinks to himself that he is in his natural element. He is invigorated by *"The dance, the sweet steel song, a sword in my hand and a foe before me"* (*D with D* 969). Whereas the pit fighter lunges at him in an unrestrained manner, Ser Barristan is able to match him through deliberate, controlled movements.

In contrast, many of Martin's knights and pseudo-knights are overcome with zeal and consequently have little regard for the aforementioned attributes and virtues that should accompany prowess. Perhaps the darkest portrayal of the institution of knighthood itself is conveyed through the words of Sandor Clegane, The Hound: repeatedly he remarks that knights are essentially killers. The Hound's brother, the brutal Ser Gregor Clegane, shapes The Hound's jaded perspective. Charles Hackney writes that "Knights of [Gregor] Clegane's mold may have been tolerated in times of invasion, but in the eleventh century, when most of the foreign invaders had been successfully repelled, king and cleric combined forces to reshape knighthood into a moral, as well as martial, force."[42] However, I would argue that Ser Gregor's cruelty is to the extent of seeming (and eventually becoming) non-human. Although technically a knight, he possesses unrestrained prowess without courtesy to such an extreme that he is portrayed as monstrous. He is reminiscent of the monster Grendel who refuses to abide by the rules of battle. Grendel is motivated solely by his hatred of the joyous music that emanates from Heorot, a hatred that drives him to kill. Grendel refuses to battle according to the rules of the Danes, preferring to attack stealthily at night (like the Sons of the Harpy) and seemingly taking pleasure in ripping apart and devouring Hrothgar's retainers. Removing him even further from the rule-governed prowess of the Danes and Geats, he refuses to pay *wergild*, or the price of a man, for those he kills.

Although the Lannisters see Ser Gregor as a loyal servant, he also kills simply because he finds pleasure in killing, not from any true sense of loyalty. Cruel from his youth, he becomes a knight who kills without question, upon command, and with unwarranted brutality. He is especially infamous for his brutality towards Princess Elia Targaryen, her young daughter, and her infant son. Lord Tywin Lannister ordered these deaths, but Ser Gregor, overcome with zeal, carries the killing too far. He reportedly bashed in the head of the infant and raped Elia with her child's blood still on his hands. Even Tywin cannot condone the brutality of these deaths and thus denies his own responsibility towards them. Tywin, however, appreciates that Ser Gregor is a useful asset to the Lannisters. He tells his son Tyrion that he is pleased with Ser Gregor's service, especially because the massive knight's scare tactics work well against his enemies (*S of S* 718). As the Lannisters engage in warfare across Westeros, Ser Gregor's reputation for rape and brutality grows with his increasingly horrific acts.

Ser Gregor represents prowess uncurbed by any concern for chivalric virtue. After he is killed by the poisoned sword of Oberyn Martell, he is transformed into something even more monstrous: Ser Robert Strong. Maester Qyburn creates, probably from Ser Gregor's corpse, this Frankenstein-like champion for Cersei Lannister. He is a fighting machine created solely to serve as Cersei Lannister's champion in trial by combat. Certainly, his impressive physical appearance in itself is intimidating. Martin describes him as over eight feet tall and powerfully built (*D with D* 941). He is both physically powerful and elaborately armored. His appearance is intended to shock and intimidate his foes. Even more terrifying than his size and mystique is the notion that this glossy exterior conceals a dead man; in essence, Ser Robert's armor contains only a corpse, an empty shell, evoking, perhaps, Italo Calvino's *The Nonexistent Knight* which features a "knight" who is, in fact, an empty armor. Malory has unknown knights, invisible knights (Garlon and, when he is given a magical ring, Gareth), and ghosts of knights (Gawain returning in a dream to warn Arthur of impending danger). Ser Robert, however, has no medieval predecessors, unless one is to count dragons and monsters that might equally be without any degree of moral compass.

In the novels, the residents of King's Landing have not yet confirmed Ser Robert's origins, but they find it odd that he does not participate in courtly life: he does not eat or drink; he is said to have taken a vow of silence; and he will not remove his helm, a hint that Ser Robert is headless. Ser Gregor's skull has been sent to the Dornish in settlement of a blood feud, making the argument for a headless knight probable. Unlike the Green Knight in *Sir Gawain and the Green Knight*, Ser Robert will not be able to reattach his head. Devoid of the capacity to reason or feel emotion, Ser Robert represents prowess unchecked by loyalty, honor, mercy, or any other kind of restraint. In the HBO series, his identity is revealed, head in tact. For readers, however, Martin implies that beneath Ser Robert's helmet lies nothing at all, rendering him incapable of curbing prowess with mercy, wit, or justice. As such, he may emerge as Martin's most evil villain, as there is no chance of redemption; nothing to redeem.

Ser Robert Strong may be Martin's most extreme example of unbridled prowess, but he certainly is not the only one. Westeros is populated by irreverent members of the Kingsguard, sellswords who kill for money rather than honor, knights who change allegiances with regard for little other than their own self-interest, and, just beyond the Wall, members of the Night's Watch who rebel against and even kill their Lord Commanders. The misbehaviors of these knights and pseudo-knights are not always due to evil or corruption. Often, they are simply misguided or overcome with thirst for glory. The quest for glory itself, while requisite, can lead ambitious knights astray. The thirst for personal glory can become such a motivating factor for the knight engaging in battle that he risks forgetting other aspects of chivalry.

Ser Loras Tyrell, young and eager for glory, has an over abundant thirst for glory that, in spite of his reputation for chivalry, leads to excessive brutality and his own disfiguring wounds. After Ser Loras successfully takes Dragonstone, Aureane Waters reports back to Cersei about Ser Loras's performance in battle, noting his bravery yet also commenting on his savage battle tactics. With proper negotiation, no bloodshed would have been required. However, the glory-seeking Ser Loras leads his men into a brutal battle that results in almost one thousand deaths (*F for C* 755). Proving herself an apt judge of human nature, Cersei has actually arranged to have Ser Loras seriously injured in this battle. She knows that he will overreach in his quest for personal glory. Later (and hypocritically), she consoles Margaery Tyrell about her brother's grievous injuries and assures her that Jaime will record Ser Loras's deeds in the White Book, and he will also live on in songs that recount his glory (*F for C* 758).[43]

Like Loras, Jon Connington suffers from overzealousness in battle. He recalls how his own thirst for glory kept him from finding Robert Baratheon, who was hidden by commoners. Myles Toyne tells Jon that, in his position, Tywin Lannister would have burned down the village. Jon, on the other hand, prefers single combat and the glory that comes along with it. However, he regrets that this decision allowed Robert to escape and ultimately confront, and kill, Rhaegar Targaryen (*D with D* 881). Too late, Jon realizes the need to curb his hunger for glory. Too much zeal can also be a liability for sellswords and pseudo-knights. Brown Benn explains to Daenerys the nature of the overzealous sellsword: "there are old sellswords and there are bold sellswords, but there are no old bold sellswords" (*D with D* 728). Similarly, Jaime's cousin Ser Daven observes that the overzealous warrior benefits those who are more cautious because "They all die young and leave more women for the rest of us" (*F for C* 697). Ser Daven speaks in jest, referring to Peck, about whom Jaime has bragged for his role at Blackwater. There is truth in these words, however. Too much enthusiasm on the battlefield can quickly prove fatal.

Some degree of enthusiasm is obviously necessary to success. Leaders often speak motivational words to inspire their warriors, even when the odds are against them. Those who fall in battle are promised that their deeds will live on through songs and stories. Even seasoned warriors sometimes have trouble separating the reality of battle from the glorified versions of battles in songs, although the two rarely match. When Stannis's men make a surprise attack on the Ironmen, one of the Ironmen, Crom, seeing the increasing numbers of the enemy, uses the thought of glory as motivation. If the Ironmen are outnumbered, he believes, songs of their exploits will be even grander. However, Asha Greyjoy acknowledges the truth of the bleak situation and wonders whether the songs will be of courage or foolhardiness (*D with D* 378). In fact, the Ironmen are terribly outnumbered by Stannis's forces, and she realizes that this will be an utter defeat that will not merit songs or written accounts by maesters: "No banners flew, no warhorns moaned, no great lord called his men about him to hear his final ringing words" (*D with D* 381). Asha is well aware of the futility of this battle and is not fooled by the promise of glory. However, she values the warrior code and vows to die fighting; bravery is, after all, one of the highest valued attributes of chivalry. When attacked at Deepwood Motte, she thinks, "*If I must die, I will die with an axe in my hand and a curse upon my lips*" (*D with D* 377). Asha understands the importance of boasting before battle even when glory is impossible. For this same reason, Jon Snow incorporates the battle pep talk when he holds the Wall to help his men face the daunting battle before them. He acknowledges to himself that these are "hollow words," yet he understands that his men need to hear them in order to keep up their courage and fight well (*S of S* 876).

In their attempts to gain glory, knights can make fatal mistakes and commit unchivalrous acts. By the same token, chivalrous acts can be found in unexpected circumstances and by seemingly unchivalrous characters. Throwing a wrench in the conventional notion that chivalry is the sole domain of knights, some of Martin's fiercest warriors and most chivalrous characters have never been dubbed and thus do not have titles. Among the non-knights who commit noble acts are Brienne of Tarth, a female "knight"; The Hound, who rebels against knighthood; and even Theon Greyjoy, accused child killer. Brienne is loyal and true to her word. Although technically she cannot be a knight because of her gender, she nonetheless values the attributes that accompany prowess and is renowned for her fighting abilities. On the other hand, The Hound is reviled for a number of atrocities which he has not actually committed when the criminal Rorge finds and dons his signature helm. Even as The Hound's vile reputation worsens because of this mistaken identity, Martin depicts The Hound committing a number of chivalrous acts.

Theon Greyjoy is arguably the most unconventional, and unexpected, hero in Martin's novels. Until *A Dance with Dragons*, Theon has displayed few admirable qualities, although readers may come to pity him. Growing up as a foster child in the Stark home, Theon lived in the shadows of Robb Stark and even of the bastard Jon Snow. When Theon returns to his homeland as emissary for Robb, his own father rejects him, and he thus becomes a turncloak to the Starks in an effort to regain his father's approval. Determined to resume his spot as his father's heir, he attempts to take Winterfell by force, which is undefended in Robb's absence. His efforts to assume control of the North lead him to kill many of those in the Stark household who served him in his childhood and also to murder two innocent peasant boys, whom he passes off as the two young Stark boys. His attempts to be brutal and prove his prowess to his father backfire as Theon finds himself the victim of brutalization. Once promising in prowess, he is, in a rare instance of karma for a

Martin character, humbled. His excessive pride and overreaching ambitions lead to a horrific fall. Theon falls into the hands of Ramsay Bolton and gets his just deserts.

Once he is broken and transformed into Reek, Theon loses both physical abilities and any sense of pride; in fact, he loses his former identity almost entirely. Thus, he is dismayed that Jeyne Poole thinks he can rescue her from Ramsay when he is broken and defenseless. He recognizes how far he has fallen. Whereas he had previously dreamed that singers would tell stories of his glory long after his death, he now believes that he will be recognized only as a turncloak, and only his treachery will live on in songs (*D with D* 538–539). Theon does, in fact, make a daring rescue with Jeyne which casts him, surprisingly, in the stereotypical role of knight rescuing damsel. Martin leaves the story at this point with readers unsure whether Theon has truly learned to value chivalry. However, in the HBO series, Theon rescues Sansa Stark (who has married Ramsay), returns home to his sister, and engages in a quest to help her win back the Iron Islands from their uncle. Most recently, a resurgence of Theon's cowardice has led to his sister's captivity, leading him on a mission to rescue her.

In his portrayal of knighthood, Martin includes unconventional characters such as The Hound and Theon whose behaviors are surprisingly chivalrous. Martin shows that non-knights can behave honorably and adhere to chivalry, while some actual knights behave deplorably. He thereby presents an array of models of knighthood through which he questions the code of chivalry. Knights have a duty to protect the realm and this duty can lead to killing. However, as The Hound ironically demonstrates, true knights measure prowess with other chivalric duties. They do not kill without just cause. They must always keep in mind their other duties: to protect the weak, to defend the kingdom and the king, to administer justice, and to show mercy. In Westeros, few actual knights live up to these ideals.

Seven

Vengeance

"So long as men remember the wrongs done to their forebears, no peace will ever last."—Hoster Blackwood, D with D 705

The Blood Feud in Chivalric and Heroic Literature

Sally Mapstone explains the significance in medieval culture of seeking compensation for the deaths of kinsmen: "In the event of the murder of a significant kin-member or person connected with the clan, the head of the clan had the obligation to seek reparation and compensation from the perpetrator and his kin."[1] In Anglo-Saxon works, compensation for a death might entail *wergild*, or "man price." In other words, the offender might make amends financially. More often, the death of a kinsman entails vengeance: "an eye for an eye." In Anglo-Saxon literature, the strongest allegiances are based on blood, and the strongest motive for bloodshed is vengeance for a loved one in the interest of family honor. If a family member is killed, the family of the deceased will often retaliate by murdering the killer or the killer's kin.

In *Beowulf*, Freawaru's doomed marriage is arranged to end a longstanding feud between her kin (the Danes) and her new husband's kin. When Beowulf returns to his home, Geatland, he tells the Geats of his adventures in King Hrothgar's court. He explains to the Geatish King Hygelac his concerns that King Hrothgar's plan to marry off Freawaru (she is Hrothgar's daughter) will not end well. When Freawaru's family visits her new in-laws, Beowulf imagines that the in-laws will see Freawaru's kinsmen adorned in swords and jewels that have been stripped from the bodies of their dead kinsmen after battle. They will be overcome by the desire to avenge their loved ones' deaths, and consequently, a fight will break out.

Vengeance drives much of the narrative of this Anglo-Saxon epic. The vengeance of Grendel's mother as she invades Heorot and kills one of King Hrothgar's most trusted retainers, Aescere, provides an interesting twist on the blood feud: a (monstrous) female taking the role of a (typically) male avenger. After her son is slain by Beowulf, she returns to Heorot for the blood price, paid by the life of Hrothgar's dearest companion. In turn, Beowulf travels to her underwater home and kills her, putting a final end to the enmity that has plagued Hrothgar's court.

The importance of settling a blood feud is equally evident in chivalric literature. Malory's *Le Morte Darthur* features a number of examples of blood feuds. Malory's Alysaundir le Orphelyne, who seeks to avenge the death of his father, carries with him the blood-stained doublet in which his father was killed. In "The Poisoned Apple," the plot is motivated by the blood feud between Sir Patryse and Gawain. Gawain has killed Sir Patryse's cousin, so Patryse seeks vengeance by attempting to poison Gawain. Gawain is associated with other blood feuds in addition to the one that motivates the events of "The Poisoned Apple." One of these feuds is predicted through a prophecy that specifically references the death of Gawain's father: "Gawayne shall revenge his fadirs dethe [kynge Lot] on kynge Pellynore."[2]

Perhaps Malory's most shocking blood feud also involves this feud between Gawain's family (the Orkneys) and the de Galys family. It commences when Gawain's father, King Lot, kills the de Galys patriarch, King Pellinore. Gawain, who avenges his father's death, later believes that Pellinore's son Lamorak engages in an affair with Morgawse, Gawain's mother, as an act of vengeance intended to shame the Orkney family. Beverly Kennedy explains that "Gawain's interpretation of Lamorak's liaison with Morgawse is completely original with Malory. Gawain seems to think that Lamorak has entered into this 'shameful' affair with their mother for the sole purpose of getting revenge for the death of his father."[3] This affair incites Gawain's brother Gaheris to kill Margawse in her bed, as he believes that she has shamed the family. Lamorak is initially spared, but subsequently, and shamefully, killed by Gawain and his brothers. The Orkney brothers, with the exception of Gaheris, ambush Lamorak, and Mordred stabs him in the back. This murder is so disgraceful that Malory relates it to readers indirectly through the accounts of other characters, including Lancelot, who are appalled by it.

Kate McClune explains that, for Malory, "Revenge cannot be contained, and the result is the inevitable conflict between kinship groups that will fatally destabilize the unity that the Round Table fellowship should represent."[4] The most disastrous blood feud in Malory's work occurs when Gawain insists on vengeance against Lancelot for Lancelot's inadvertent killing of Gawain's favorite brothers, Gareth and Gaheris. This blood feud ultimately leads to the downfall of the Round Table. Gawain ignores Lancelot's attempts to atone, and he ignores Arthur's pleas that he should forgive Lancelot. Gawain will not let go of his desire for vengeance. He places his desire for vengeance above the good of the kingdom and above all other aspects of chivalry.

Perhaps foreshadowing the disastrous blood feud between Gawain and Lancelot, one of Malory's early tales, "The Knight with the Two Swords," depicts Balin placing his desire to seek vengeance over his duty to King Arthur. When the Lady of the Lake appears in Arthur's court, she asks for Balin's head in recompense for the death of her brother. Balin, on the other hand, seeks to avenge the death of his mother at the hands of the Lady of the Lake. He faces a dilemma: the Lady of the Lake is under Arthur's safe conduct. He chooses to seek vengeance against the Lady of the Lake by striking off her head ignoring that, as a guest in Arthur's court, Arthur has a duty to protect her. Nevertheless, Arthur seems to understand Balin's need for vengeance and chastises Balin not for the murder, but for committing the act in his presence with the Lady under his protection. Rather than putting Balin to death for the act, he banishes him. Balin's choice of vengeance then sets off a series of adventures that result in his striking the Dolorous Stroke and the maiming of King Pellam.

The Dolorous Stroke itself results from an act of vengeance. Balin, a guest in King Pellam's castle, sees his enemy Garlon who has killed two men under Balin's protection. When a fight breaks out between the two, Balin kills Garlon. King Pellam, Garlon's brother, strikes out against Balin for the death of his brother, and also because Balin has dishonored him by ignoring rules of hospitality. In the ensuing fight, Balin comes upon a sacred sword and, not knowing its value, uses it against King Pellam. This incident results in a wasteland, the complete devastation of Pellam's kingdom. Pellam himself remains injured until the perfect holy knight, Galahad, cures him of his wounds.[5] Balin has acted out of an obligation to avenge the deaths of those he swore to protect; he could not predict the widespread effect of his actions.

The Blood Feud in Westeros

Martin seems to draw heavily from the chivalric code of conduct to portray the kinds of tensions that result when loved ones must be avenged. His novels illustrate that honor frequently depends upon upholding this duty. As the Tully family motto declares, "family, honor, and duty" are deeply entwined with each other and are integral components of the chivalric code. The first point-of-view chapter that is told from the perspective of Daenerys Targaryen in *A Game of Thrones* summarizes the blood feud that serves as a backdrop to the series: the Targaryens, long-time rulers of Westeros, have been displaced by the Baratheons, setting off a series of murders and disputes requiring vengeance. The current ruler, King Robert Baratheon, is so overcome with hatred for and fear of the Targaryens that he seeks to kill Daenerys, her older brother Viserys, and when she marries, her unborn son.

Daenerys has lived a life of exile because of this threat. Robert will not listen to the rational voice of his Hand, Eddard Stark. Eddard tries to convince Robert that Daenerys, a young teenager who lives far across the Narrow Sea, is not a threat, but still, Robert makes attempts on her life. The motivation behind Robert's vengeance is complex. It is not for the death of a kinsman, but rather for the death of his betrothed, Lyanna Stark, whom he believes to have been kidnapped by Rhaegar Targaryen, Daenerys's oldest brother. Further, he is fearful that the surviving Targaryens will attempt to reclaim the Iron Throne, so his motivation is also political. Eddard has a better cause for a blood feud with the Targaryens because Lyanna's apparent abduction led to the deaths of his father and brother and perhaps Lyanna herself, who is Eddard's sister. However, he maintains a level head and is not driven by vengeance.[6]

In addition to this major feud, Martin depicts numerous other blood feuds that complicate the politics of Westeros. These blood feuds may be settled in a number of ways, but for the Westerosi, feuds most often entail violence and have longlasting repercussions well beyond the immediate cause. In medieval romance, a duel generally settles the matter. In some versions of Arthurian legend, including Malory's *Le Morte Darthur*, Gawain's feud with Lancelot leads to a war between Arthur's men and Lancelot's. However, as the war wages on, Gawain and Lancelot agree to face off in single combat. During this duel, Gawain receives an injury that later leads to his death.

A similar situation occurs when Oberyn Martell faces off against Ser Gregor Clegane to settle their long-standing blood feud. Oberyn has a grudge against Ser Gregor for the brutal murder of his sister, Elia Martell, bride of Rhaegar Targaryen. Ser Gregor has reportedly brutally killed Elia's daughter and infant son and then, with her infant's blood still on his hands, raped and killed Elia. Years later, when Tyrion Lannister is put on trial for the murder of King Joffrey, Cersei Lannister chooses Ser Gregor Clegane as her champion. Although Tywin Lannister has tried to prevent a duel between Ser Gregor and Oberyn, Oberyn seizes the opportunity to avenge his kinsman's death by agreeing to champion Tyrion. Oberyn is killed in the battle, but he succeeds at vengeance: he has tainted the point of his spear with a poison that eventually kills Ser Gregor. For Oberyn, vengeance comes with a high price: his own death.

Martin's characters, like Malory's, are sometimes challenged by other obligations that complicate their ability to settle blood feuds. In Malory, as previously mentioned, Balin's loyalties are torn between King Arthur and the kin he must avenge, and Arthur's loyalties are torn between his nephew Gawain and his best knight Lancelot. Among the most conflicted of Martin's characters is Jon Snow, whose service at the Wall requires him to sever family ties and thus should prevent him from avenging the deaths of his loved ones.

Early in the narrative, Jon learns about his father's death at the hands of the Lannisters. He seriously considers leaving the Night's Watch and even attempts to do so in order to avenge this death. He weighs the importance of his vows to the Watch with his loyalty to his family and decides that vengeance has greater significance. He determines to break his vows to the Watch, reasoning that "it made no matter" because he feels so compelled to aid his brother in avenging his father's death (*G of T* 775). Later, when Lord Commander Mormont questions him about the near-desertion, Jon says, "They killed my father. Did you expect me to do nothing?" (*G of T* 782).

Jon returns to the Wall, but he never abandons his desire to avenge his father's death (and later the deaths of his brothers). Jon's thirst for vengeance becomes particularly problematic when Janos Slynt is assigned to the Wall. Jon has long standing animosity towards Janos Slynt and, once Jon becomes Lord Commander, re-assigns Slynt to Castle Greyguard. He reasons with himself about Slynt's potential as an enemy, acknowledging the blood feud between them. Slynt was a participant in his father's death. Additionally, Slynt has tried to kill Jon, giving Jon yet another reason to have a personal vendetta against him (*D with D* 188). When Slynt refuses the assignment, Jon has him put to death. This death is the consequence for Slynt's blatant refusal to obey an order, and Jon must go through with it in order to exert his own authority. Although his first thought is to hang Slynt, Jon reconsiders and beheads him, just as Eddard Stark was beheaded. Jon does the deed himself, as his father taught him. Ostensibly, this beheading is performed because Slynt has defied the orders of the Lord Commander, but it also serves to settle Jon's blood feud against him.

Blood ties again become problematic for Jon when Alys Karstark asks for protection against her uncle's attempts to marry her off as a peace weaver. When she escapes to Castle Black, she first appeals to Jon by invoking family ties (they are distant cousins), reminding him that their families are joined by blood ties and that Jon has a familial duty to render aid to her (*D with D* 646). Jon explains that the situation is more complicated than Alys implies: Jon's brother Robb killed Alys's father for his slaying of two young Lannister hostages, so in fact, Alys and Jon should themselves be opponents in a blood feud. Alys dismisses this feud, reminding Jon that both Robb and her father are now dead. Jon tries to exempt himself from involvement and claims that, as a man of the Watch, he cannot engage in any feuds, regardless (*D with D* 647). Jon does, in the end, come to Alys's rescue by marrying her off to Magnar of Thenn. However, regardless of his statement about "putting feuds behind him," Jon has not earnestly severed family ties. He still feels the pull of blood ties to his immediate family. Soon after, he determines to return to Winterfell and exact vengeance against Ramsay Bolton, who has taken over his father's castle. In the HBO series, he does so successfully. He abandons his post at the Wall to avenge the brutal treatment of his sister Sansa and to reclaim Winterfell in his family's name.

As a bastard, Jon Snow never imagined that he could become lord of Winterfell, much less, as he is dubbed in the HBO series, "King of the North." His older and legitimate half-brother Robb is proper heir to Winterfell. Thus, in the early novels after their father's death, Robb has the duty of settling the blood feud between his family and the Lannisters. Robb's deep-seated feelings against the Lannisters emerge early in *A Game of Thrones* when Robb learns that a Lannister (Tyrion, he initially believes) may have thrown his younger brother Bran from a tower causing the boy to be crippled. He immediately declares his determination to avenge this act of violence. He pulls out his sword and vows to kill Tyrion himself if this rumor is proven true (*G of T* 137). Later, after hearing of his father's murder, Robb is motivated by an intense thirst for vengeance. His foster brother Theon Greyjoy encourages him to declare war against his enemies: "call up the banners.... Blood for blood" (*G of T* 400).

Hailed as King of the North, Robb decides that he must engage in battle against the Lannisters, but his youth, overzealousness, and inexperience lead him to make mistakes. He refuses his mother's advice to yield once it becomes clear that winning against them is unlikely. She tells him, "You would not be the first king to bend the knee, nor even the first Stark.... Torrhen Stark bent the knee to Aegon the Conqueror rather than see his army face the fires." Robb remains unmoved, reminding her of his duty to avenge his father. He counters with a rhetorical question that makes clear the significance of avenging the death of one's father: "Did Aegon kill King Torrhen's father?" (*S of S* 482). Ultimately, Robb's own death results from a feud with the Freys when he breaks a marital arrangement with one of the Frey daughters. The Starks desperately need the Freys to align with their cause rather than with the Lannisters, and Robb soon realizes that by breaking this marriage contract, he has made a strategic error that threatens this alliance. He offers up his uncle as a marriage prospect for the Freys, instead. The Freys agree to a marriage between Robb's uncle and one of the Frey daughters, but they betray Robb. They kill him, with the backing of the Lannisters, at his uncle's wedding feast, spurring a new blood feud that pits Starks against Freys.

Preserving family loyalty and honor are vital aspects of chivalry; the deaths of blood kin must be avenged. However, the blood feud can lead to a dangerous obsession with vengeance. Catelyn and Arya Stark are so consumed with their quests for vengeance that they transform into cold-blooded killers. Their obsessions with vengeance prevent them from acting in accordance to accepted behaviors for women of high birth. From the early pages of *A Game of Thrones*, Catelyn has a sense of foreboding about the Lannisters. After her husband is killed at their instigation, she is caught between her desire for vengeance and her concern for her children, who are in Lannister custody. When her son Robb captures Jaime Lannister, she warns Robb that if Jaime is harmed, Cersei will seek revenge by "[paying] us back blood for blood—" (*C of K* 113). Catelyn knows that Cersei will retaliate by putting the Stark sisters to death if Jaime is harmed, and she urges Robb to act with restraint and caution.

Once her family members begin to die, Catelyn becomes less restrained. She later has a blood feud against Theon Greyjoy for the supposed deaths of her sons Bran and Rickon. At this point in the series, her son Robb is still alive. As a woman, she must count on him to exact vengeance, but she expresses her desire to do the killing herself: "Robb will avenge his brothers. Ice can kill as dead as fire. *Ice* was Ned's great sword.... The Starks do not use headsmen. Ned always said that the man who passes the sentence should swing the blade, though he never took any joy in the duty. But *I* would, oh, yes" (*C of K* 786). Catelyn soon must take matters of vengeance into her own hands, an unusual role for a woman that places her in the tradition of Grendel's mother. When the Freys are about to kill Robb, she seizes the Freys' mentally disabled son Aegon and holds him at knife point. As soon as Robb is killed, she retaliates without hesitation, killing the Frey son on the spot. In turn, one of the Freys slits her throat. When she is subsequently revived by Thoros and Beric Dondarrion, Catelyn appears to have no remaining human emotion other than an all-consuming and merciless desire for vengeance. She is vengeance incarnate.

Similarly, Arya Stark is so consumed with vengeance that it becomes her defining feature. Like her mother, she is transformed to such an extent that their behavior seems monstrous. Each night she recites the names of those who have wronged her family and friends in what is for her a prayer of vengeance. Arya first kills out of necessity, murdering a stable boy in her attempt to escape King's Landing. She subsequently engages in a series of murders, again, all out of necessity. Caught in a number of difficult situations while on the run for her life, Arya becomes increasingly hardened. Vengeance is requisite if a kinsman is killed or if one is engaged in war, but senseless killing is not part of the chivalric or heroic code. Still, Arya begins to kill without regret or true motive. When she kills Dareon, a deserter from the Night's Watch, her life is not at stake, nor is she exacting vengeance for the death of kin. Further, while deserters are typically put to death, it is not the duty of a young girl to do the act. When her father was warden of the North, his duty entailed putting to the sword any deserters who made their way into his land. Arya, however, has no such obligation, yet she sees the opportunity to kill and strikes. Because Dareon has deserted the Night's Watch, Arya finds his death well deserved. Though the killing is motiveless, she has no remorse for her actions (*D with D* 656).

Arya's unwavering quest for vengeance and her penchant for murder ultimately lead her to become one of the Faceless Men, who are paid assassins. Before Arya becomes an assassin, the kindly man who is in charge of her training challenges her abilities to join them, as they kill without personal interest or passion. He chastises her, accusing her of committing murder for vengeance and pleasure (*D with D* 915). He explains that if vengeance is her motive, she cannot be one of the Faceless Men: "Death holds no sweetness in this house.... We never give the gift to please ourselves. Nor do we choose the ones we kill" (*D with D* 915–916). The Faceless Men view death as a merciful act. For a high price, they will kill anyone, and they will do so without motive or emotion. Arya insists that she can leave aside her personal need for vengeance and join them, but old wrongs to her family continue to pull her away from her new commitment to the House of Black and White.

Unable to maintain her resolve, Arya continues to whisper the names of those who have wronged her and her family, even while she is in the House of Black and White: "*Ser Gregor, Dansen, Raff the Sweetling, Ser Ilyn, Ser Meryn, Queen Cersei*" (*D with D* 924). Like her half-brother Jon, she cannot truly abandon her former life or her quest to avenge her loved ones. In the HBO series, she leaves the Faceless Men and returns to Westeros. Her first act upon returning is vengeance for her brother Robb's death: she bakes Frey's sons in a pie and serves it to him before slitting his throat.[7] Frey's death provides poetic justice as both Robb and his mother have died from a similar cut to the throat. Subsequently, Arya returns to Winterfell, joining forces with Sansa and Bran to bring Littlefinger to justice.

Cycles of Vengeance and the Martell/Lannister Blood Feud

The previous examples focus on individuals seeking to avenge their kin, but the blood feud affects entire families and can be long lasting. Hoster Blackwood explains to Jaime Lannister how peace between the Blackwoods and Brackens is always precarious because of a long-standing blood feud that dates back past memory. As long as family stories are passed down from one generation to the next, "no peace will ever last" (*D with D* 705). Thus, he explains, the feud continues for many generations. Jaime counters that a peace can be possible because those involved are dead and cannot retaliate. Hoster, however, reminds Jaime of the duties of kin, telling him that the dead men's sons will be compelled to seek vengeance on their behalf (*D with D* 705). As the Bracken/Blackwood feud demonstrates, accounts of old wrongs are passed down from one generation to the next in a seemingly never-ending cycle. Violence between the two families re-erupts periodically with no hope for reconciliation.

A blood feud entraps the Martells of Dorne in a cycle of vengeance that spans several generations. This feud, referenced earlier, begins when Ser Gregor Clegane, under the command of Tywin Lannister, murders Elia Martell and her children. Elia's brother Oberyn Martell waits years to challenge Ser Gregor in a duel that results in the deaths of both himself and his opponent, but still the feud continues. It is then resumed by Oberyn's illegitimate daughters, the Sand sisters, who are unsatisfied by Ser Gregor's death and must be temporarily imprisoned by their cautious uncle, Prince Doran, to prevent rash vengeance against the Lannisters. Like Grendel's mother, Obara Sand takes vengeance in her own hands. Obara begs her uncle to let her personally avenge her father's death (*F for C* 46). She is not appeased by her uncle's promise that Lord Tywin will deliver Ser Gregor's head to the family as proof of his death. She asks, "And who will deliver us Lord Tywin's head?" (*F for C* 470). When Balon Swann brings (what appears to be) Ser Gregor's skull to Dorne, Prince Doran is appeased and claims that the Lannisters have now paid off their blood debt. The Sand sisters, however, are still unsatisfied. Prince Doran indicates that the death of Ser Gregor ends the feud. For Obara and her sisters, as long as the Lannisters live, vengeance has not been properly served. Ser Gregor may have killed both Elia and Oberyn, but he did so under the Lannisters' orders. The feud cannot be resolved, in their view, until Lannister blood is shed.

Another of Oberyn's daughters, Nym Sand, asks her uncle to allow her to exact vengeance against the Lannisters, claiming to use as ruse "only one sweet sister," Tyene (*F for C* 55). She explains how her sister Tyene, who appears docile but is in fact a ruthless killer, can be an effective tool for vengeance. Nym goes so far as to quantify the Lannister lives she requires as recompense for the death of her father: "Four lives will suffice for me. Lord Tywin's golden twins, as payment for Elia's children. The old lion, for Elia herself. And last of all the little king for my father" (*F for C* 55). She explains her desire to kill King Tommen, although he is only a child, arguing that only royal blood can serve as compensation for the death of her father. She suggests that her sister Tyene can best perform the murder by charming her way into the Lannister's trust (*F for C* 56). For Nym, vengeance must be paid life for life: the Lannisters are responsible for the deaths of four of their kin. In retaliation, she wants the deaths of four Lannisters. Ser Gregor is merely an agent for the Lannisters. His death does not settle the feud according to the vengeful Sand sisters.

Prince Doran's daughter, Arianne, is also disgusted that her father doesn't take strident measures to avenge the death of his brother. She accuses him of "meekness" that "shames all Dorne" (*F for C* 854). Prince Doran, however, remains passive and appears to fear the consequences of vengeance, leading the Sand sisters to take matters into their own hands. When the Sand sisters suggest subterfuge and trickery as vengeance, Doran argues that Oberyn died in single combat and such methods would be dishonorable. Still, the Sand sisters are determined to avenge their father's deaths. Although their father waited seventeen years for vengeance, they insist that they will not do the same (*F for C* 56). Oberyn's paramour, Ellaria Sand, fears for her own young daughters and wants to end the feud before it spans another generation. Distressed over this cycle of vengeance, she asks the older Sand sisters when it will end. If they are killed, will her own children be required to seek vengeance? She fears that vengeance will go "round and round forever," and she asks, "*where does it end?*" (*D with D* 559). The older Sand sisters, citing family honor and their unsatisfied thirst for vengeance, remain unmoved by Ellaria's pleas to spare their half-sisters from this cycle of vengeance.

The Sand sisters see no alternative but a seemingly endless cycle of vengeance. However, blood feuds can be settled, or forestalled, without violence. One non-violent solution to settling blood feuds, hostage taking, can deter, but usually not prevent, confrontations. Hostage taking can be a significant tool for negotiating peace, although in such arrangements, peace is usually tenuous. Myrcella Baratheon is sent to Dorne as part of a marriage contract, yet she is equally a hostage. As long as the Dornish hold her, the Lannisters will have to negotiate with care.[8] Likewise, Sansa Stark is held captive by the Lannisters who value her not only for her worth as apparent heir of Winterfell, but also because of the potential power they might wield over the Starks while she is in their custody. Subsequently, the Starks temporarily hold Jaime Lannister, but Catelyn Stark releases him in hopes of an exchange for her daughters. This move is condemned by Catelyn's son Robb and the men who support him, for young girls are not nearly as valuable an exchange as a knight of Jaime's caliber.

Fostering may be another form of hostage taking. This is the case for Theon Greyjoy. He is surrendered by his family to the Starks and becomes their foster son after his father rebels against the Baratheons. His position in the Stark household ensures that the Greyjoys will not attempt another rebellion; Theon is his father's only surviving son. The Martells have also used fostering to assuage violence. In addition to their longstanding feud with the Lannisters, the Martells have been involved in another blood feud, which also took place before the events in Martin's novels. This feud once again involves Oberyn Martell, who, in this case, defeated Edgar Yronwood in a duel. Although both Oberyn and Edgar were injured in the duel, Edgar's wounds festered and led to his death. The Yronwoods believe Oberyn poisoned the tip of his sword (a likely possibility since he does just this in his duel with Ser Gregor). Prince Doran has attempted to resolve this feud by sending as payment his oldest son, Quentyn, to be fostered by the Yronwoods. Prince Doran's daughter, Arianne, recalls the impact this blood payment had on her mother, who mourned over the loss of her young son. Prince Doran explained to his wife the nature of the blood debt: "Quentyn is the only coin Lord Ormond will accept" (*F for C* 428). His wife challenged the notion of using a human life as collateral. She asked what kind of man would make such a callous bargain. Prince Doran responded, "The princely sort" (*F for C* 428). For Prince Doran, this exchange is difficult, but a necessary part of his duties.

Despite his posturing, Prince Doran is not as passive as he has appeared to his wife and later to his daughter. He has fostered his son to Lord Ormond not only as a resolution to the blood feud, but also to keep his son safe so that one day he might align with the Targaryens and get vengeance on the Lannisters. He remains in communication with his son and charges him with the duty of winning over and ultimately marrying Daenerys Targaryen. Prince Doran eventually explains his intentions to Arianne, telling her that her brother Quentyn has gone abroad for "Vengeance.... Justice.... *Fire and blood*" (*F for C* 863). Rather than being passive and weak as his family perceives him, Prince Doran demonstrates patience as he waits for the proper instrumentation of vengeance against the Lannisters: this alliance with the Targaryens. Unfortunately, this alliance does not come about, as Daenerys is unimpressed with Quentyn. Quentyn, in an attempt to follow through with his father's orders, is killed while trying to tame one of Daenerys's dragons.

As previously mentioned, another peaceful method of settling the blood feud is *wergild*. In *Beowulf*, Grendel's crimes are particularly loathsome because of his refusal to pay the price for the men he has killed. Martin mentions only one instance of this method of settlement. Daenerys Targaryen uses the equivalent of *wergild* after her dragon Drogon kills a peasant girl. The Shavepate suggests that, to silence the father of the girl, Daenerys should rip his tongue out. Daenerys, however, opts to pay the Westerosi equivalent of *wergild*. She makes a decision to pay "the blood price" (*D with D* 174). When she cannot place a monetary value on the man's daughter, she determines to pay the equivalence of one hundred lambs. She chooses to pay this *wergild* as a means of justice and atonement. As one who administers justice, she realizes that the peasant father has no means of retaliation against her. This incident makes her keenly aware of the potential danger of her dragons; she has difficulty controlling them, and she knows that she cannot continue to pay "the blood price" if their killing becomes rampant. Thus, she chains the remaining two dragons that are still in her custody.

Those who are prevented from seeking vengeance because they lack political power might settle blood feuds by changing alliances. When Ser Davos visits the Manderlys at White Harbor to solicit support for Stannis Baratheon. Ser Davos uses the blood feud as a reason the Manderlys should align with Stannis. When asked how this alliance might benefit them, Ser

Davos tells him that Stannis will help them avenge the deaths of their family members and the death of their king (*D with D* 273). Wayman Manderly's kinsmen have died at the hands of the Lannisters. His kinsmen are not powerful enough to stand alone against them. Vengeance is further problematized for Manderly because the Lannisters hold his son Wendel. He cannot avenge the deaths of his other loved ones without risking the death of his son.

Manderly's granddaughter Wylla offers another good reason for a change in alliance: vengeance for the death of Robb Stark, the Manderlys' king, who has died at the hands of the Freys, at the instigation of the Lannisters. She explains that the Lannisters are responsible for the deaths of members of the Stark family, especially Robb, who was their king and whom she admired. She maintains that this is sufficient reason for the alliance. She urges her grandfather to join Stannis if he will offer vengeance on her family's behalf (*D with D* 273–4). Manderly cannot openly agree to this new alliance even though the Lannisters have brought about the deaths of both his king and his kin. He imprisons Ser Davos and claims to have put him to death. Secretly, however, he promises Ser Davos that if Rickon Stark returns, he will declare for Stannis.

Manderly is not able to direct his vengeance against the Lannisters. He does, however, get some part of the vengeance he desires. When Manderly arrives at Ramsay Bolton's wedding, he serves the Frey patriarch three of Frey's own sons baked into a pie. In the HBO series, the pies are served to Frey by Arya Stark, transforming the scene solely into blood vengeance rather than vengeance for one's lord. The novels, on the other hand, emphasize the bond of loyalty between lord and thane as Robb's kinsmen and retainers in the North rally to avenge his death.

With no known living relatives, Daenerys Targaryen must build her own band of followers in order to exact vengeance on behalf of her family and to reclaim the kingdom that was taken from them. She understands the implications of a longstanding blood feud as her own family's feud has haunted her from birth. She was conceived during Robert's Rebellion and has lived her entire life as an exile, always on the run from assassins sent by Robert Baratheon to ensure that he will keep the Iron Throne. Her brother Viserys is so motivated by his desire for both vengeance and power (to be acquired by retaking the Iron Throne) that he overreaches. He pushes too hard to take control of the Dothraki band of warriors to whom he has married off his sister. When they retaliate and put Viserys to death, Daenerys takes over the quest to retake the Iron Throne and to avenge the deaths of her father and brother Rhaegar.[9] Ser Jorah warns her that, even though King Robert is dead, Robert's heir, King Joffrey, remains a threat. He tells her that Joffrey will settle this blood debt because "a dutiful son pays his father's debts" (*S of S* 115). Daenerys, meanwhile, moves forward with her attempts to form an army that can help her regain her family's realm and exact long-awaited vengeance.

As Daenerys's experiences in Essos illustrate, the blood feud inspires, for Martin's world, a universal code of vengeance. Daenerys's happiness with her Dothraki husband, Khal Drogo, is upended when the Lhazareen Mirri Maz Duur kills Daenerys's child to avenge the deaths of her people, whom the Dothraki have brutalized. She tells Daenerys, "Only death may pay for life" (*G of T* 710), implying that she has had to kill Daenerys's infant son in order to save the gravely injured Khal Drogo. In fact, Mirri wants vengeance for the deaths of her people. More accurately, she might have stated "only death may pay for death." Daenerys has saved Mirri from rape, but Mirri is called to avenge the mistreatment and deaths of her people at the hands of the Dothraki. She also wants to ensure that Khal Drogo will have no heir to continue the brutal traditions of the Dothraki.

This tragedy puts Daenerys on a trajectory towards regaining the throne, but in doing so, she makes many enemies and finds herself the frequent target of vengeance. When the Sons of the Harpy attack the people she has saved, the Shavepate suggests vengeance that is reminiscent of the blood feud. He suggests killing one man from each offending family because "blood must pay for blood" (*D with D* 42). Daenerys rejects this idea, as does her seneschal, Reznak. Reznak refers to this solution as savagery that would offend the gods. Ultimately, Daenerys's solution is a marriage contract rather than violence. Although Daenerys does exact vengeance when necessary (such as her vengeance on the Meereenese for the hanging of slave children), she tends to favor peaceful solutions in her conquests in Essos. However, she is well aware that claiming the Iron Throne will require bloodshed, and she works hard to build an army towards this end.

Kin Killing and King Killing

The worst kind of blood feud is internecine, resulting when one family member kills another or when one clansman kills another. Two of the worse violations of the chivalric and heroic codes are king slaying and kinslaying, crimes against king and blood. Kin slaying is particularly problematic because of its potential to split families apart. How can one exact vengeance against a kinsman in a society that places such a high value on strong bonds of kinship? In one of the more memorable narrative digressions in *Beowulf*, the author poignantly describes the ramifications of kin killing through the narrative of Haethcynn's incidental slaying of his brother Herebeald. Their father, King Hrethel, is left in the difficult position of having his oldest son's death left unavenged, as he cannot shed the blood of the killer, his second son. Neither *wergild* nor vengeance serve when one kinsman kills another. King Hrethel is left grief-stricken. He blames his second son, yet he has no recourse to avenge the death of his oldest son: "wihte ne meahte/on ðam feorh-bonan fæghðe gebetan;/no ðy ær he þone heaðo-rinc hatian ne meahte/laðym dædum, þeah him leof ne wæs" (not a wit might he settle the feud of that slayer, nor might he seek vengeance on the killer, though he was no longer dear to him).[10] Regardless of the significance in Anglo-Saxon culture of settling blood feuds, the king cannot exact vengeance on Haethcynn, who succeeds his brother as heir.

A similar passage occurs in *A Dance with Dragons*, altered by the facts that the mourning father, Roose Bolton, is one of Martin's more despicable characters and that, unlike the death of Herebeald, the death of the Bolton youth is no accident.[11] Roose Bolton recognizes that his bastard son Ramsay has killed his true heir, yet he must overlook the crime since he has no other sons. He tells Ramsay's creature Reek about the deaths of his son Domeric and his other infants at the hands of Ramsay. He implies that Ramsay has killed other legitimate heirs while they were still infants, and he asks, "If the kinslayer is accursed, what is a father to do when one son slays another?" (*D with D* 473). These words echo those of *Beowulf*'s Hrethel. Martin skillfully adopts and adapts this father's lament, recasting it in the context of the vile Ramsay Bolton as killer. In the HBO series, Ramsay takes kin killing a step further, first slaying his father and then feeding his stepmother and newborn half-brother to his starving dogs. Audiences rejoice at how fate ultimately treats the much-loathed Ramsay for these atrocities as he is ultimately killed by these same dogs.

Kin killing is also reviled in the romance tradition and is especially prominent in Malory's *Le Morte Dathur*, perhaps because Malory was writing during the War of the Roses. Thus, he was very familiar with real-life internecine struggles as cousins from the York and Lancaster families vied for the throne. In fact, Malory's work culminates with the battle between Arthur and his bastard son Mordred in which each slays the other. The depiction of good and evil is clear cut in this battle, but elsewhere in Malory, incidents of kin killing are more ambiguous regarding motives and culpability. Gaheris's killing of his own mother is, as Kate McClune describes it, "a serious breach of normal blood loyalties, one which, in its culmination, raises serious questions about the whole blood-feud system" since her death is left unavenged and is seen by Gaheris as an attempt to reduce the family's disgrace at her affair with their enemy.[12] For Gaheris, this death of a family member is, ironically, necessary to uphold family honor. On the other hand, Malory's tale of Balin, "The Knight with the Two Swords," involves a case of accidental kin killing that is viewed as tragic by the two brothers who engage in mortal combat against each other. Balin slays his beloved brother Balan in a case of misidentification as neither bears familial arms in the fatal battle. Balin accepts a challenge with good faith and according to the rules of chivalry. He is told that he cannot pass through a kingdom unless he "have adoo with but one knyghte." Balin comments that this is "an unhappy custom," but he agrees to follow it.[13] He is also agreeable when asked to exchange his worn armor for another, for such offerings are a typical sign of hospitality.

Balin is sometimes criticized for the fact that he ignores numerous warnings that could prevent his fate. He does not heed the death blast from a horn, an engraved cross with a message that no unaccompanied knights should pass, nor an old man who explicitly tells Balin to turn back. Ignoring these warnings, Balin proceeds to the encounter. Scholars such as Felicia Ackerman conclude that Balin is flawed for proceeding despite these ominous warning. Ackerman questions Balin's judgment and, by extent, Malory's view of worship and prowess: "to Malory, a man of worship and of prowess is a man of poor judgment."[14] Certainly, neither brother questions the typical *modus operandi* in which a challenge is accepted without question. Their refusal to question the situation is not so much a lack of judgment as it is a strict adherence to codes and customs. The chivalric code of conduct does not allow Balin to consider finding a way out of this battle; he follows through with this adventure anticipating a typical battle against an anonymous knight. Balin has no intention of harming his beloved brother. He moves forward, believing that he "maye not torne now agayne for shame"[15]

Malory is quick to excuse this kin killing as an accident. He concludes this narrative with praise for the hero. Balin's sword is reserved for "the best knight in the world," and in the final lines, both Balin and his brother are described as "two passynge good knyghtes as ever were in tho dayes."[16] Martin seems to give a direct nod to Malory's tale of Balin by making several brief references to a Westerosi legend that similarly involves the deaths of two brothers at each other's hands, Erykk and Arykk Cargyll (whose similar sounding names in themselves evoke the names of Balin and Balan). The Cargyll brothers also find themselves caught in a chivalric code that demands loyalty to both king and kin. They align themselves with opposing Targaryens who claim the throne, forcing a breach in their blood connection. The Westerosi legend holds that the two fight to the death, but versions of the legend differ as to whether the two reconcile in their final moments as Balin and Balan do.[17]

Martin's kin killers are rarely honorable and generally perform kin killing deliberately rather than accidentally. The death of Renly Baratheon at the hands of his older brother is one of the more prominent examples of deliberate kin killing. After the death of King Robert, the surviving Baratheon brothers, Renly and Stannis, are pitted against each other as they each aspire to the throne. Catelyn Stark tries to intervene to prevent their battle, but the brothers insist upon facing each other in combat at an appointed time. In a display of misplaced chivalry and misdirected familial honor, Stannis, the elder but less popular brother, pretends to show some concern for the prevention of the desecration of his brother's body if his brother is defeated in battle. He insists that "no assault is done to his corpse" and that his head is not to be "paraded about on a spear" (C of K 500). Even as he plots his brother's death, Stannis cannot deny the bonds of kinship: "He is my own blood" (C of K 500). However, Stannis's sole concern seems to be his reputation rather than a sincere respect for blood ties. He is most concerned about how he might be perceived if his men flaunt Renly's death, and he is fearful that Renly might defeat him. Thus, rather than engaging in a proper battle, Stannis resorts to subterfuge. He employs the dark arts of his red priestess Melisandre to have his brother put to death before the battle begins

Stannis goes even further with kinslaying while under the guidance of Melisandre. The chivalric and heroic codes place a value on blood ties for their ability to bond together kinsmen. Melisandre, on the other hand, values blood because she believes blood is key to Stannis Baratheon's ascendancy to the throne and because she believes that Stannis may be Azhor Ahai, the prince who was promised. Under the impression that she needs king's blood to enable Stannis's powers, she encourages Stannis to commit more kinslaying. She goes after the blood of Stannis's deceased brother, King Robert, through Robert's bastard child, Edric Storm. In this instance, Ser Davos prevents the kinslaying, helping Edric escape. In the HBO version, it is another of Robert's bastards, Gendry (in Edric's role here), who escapes, but Melisandre resorts to an even greater form of kinslaying: Stannis's own daughter is sacrificed to the fires in an attempt to end the snowstorm that plagues Stannis's troops.

Kinslaying is, obviously, self destructive to the family unit; vengeance is out of sorts when family members turn on each other. Equally taboo is the murder of one's lord or king. Killing one's lord is an egregious offense to chivalric and heroic culture, as knights and warriors swear oaths that their priority will be their lord's protection. When one's lord is also a blood relative, the magnitude of the crime is compounded. In Malory's Le Morte Darthur, Mordred's violence against his father (also uncle) leads to the deaths of both men. Mordred, simultaneously kingslayer and kinslayer, is doubly villainous for the killing of his father/king.

The Lannisters are infamous for both kin killing and king killing. Even though he has good reasons for doing so, Jaime Lannister is reviled for his slaying of the Mad King Aerys. King Aerys had threatened to kill Jaime's family, and his instability threatened the entire kingdom. Jaime felt that he had to stop the irrational acts of a mad king. Still, few in Westeros understand Jaime's motives, and he must live with the label "kingslayer" and the reputation that follows it. Like Malory's Mordred, Jaime's brother Tyrion is known as both kinslayer and kingslayer. Unlike Malory's villain, however, Tyrion has emerged as one of Martin's most likable characters. Tyrion is labeled kingslayer/kinslayer for the death of his nephew/king, but he is wrongfully accused of this murder. He is put in the Red Keep to await trial for the crime. Tyrion is never a kingslayer, but he earns his reputation as kinslayer when he later kills his own father. Jaime frees Tyrion from the Red Keep after he tells Tyrion the truth about Tyrion's first wife, Tysha. Tyrion is so angered by the revelation that she was not a whore as his father told him, that he swears vengeance against his father, citing the family motto, "A Lannister always pays his debts" (*S of S* 1065). This leads him to confront, and murder, his father, whom he finds and kills on the privy.[18]

When Cersei realizes that Tyrion has killed their father and, she believes, her son, she wants vengeance against her younger brother. She claims that she needs "*Tyrion's blood, the blood of the* valonquar" (*F for C* 79). Cersei has never loved her younger brother and recalls the words of a maegi that indicated the *valonquar*, or little brother, would one day kill her. She feels none of the bonds of kinship that might prevent her from shedding her brother's blood, and she fears that he will kill her if she doesn't act first. Jaime, however, is torn when he hears of his brother's patricide. Earlier in the series, when his sword hand is taken, Jaime's ties to his family give him a reason to survive the grave injury: "*live for Cersei, live for Tyrion. Live for vengeance*" (*S of S* 416). His close relationship with his brother leads Jaime to tell Tyrion the truth about Tysha. Thus, Jaime feels complicit in his father's murder, both for this confession and for his role in freeing Tyrion. He struggles with this decision, thinking to himself that he was unaware of Tyrion's intent to kill their father. Had he known, he would have killed Tyrion rather than setting him free. Had that happened, he thinks, "*I would be the kinslayer, not him*" (*F for C* 167). As he stands vigil over Tywin's rotting corpse, he finds irony in his position, "*standing vigil for a father I helped to slay, sending forth men to capture a brother I helped to free...*" (*F for C* 175). Jaime's guilt, however, seems to be part of Martin's larger move to redeem him. At this point in the novels, Jaime does not rush to his sister's aid when she asks him to be her champion. Once he returns to King's Landing, he refuses her advances and shows no sign of resuming their relationship. Kin killing, albeit indirectly through the murderous actions of his brother, may help Jaime sever ties with his evil sister and leave behind the vile family legacy his father has bequeathed him. Once her father is killed, Cersei Lannister begins a ruthless pursuit of power that drives Jaime further from her.

Meanwhile, Tyrion is on the lam, embarking on a new series of adventures after fleeing King's Landing. However, his reputation as kinslayer follows him even when he travels across the Narrow Sea. He is painfully aware of the magnitude of this crime, frequently repeating, in the opening chapters of *A Dance with Dragons* that kin killers are the most accursed of all men. Ser

Jorah Mormont, who has himself been exiled for his crimes, chastises Tyrion. Ser Jorah has committed shameful acts that have disgraced his family and ultimately brought about his exile. These acts seem trivial compared to Tyrion's crime of patricide. He marvels at the fact that any man could commit crime as atrocious as kin killing (*D with D* 386). Ser Jorah's shock at Tyrion's behavior demonstrates the revulsion of the Westerosi for this taboo act.

The pirate-like Ironmen also engage in kin killing. Asha Greyjoy strongly suspects that her uncle Euron has murdered her father, Balon, who has mysteriously fallen to his death. Euron vehemently denies the accusation and pretends to want vengeance against his brother's killer. He asks his niece for the name of the killer so that he might himself exact vengeance (*F for C* 373). Asha, however, does not fall for this ploy. With the death of Balon, the surviving Greyjoy brothers (with the exception of the Damphair, who serves as the Drowned Priest) vie for the Seastone Chair, along with Asha. When Euron wins, the youngest brother, Victorion, knows that he must yield to Euron's rule or fight and possibly become a kinslayer. He is appalled at the prospect of slaying his older brother and of killing a fellow Ironman. The feud between the two is less significant to Euron than the shame that would come from killing his own brother (*F for C* 363).

In fact, Victorian has good reason to want vengeance against Euron, who slept with and impregnated Victorian's wife. Notwithstanding his hatred of this brother, he restrains himself, once more citing that those who kill kin are "*accursed in the eyes of gods and men*" (*F for C* 365). Victorian explains to Asha how Euron betrayed him and how Victorian subsequently killed his unfaithful wife. Had Balon allowed him to do so, he claims that he would have killed Euron as well. To prevent one brother from killing the other in his hall, Balon exiles Euron (*F for C* 378). Years later, Victorian is still tempted to kill his brother, but he fears the consequences. Euron himself does not want to be labeled a kinslayer. He first denies the death of his older brother, and later that of his younger one, the Damphair. When the Damphair disappears, Asha and her companions strongly suspect Euron. Tristofer Botley tells Asha that he believes the Damphair has been murdered and that Euron is pretending a search for him to hide the crime because he hopes to evade the stigma of kinslayer (*D with D* 374). He is openly treacherous, yet even Euron, who has likely murdered two brothers and is deserving of this label, does not want the stigma associated with kin killing.

Other kinslayers fill the pages of Martin's novels and make up much of the back story. The Targaryens have a long history of internecine war as they battle against each other for the Iron Throne. Much of this pseudo-historical fighting was sparked when King Aegon IV legitimized his bastard children. These children and their offspring then began to compete for the Iron Throne, resulting in a series of Blackfyre Rebellions that pitted half-siblings against half-siblings. Family ties are critical to the intricately connected world of Westeros. Westerosi history shows that, when those ties are broken through internecine struggles, vengeance is out of sorts.

The deaths of one's brothers in arms, whether kinsman or not, can also inspire vengeance. A loyal thane will seek to avenge the death of his lord, and a loyal brother in arms will seek to avenge the deaths of his companions. In Anglo-Saxon literature, a warrior's companions would likely include some of his kinsmen. Arthur's knights are a more eclectic group, though Arthur ultimately aligns himself with Gawain, a kinsman, rather than Lancelot, with whom he has no shared blood, when Gawain and Lancelot become enemies. Examples of vengeance for one's brothers in arms are less common in Martin's work but perhaps felt most strongly by the men of the Night's Watch. These men must abandon all other allegiances except their allegiance to the realm itself. Without the distraction of loyalties to family or king, their strongest personal bonds are to their companions in the Watch. For this reason, some of the men of the Night's Watch find Jon's decision to allow the Wildlings to cross the Wall unforgivable.

Traditionally, the Wildlings have fought and killed many men of the Night's Watch, and Jon's conciliatory actions towards them aggravate the urge for vengeance by some of the Brothers. Bowen Marsh asks if Jon will allow a particularly infamous Wildling, the Weeping Man, to cross the Wall even though the Weeping Man has killed some of Jon's companions. Jon replies that he will not be pleased to do so but sees no other option. He remembers the horrors done to his brothers by the Weeping Man, and he regrets that he cannot avenge them. All he can do, he claims, is honor their memory by remembering their names (*D with D* 779). Jon does value his companions, but he also understands the significance of his duty to protect the realm. He knows that, in this instance, he must put aside his personal desire for vengeance for the greater cause of the kingdom: the impending threat of invasion by the Others.

Clearly, blood feuds motivate much of Martin's plot. Various kingdoms of Martin's pseudo-medieval society are precariously bound together through bonds of loyalty and family ties. The struggle for the Iron Throne pits kingdom against kingdom and sometimes brother against brother, straining and often breaking tenuous bonds of loyalty. Ultimately, however, the Westerosi may not survive against the impending threat beyond the Wall without unifying and putting aside feuds, joining not only with each other, but also with the Wildlings. In Martin's world, of course, such unification is unlikely.

Eight

Peace Weaving

*"My Joff and your Sansa shall join our houses, as Lyanna
and I might once have done."*—Robert Baratheon, G of T 48

Medieval Peace Weavers

Much of the burgeoning scholarship on Martin's *A Song of Ice and Fire*
focuses on his portrayal of women. Some praise Martin for his depiction of
strong women; others condemn him as misogynistic for the brutal circumstances in which his females are sometimes placed. The HBO series, in particular, has been criticized for its brutality towards women. Certainly, Martin's
portrayal of women has inspired a variety of responses, and scholars approach
the topic of Martin's women from a number of angles. Caroline Spector calls
Martin's works "subversively feminist" by "establish[ing] medieval fantasy
tropes and then destroy[ing] them."[1] Although Martin has proclaimed "My
work is not an allegory to our days,"[2] some critics and commentators, including T.J. West, consider Martin's women in a contemporary context. West
claims that the novels and HBO series provide "commentary on not only the
highly precarious position women—especially those in power—occupy in
American society, but also the contradictions and complexities inherent in
the representation of sexual and gender violence."[3]

Martin's women have also been compared to historical figures. Valerie
Estelle Frankel links them to women involved in the War of the Roses.[4] However, Martin does not duplicate history to create his stories. He explains on
his website that his reliance on history is loose, at best: "There's really no
one-for-one character-for-character correspondence."[5] Still, all of these perspectives have some merit and point to the potential for more research on
Martin's women. For medievalists and scholars of medievalism, however, the
most provocative aspect of Martin's portrayal of women is in the context of
the medieval peace weaver.

The marital exchanges in Westeros are largely reflective of those in medieval literature. In most versions of Arthur's birth. Ygraine's marriage to Uther is a kind of peace exchange to end the strife caused by Gorlois' death, and even Guinevere's marriage to Arthur offers a political alliance by securing Arthur's friendship with Leodegrance, Guinevere's father. Christian romances, including the tales of Constance and Griselda in Chaucer's *The Canterbury Tales*, also feature exiled women who are sent from their homes to be married off in peace exchanges.

Peace weaving exchanges tend to be even more prominent in Anglo-Saxon literature and align closely with Martin's portrayal of marital alliances. In Anglo-Saxon literature, Germanic women of the highest rank sometimes served as peace pledges in order to bind men together and ensure alliances. Usually the daughter of an important warrior or king, the woman would be married off to a man of high status who might be perceived as a potential threat to her kin in hopes of forming or strengthening an alliance and possibly preventing conflict. Peace weaving is prominent throughout *Beowulf*, illustrating an array of both positive and negative repercussions, through the portrayals of such characters as Wealhtheow, Hygd, Thryth, Hildeburh, and Freawaru. Peace weaving women also feature prominently in the Anglo-Saxon elegies "The Wife's Lament" and, arguably, "Wulf and Eadwacer."[6]

Peace weaving women of medieval literature may be passive or rebellious as they react to the political marital exchanges about which they have little or no choice. Jane Chance delimits their important role: "either biologically through her marital ties with foreign kings as a peace pledge or mother of sons, or socially and psychologically as a cup-passing and peace-weaving queen within a hall."[7] Martin's women illustrate the full array of possibilities for the peace weaver, all which, to some degree, echo these medieval texts. He explains, "I wanted to present my female characters in great diversity, even in a society as sexist and patriarchal as the Seven Kingdoms of Westeros."[8] Martin does not intend direct comparisons to these Anglo-Saxon and medieval texts, but he clearly understands the importance of medieval peace weaving, and his novels thus vividly evoke various situations in which literary peace weavers might find themselves.

In Anglo-Saxon texts such as *Beowulf*, marriages are gift transactions in which women (and sometimes sons and men) are exchanged to forge unions and prevent hostilities. The woman who is exchanged is called *freoþuwebbe*, an Anglo-Saxon compound word meaning "weaver of peace."[9] Although the peace weaving woman might be seen as merely an object of exchange, she could find power within the system. The peace weaver could become, in the best of situations, a sort of diplomat, participating actively in the politics of her husband's kingdom, advising him, and sometimes ruling on her own. At its best, peace weaving offers women opportunities to use their diplomatic skills as tools to forge peace. However, if the exchange is not successful, she could find herself in a precarious, and potentially dangerous, situation. In a society that values warfare, especially one in which a game of thrones is involved, marrying off women as a means to ensure peace could turn out badly, in such cases reducing the peace weaver's status to object of exchange.

Anglo-Saxon authors were well aware of the pitfalls of peace weaving. Although its language is vague, the poignant elegy "The Wife's Lament" appears to depict a peace weaving arrangement gone awry. The narrator, perhaps a foreign bride, joins her new husband in his kingdom, but he is either exiled for a crime or perhaps gone away to fight in a war, possibly a war against her own kin. Regardless, she finds herself at the mercy of hostile in-laws who perceive her as a threat and hold her captive: "heht mec mon wunian on wuda bearwe,/under actreo in þam eorþscræfe" (someone sent me to dwell in the woods under an oak tree in an earth cave).[10] Upon her husband's departure, his kin apparently turn on her, refusing to integrate her into their family and plotting against her: "Ongunnon þæt þæs monnes magas hycgan/þurh dyrne geþoht" (that man's kinsmen began to conjure secret thought).[11] Much of the poem reflects the narrator's grief as she is separated not only from her own kin, in the way that the marital exchange would necessitate, but from her new husband and his kin, as well. She complains, "Þær ic sittan mot sumor-langne dæg/þær ic wepan mæg mine wræcsiþas" (There I must sit through the long summer's day; There I must weep my exile).[12] Stripped of hope, deprived of mobility, and apparently rejected by her in-laws, she sits in her earth cave and grieves.

Another peace weaver who finds herself surrounded by enemies in her husband's home is Hildeburh, whose story is related in *Beowulf* and "The Finnsburg Fragment." Although Hildeburh appears to be initially successful in her new husband's hall, she suffers great loss when her family and her in-laws conflict. Married off to Finn, she is visited by her brother, Hnæf. Hildeburh's marriage has not brought peace between her husband's tribe and her own, for her brother and son are attacked and killed during the night by a band of her husband's men.[13] These examples illustrate that marital exchanges were necessary to Anglo-Saxon social structure, yet not always beneficial to the peace weaver.

Westerosi Peace Weavers

Peace weaving is also essential to the power struggles in Martin's novels. Much of the narrative tension in *A Song of Ice and Fire* involves these marital exchanges. Through marital pacts, Lannisters attempt to align themselves with Tyrells and Martells; Martells attempt to align themselves with Targaryens;

Starks attempt to align themselves with Baratheons and Freys—the alliances go on and on. In the divided and politically complex kingdom of Westeros, such marital arrangements are critical to the game of thrones. Within the present and past of Martin's novels, these marital alliances are decisive factors in determining the distribution of power and, especially, in determining who sits upon the Iron Throne. Peace weaving is foremost a means to gain status and power. In *The World of Ice and Fire*, the maester who narrates presents as a sign of esteem the fact that House Arryn was twice "deemed worthy of marriage with the blood of the dragon."[14] In Anglo-Saxon literature as in Martin's novels, marital pacts serve to align clans; they involve oaths, and if broken, the consequences could be dire. His novels reflect the variety of possibilities that could occur when women (and men and children) are used to forge alliances.

Much like the helpless women from Anglo-Saxon poetry, Sansa Stark is, in the first of Martin's novels, a passive pawn in the game of thrones who finds herself at the mercy of (almost) in-laws. She, like her Anglo-Saxon predecessors, illustrates what can happen when marital alliances go awry. Sansa comes to King's Landing as a naïve young girl filled with romantic dreams. She longs for true love as she has envisioned it from the idealized heroes depicted in the lore of Westeros, and she believes that her arranged marriage to young Joffrey Baratheon, her "prince," will be the fulfillment of her dreams. The harsh reality in which she finds herself, however, leaves Sansa increasingly disillusioned. She witnesses knights behaving poorly, at odds with her notions of gallantry. Initially, when she sees behavior that does not meet with her expectations, she exclaims that the offender is not a true knight. As she becomes more attuned to her own role as peace weaver, a pawn in the game of thrones, she gradually becomes skeptical of true love and knightly virtue. Increasingly, she bemoans what seems to be her newfound reality: there truly are no "true" knights in Sansa's experiences.

Sansa has dreamed of becoming a princess, and her arranged marriage to Joffrey Baratheon promises to bring this dream to fruition. Sansa may have a romanticized vision of this marriage, but in fact it is a political arrangement. This proposed marriage is intended to forge an even closer relationship between King Robert Baratheon and Sansa's father, Eddard, who serves, reluctantly, as the King's Hand. The politics behind this marriage are much more complex than Sansa or her family realize. At the time the marital pact is arranged, the Starks do not know that Joffrey is not King Robert's legitimate son; rather, he is the product of an incestuous relationship between his mother, Cersei, and her twin brother, Jaime. Thus, he is an imposter to the throne. Further, Sansa begins to see that her "knight in shining armor" is actually cruel and sadistic.

Sansa's arranged marriage to Joffrey is threatened, and ultimately dissolved, when both her father and King Robert are murdered at the hands of the Lannisters. Much like the helpless narrator of "The Wife's Lament," Sansa finds herself surrounded and held captive (though not in an earth-cave) by hostile (almost) in-laws, Joffrey Baratheon's relations. Unknowingly, Sansa also becomes an object of another kind of political exchange, one intended to rescue her from this dangerous situation. Her mother, Catelyn Stark, is fearful for Sansa's life. She tries to free Sansa from the Lannisters through bargaining. Catelyn frees her son's hostage Jaime Lannister hoping for an exchange with the Lannisters that will bring both Sansa and her sister Arya home to Winterfell. Even with Jaime's increasingly good intentions, this exchange does not come about.

Left in the custody of the Lannisters, Sansa is displaced as Joffrey's intended bride, and Margaery Tyrell steps in as peace weaver to forge what the Lannisters see as a more advantageous relationship which will bring to the Lannisters the support of Highgarden, the seat of the powerful Tyrell family. During the marital negotiations that will align Tyrells with Lannisters, Littlefinger (who has motives of his own) comments that since Sansa's family has fallen from power, she has little to offer other than her body. Margaery Tyrell, on the other hand, brings an alliance with the powerful Highgarden family which offers both financial and military benefits (C of K 532). As in the peace weaving of Anglo-Saxon literature, marital exchanges are about power; they have, as Martin's characters might say, "little and less" to do with the kind of romantic love Sansa has envisioned.

Sansa's replacement, Margaery, is much savvier than Sansa. Although she is not as aggressive in her pursuit of power as the HBO series depicts her, Margaery serves as foil to Sansa in the novels in several ways. Whereas Sansa's family members have been lost to her or murdered, Margaery has the powerful Tyrells at her back, freeing her to exert power successfully within the Lannister household. Margaery is cunning and much better equipped than Sansa to find power within the system of exchange; however, she is still a pawn. A serial peace pledge, she is married off first to Renly Baratheon; then to Joffrey; then to his younger brother Tommen. Her multiple marriages carry on a tradition implied in the Finnsburh fragment when, after Hildeburh's husband and son are killed, her family brings her home, probably in hopes of a new marital arrangement.

Margaery has a clear sense of agency and seems in control of her situation, an attribute that neither Hildeburh nor Sansa seems to possess. When Catelyn meets Margaery at Renly's camp, she observes that this marriage, Margaery's first, is "the mortar that held the great southron alliance together" (C of K 341). Martin insinuates strongly that Renly is homosexual, making the marriage a political arrangement and nothing more.[15] After Renly's death when Margaery marries into the Lannister family, she, like Sansa, must contend with the Lannisters as hostile in-laws. When Joffrey is killed, she marries the more malleable Tommen and begins to exert a strong influence over him. When Cersei becomes fearful and resentful of Margaery's power as queen, Cersei tries to show that Margaery has been unfaithful to Tommen (*F for C* 825–7). Readers learn in Martin's most recent novel that she will have to face a trial and might assume that the clever Margaery will emerge unscathed. If the novels reflect the HBO series, which is ahead of Martin with this storyline, Margaery's shrewd diplomatic skills will not save her.

Margaery takes Sansa's place as peace pledge, yet Sansa is not allowed to return home; she is too valuable a commodity and is still held captive. Sansa is released from her arranged marriage to Joffrey, but she soon learns that Joffrey, as king, still has power over her. He tells her that his position frees him to sleep with whomever he wants. He mentions his own father, known for adulterous affairs, as an example, and also a Targaryen king notorious for womanizing. He flaunts his power, warning her that he can order her to sleep with him at his will (*S of S* 390). Further, even with Joffrey's new alliance with Margaery, Sansa is not relieved of her role as peace weaver. The Lannisters still see her as useful in their own quest for power. Once her oldest brother is killed and her younger ones are presumed dead, Sansa, as heir to Winterfell, is more than ever a valuable object of exchange. The Lannisters thus marry her off to Tyrion, Joffrey's dwarf uncle whom Sansa finds repulsive even though he is kind and compassionate towards her and even though this marriage protects her from becoming Joffrey's victim. Tyrion is himself a pawn in the marital arrangements set up by his father. He secretly wishes that he could please Sansa and that she could learn to love him. He acknowledges the benefits of gaining Winterfell, yet he feels true affection for Sansa, and he wants her to be more to him than simply an object of exchange (*S of S* 427). Sadly, Sansa cannot see beyond Tyrion's physical defects nor his status as a Lannister. When Joffrey is killed by the Tyrells (at the instigation of the Tyrell matriarch who fears that he might be cruel to Margaery), Sansa and Tyrion are accused of murder, and Sansa manages to flee.

Even after Sansa escapes from King's Landing, she still finds herself in the position of a pawn. Once she arrives at the Eyrie, thinking she has found refuge, she realizes her aunt Lysa's intent to marry her off to her cousin, Lysa's sickly son Robert. Sansa begins to recognize her position as a commodity. Like the Lannisters, Lysa is uninterested in Sansa as a person. She views her simply as a way to claim Winterfell (*S of S* 944). Sansa fears that she will not be able to marry for love, as she has always dreamed of doing. She is stunned by her aunt's own ruthlessness at making *herself* an object of exchange. She observes as Lysa complains to Littlefinger about the many suitors vying for her attention (in a misguided attempt to make Littlefinger jealous): "And the others all swarm around me, … but none of them truly love me. Only you,

Petyr" (*S of S* 938). Lysa then turns the tables on the peace weaving process and "commands" Littlefinger to wed her (*S of S* 938). Cunning Littlefinger is actually in control of this plan, seeing the usefulness of marrying Lysa Arryn. Sansa is dismayed by this proposed marriage, stunned by the prospect of Littlefinger becoming The Lord of Harrenhal (*S of S* 929). She watches and learns as these exchanges take place before her, gradually becoming less naïve and more aware of her own role as a valuable commodity in the politics of peace exchanges.

As Sansa comes to understand the power struggles associated with marital arrangements, she gradually lets go of her dreams of true love. Even after her aunt Lysa dies and she assumes the role of Littlefinger's natural daughter, Sansa is still an object of exchange. Littlefinger sees a new opportunity for Sansa, who assumes a new identity as Alayne. He plans to marry her off to Harrold Hardyng, Robert Arryn's heir. Her "father" tells her that he has made a marriage contract for her. He explains to her that it is only a betrothal. An actual wedding must wait until Tyrion, still legally her husband, is dead (*F for C* 893). Sansa balks initially at the notion of a marriage to Hardyng, who has only recently been made a knight and who has an illegitimate daughter with one of the small folk (*F for C* 893). Once Littlefinger explains Hardyng's relation to Jon Arryn, Sansa/Alayne understands that Hardying is her cousin's heir, and that if Robert were to die, she and Hardyng would inherit the Arryn titles and land. She realizes that this marriage could unite the houses of Arryn and Stark. It would bring her to a position of great power, power that can only come to fruition from a carefully arranged marriage.

Littlefinger plans to reveal Alayne's true identity after the marriage. He explains that the alliance would win both the Eyrie and Winterfell and that the knights of the Vale would aid Sansa in winning back Winterfell (*F for C* 896). The social-climbing Littlefinger is clearly using Sansa to help advance himself, but Sansa/Alayne now seems less a pawn, more in control of her own destiny as peace weaver. In an excerpt from the forthcoming *Winds of Winter*, readers see her, much more confident in her own powers, humbling and then beginning to win over Hardyng.[16] She is realizing the potential to exert power from within the very patriarchal power system that has previously made her victim.

Although she seems to be emerging as ever more capable and independent, thus far in Martin's novels, Sansa remains among the most passive of his peace weavers. Caroline Spector calls Sansa a "passive pawn," claiming that she "fills the role of the traditional princess of medieval fantasy. But in assigning her that role, Martin is making a powerful point about the dangers inherent in fantasy: how fanciful myths hide—and perpetuate—a fundamentally oppressive social structure."[17] Spector, like many of the scholars who discuss Martin's women, does not acknowledge the important theme of medieval peace weaving embedded in Martin's work. The social structure depicted in Anglo-Saxon literature, mirrored by Martin's Westeros, is fundamentally oppressive and patriarchal. There is nothing fanciful in the portrayals of either Hildeburh, the narrator of "The Wife's Lament," or Sansa Stark. To understand fully how women might survive, even thrive, in these circumstances, one must understand the complexity of the social situation of the peace weaver.

In the novels, Sansa herself appears to be working towards an understanding of how she might succeed in this oppressive social structure. Her trajectory in Martin's writing takes a dramatic turn from the HBO series, although both depict Sansa gaining autonomy. The series was harshly criticized for marrying Sansa off to Ramsay Bolton and insinuating a rape scene in Season Six. In the novels, Jeyne Poole, who is not a point of view character, takes on the role as "fake Arya" and wife to Ramsay. By substituting Sansa as Ramsay's wife, Sansa is, even more so than in the novels, a victim of peace weaving. After Theon helps her escape from Ramsay and Brienne reunites her with her half-brother Jon Snow, Sansa exerts her authority as the oldest surviving Stark child and advises Jon in his battle plans against Ramsay. Once Ramsay is defeated, she herself chooses his method of death and watches as his dogs devour him. When Jon leaves Winterfell to seek an alliance with Daenerys, Sansa has assumed a position of power and is left to rule Winterfell in his absence.

Whereas Sansa Stark is, at least in the first books, a passive pawn who gradually learns to exert some power, Cersei Lannister is an aggressive and avaricious predator. Cersei's marriage to Robert Baratheon brings with it a crown and the potential for great power. The Lannisters have previously been aligned with the Targaryens; when the Targaryen king falls and Robert Baratheon usurps the throne, the Lannisters seek favor from the new ruler. This marriage is seen as an assurance of that favor. Cersei's missed potential to use this position positively is obvious when she is considered alongside exemplary Anglo-Saxon peace weaving queens, including *Beowulf's* Wealtheow and Hygd, both who wield great power and influence through their marriages to kings.

Wealtheow is a successful peace pledge whose marriage has, apparently, brought peace between her husband's tribe and her own. She has balanced or shifted her loyalties and assumes an important role in her husband's hall, distributing mead and gold rings to her husband's thanes and actively participating in forging political alliances. Her actions in the mead hall enable her to empower her husband's men; those she serves first are placed in a position of privilege. Wealtheow also exerts diplomacy and power when she speaks at court. Through her words, she attempts to ensure her sons' succession, and she offers advice to her husband. L. John Sklute explains that her "presence and actions help the lord at his task" of preserving peace. He adds, "If [her role] reflects anything of the social system of the Anglo-Saxons, it is that of the diplomat."[18] It is difficult to perceive Wealtheow as merely an object of exchange: she has established a vital role in her husband's hall occupying a position that enables her to participate in king-making decisions. Hyglac's wife, the young Hygd, also uses diplomacy to exert her power as peace weaver. Upon her husband's death, she appears to have the power to choose who should rule in her son's minority. She appoints Beowulf to this position (he refuses but promises to aid and advise Hrothulf while he is young). Both Hygd and Wealhtheow participate in negotiations in the mead hall, not hesitating to intervene in political matters, particularly those concerning the futures of their sons as kings.

Similarly, Cersei Lannister wields great power through her role as peace weaver, but she does so foolishly and selfishly, in ways that threaten to topple the social alliances of Westeros. Cersei deeply resents the social system that has placed her in an unhappy marriage but has also made her queen. At a young age, her hopes are dashed when King Aerys Targaryen rejects Tywin Lannister's plans to marry her off to Aerys's son Rhaegar, whom she loves. Her uncle Kevan Lannister contemplates the failed marital pact between Rhaegar Targaryen and Cersei and muses about the hostilities that could have been prevented if Aerys had agreed upon this marriage: "*how many deaths could have been avoided?*" (*D with D* 1043). Cersei's marriage to Robert Baratheon, an exchange not looked upon favorably by either Cersei or Robert, shows that men, too, were pawns in such alliances. Robert explains that his marriage to Cersei was a political necessity about which he had little choice. He blames his Hand, Jon Arryn. After the death of his beloved Lyanna Stark, Robert was not interested in marriage at all. However, Jon convinced him that marriage is important for the kingdom as Robert will need an heir. A marriage to Cersei Lannister would ensure that the Lannisters would back Robert if Viserys Targaryen were ever to reclaim the throne (*G of T* 310). Robert and Cersei prove incompatible. Both mourn for their lost loves, and their marriage is further challenged by Cersei's incest with her twin brother and Robert's drinking and womanizing.

Cersei becomes a queen through this marriage to Robert as he usurps the throne from the Targaryens, but her greatest opportunity to exert power is through her children. Like Wealhtheow and Hygd, Cersei's role as mother allows her to be a king maker. However, whereas she is sometimes admired by readers for her seemingly fierce dedication to her children, Cersei's ruthlessness is more often self-centered.[19] As Frankel describes her (and some of Martin's other mothers), she "play[s] the game of thrones on behalf of [her] sons, all the while succumbing to clichéd irrationality."[20] Cersei is not merely irrational, but dangerous to the social order of Westeros, for her children are illegitimate and thus imposters to the Iron Throne.[21] Ruth Lexton explains that "The power of queenship inhered in the position of the queen consort as the king's wife and the mother of his heirs; her chastity was integral to her role so any hint of accusation of sexual transgression could seriously damage her position and affect the king."[22] Cersei places the kingdom at risk through her incestuous affair with her brother and their attempts to pass off their children as legitimate heirs.[23] As with Malory's depiction of Arthur and his nephew/son Mordred, the complicated familial connections resulting from Cersei and Jaime's incest lead to political confusion. About the incest in Malory's work, Ruth Lexton writes that "The ambiguity surrounding the father-son/uncle-nephew relationship puts familial discord at the center of the struggle."[24]

In a discussion of the traffic of women, Gayle Rubin explains that the "weight of the entire system may come to rest on one woman kept in a miserable marriage."[25] Cersei refuses to be kept in her miserable marriage to a drunken, unfaithful husband, particularly once she has reason to fear that her children's illegitimacy will be revealed. Thus, she arranges her husband's murder, seeing his death as an assurance for her children's ascendancy to the throne and also as a means for her own greater power. The death of the king and the subsequent accession of her bastard son threatens the entire social order of Westeros and leads to a struggle between claimants to the Iron Throne. Further, she is dismayed to find that, even with her husband dead, her powers are limited; her father, Tywin Lannister, still sees her as a commodity of exchange. Cersei is outraged when she learns that her father plans to marry her to Willas Tyrell, both to forge ties between Lannisters and Tyrells and also to dispel (true) rumors of her incestuous relationship with her twin brother. She vehemently objects to this marriage proposal: "I am queen of the Seven Kingdoms; not a brood mare" (*S of S* 266). Despite her objection, Cersei understands that she will have to go through with this arrangement. "Remember your duty," her father tells her (*S of S* 267), reminding her that such marital exchanges are critical to the politics of Westeros. Later, Tywin exerts his patriarchal power over her more forcefully, telling her that as her father, he has the right to marry her off in any way he chooses: "You'll marry the pig boy if I say so, and bed down with him in the sty" (*S of S* 384).

After Tywin's death, Cersei is freed from his political manipulations and eager to begin her own regime with more forcefulness. She believes she has at last found true power and the freedom to exert it. Having assumed the role of Regent while her son Joffrey is in his minority, Cersei, drunk with her newly assumed power (and wine), contemplates the potential of her role. She intends to hold on to the position of regent until Tommen is of sufficient age. She is clearly frustrated with the duties placed upon her as a female from a powerful family and her long wait to ascent to a position of power. She has been a "dutiful daughter," a "blushing bride," and a "pliant wife" who has suffered the indignities of a drunken husband, a jealous brother, and the machinations of numerous men who control the kingdom, including Stannis, Varys, Jon

Arryn, and Ned Stark. Most of all, she sees her new position as an opportunity to seek vengeance on her loathed younger brother, Tyrion (*F for C* 491).

Cersei has no concern for the kingdom, only for her own power, which she wields carelessly. She is, however, aware of the limits of her power as a woman. She is displeased that she does not get the respect from her council that her father commanded. She resents that the men on the counsel question her authority and sometimes refuse to do her bidding, and she blames this disrespect on her status as a woman: "*It is all because I am a woman. Because I cannot fight them with a sword*" (*F for C* 507). She becomes a key player in politics, but resorts to subterfuge and quickly oversteps her boundaries. Cersei is in a position of authority; had she ruled and acted wisely, using diplomacy rather than trickery, she could have been a Wealhtheow or Hygd. Instead, she overreaches and is briefly humbled once the Warrior's Sons, whom she has equipped with arms, imprison her and then force her to a walk of atonement.

Feminist scholars make much of Cersei's struggle for power; she is a woman who desires to possess the political and sexual powers of men. Sexually promiscuous, Cersei sleeps with a series of men who she thinks might be useful to her, ignoring her commitment to her brother Jaime. Her sexual relationship with a woman, Taena of Myr, illustrates Cersei's desire for dominance and for the power her society only allows to men. In bed with Taena, Cersei assumes the role of man, using her friend as she feels she herself has been used. Cersei cannot change the patriarchal system to which she has fallen victim. Her primary failure is her inability to understand how she might exert power within that system. In her rebellion, she evokes both Grendel's mother and Thryth, the latter who serves as a foil to the effective queen Hygd. Her very name, if one accepts the popular reading that the description *mod þryðo* includes her name, has been interpreted to mean "arrogance." One popular reading of the episode depicting Thryth is that she is (initially) unwilling to participate in the peace exchanges arranged by her father. She puts to death potential suitors as an act of rebellion. Although the *Beowulf* poet does not directly link her rebellion to peace weaving, certainly her unwillingness to marry would prevent alliances that could be valuable to her kingdom. Her rebellion against the system of peace weaving is not only detrimental to the men she cuts down, but could equally be a danger to her people. The poet does not indicate hostility between her family's tribe and her new husband's tribe, yet marriage to Offa, whom the poet praises and who may be based upon a real-life King Offa, would surely be advantageous.

Like Thryth, Cersei's resistance to peace weaving poses a real danger to the kingdom. Her incestuous relationship with her brother is particularly reprehensible because it is a serious threat to the political order.[26] Foremost, the offspring of this relationship become imposters to the throne. Secondly, as her father recognizes, his children's incestuous affair prevents important alliances that could prove advantageous to the Lannisters. Cersei's encouragement of Jaime to join the Kingsguard is for selfish reasons and prevents him, too, from a politically advantageous marriage. Once she is freed from her marriage and from her father, she embarks on a quest for power. Thus far in the novels, her power seems to be exerted on behalf of her sons. However, the HBO series at the end of Season Six makes clear that that Cersei's thirst is for personal power.[27] Cersei is a dangerous woman, threatening the very fiber of social order in Westeros.

Cersei's daughter Myrcella, who is much milder in temperament than her mother, is more easily resigned to her own position as a peace weaver. When she leaves her family behind to travel to Dorne for an arranged marriage to Trystane Martell, Myrcella puts on a brave face. Tyrion admires her courage as she boards the ship that will carry her away from her family: "her smile was a shade tremulous … but the girl knew the proper words to say, and she said them with courage and dignity" (*C of K* 587).[28] Ser Aerys notes that Myrcella is far braver than the young King Tommen. He recalls Tommen weeping when Myrcella leaves for Dorne, and he also notices that Myrcella does not cry despite the fact that she is being forced to leave her home and enter into a potentially dangerous alliance with a stranger. Nevertheless, she is happy once in Dorne, adapting readily to her betrothed as well as the strange new customs and even the spicy food that await her in this foreign kingdom.

Unfortunately, Myrcella finds herself amidst the schemes of Trystane's older sister, Arianne. Arianne is herself a sort of Thryth character as we learn that she, like the unwilling *Beowulf* peace weaver, has rejected the suitors her father chooses for her. Thryth is "firen ondrysne" (terribly wicked).[29] She goes so far as to put to death the men whom her father chooses for her, finally finding a satisfactory husband in Offa. Although Arianne does not kill potential suitors, she complains bitterly of her father's attempts to align her with old men, all of whom she rejects. Although her father did not insist on the marriages, Arianne is insulted by the offers which "prove how little he regarded me" (*F for C* 279). She mulls over her status as peace weaver and her helplessness to choose her own spouse. She was brought up with the understanding that, since she is a princess, her father would choose her husband. She is envious of her cousins, the Sand sisters, whose father Oberyn told them that wedding was not necessary and that they should emphasize pleasure over matrimony (*F for C* 850). Arianne does not initially know that she was secretly promised to Viserys Targaryen, and her father's attempts to marry her off to old men in Dorne are simply a ploy, as he knows she will refuse them.

Unaware that her father has other plans for her, strong-willed Arianne has no difficulty in making plans for herself. In Dorne, women are allowed to ascend to the throne. Arianne fears that her father is bypassing her for her brother Quentyn. Thus, she conspires against her father, whom she sees as weak. Citing the Dornish law of succession which allows women to hold the throne, Arianne kidnaps Myrcella and plans to have her claim the Iron Throne. These plans go awry when Arianne's father learns of them, and Myrcella is injured when Doran's men intervene. Ser Aerys, the Kingsguard from King's Landing assigned to watch over her, is killed in the fray. Arianne's rash actions could lead to increased enmity between the Martells and Lannisters, but Myrcella uses her position to negotiate. When a new representative from King's Landing arrives, Myrcella blames her injuries on the renegade Dornish knight Ser Gerold Dayne, but she does not mention the raucous events that actually ensued. She realizes that she is in a potentially dangerous situation, and she recognizes her own power and ability to keep the peace. She lies to preserve this precarious peace between her new in-laws and her kin in King's Landing. The HBO series underplays Myrcella's cleverness.[30] So far in the novels, Myrcella is skillfully managing a very dangerous peace exchange. Even at her young age, she appears to understand the repercussions that can follow when peace weaving fails.

When peace weaving goes awry, the woman who has been sent abroad to a new family may find herself in a most dangerous situation. Bruce Mitchell and Fred Robinson describe the difficult social predicament of the Anglo-Saxon peace pledge, who was "given in marriage ... to patch up a blood feud [and thus] was involved in ... conflict between loyalty to her lord, her husband, on the one hand, and her family on the other."[31] Beowulf predicts that Freawaru's arranged marriage will not suffice to amend the longstanding troubles between her new husband's kin and her own. He fears that Freawaru's new husband and his kinsmen will resent the young bride and war will ensue: "Þonne bioð abrocene on ba healfe/að-sweorðe eorla; syððan Ingelde/weallað wæl-niðas ond him wif-lufan æfter cear-wælmym colran weorðað" (Then will the oaths sworn by both leaders be broken; then Ingeld will be filled with hatred for his wife's kinsmen and his love for her will diminish)."[32] Freawaru will be hopelessly and helplessly caught in the conflict. The *Beowulf* poet predicts, but does not give us the actual outcome, of Freawaru's marriage. On the other hand, Martin's female peace weavers show a variety of responses to such delicate arrangements. Some manage these tricky situations artfully, as does Myrcella thus far (in the novels); others, like Sansa Stark (again, in the novels), do not fare as well.

Children and Men as Peace Weavers

While it is easy to see how marital exchanges affect women, children and men may also be objects of exchange. In Anglo-Saxon literature, the sons produced from peace exchanges might be sent back to the woman's family in order to seal the peace pact more completely. If a peace exchange is not successful, the son, once given to his mother's kin, could become estranged from her and even endangered. In the Finnsburgh fragment, this is likely the case. Hildeburh's son dies in the conflict between his father and his uncle, probably fighting on his uncle's side. This exchange of sons could also be a possible scenario for the Anglo-Saxon elegy "Wulf," if we accept that Wulf is the narrator's child.[33] This poem depicts a peace weaver mourning about her separation from Wulf. In the poem, she makes a direct plea to Eadwacer, whom I take to be her husband, urging him to recognize that their child might be in danger. This reading of the elegy was first made legitimate by Marijane Osborn who explains that the narrator's grief "[suggests] the apprehension that such a mother as 'peace-weaver' might well feel when sending her son away to fulfill his destiny in her native land."[34] The narrator's actions and language indicate that she may be a peace pledge whose exchange in marriage has unhappy consequences for herself and her son. Osborn explains that "It was a Germanic custom to try to ensure peace between feuding tribes, to 'settle the feud,' by arranging a marriage between the daughter of one ruler and the son of the other; when a son was born of that union he would be sent at about the age of seven to be brought up by the mother's people."[35] Beowulf himself, brought up in his uncle's kingdom, could be an example of such an exchange.

In *A Song of Ice and Fire*, Jon Snow negotiates an exchange of male children to ensure that the Wildlings will be peaceful once he allows them to cross the Wall. While this exchange does not involve marital arrangements, it is, nonetheless, a political exchange in which children are used as commodities to ensure peace, and it is also an exchange that profoundly affects women. The Magnar of Thenn, with whom Jon has sealed this pact, points out to Jon the devastating effect this exchange will have on the Wildling women. He refers to the exchange as Jon's "blood price" and notes the "the wailing o' their poor mothers" that might "haunt [Jon's] dreams at night" (*D with D* 846). In a different situation, another mother, the Wildling Gilly, must exchange her son for Mance Rayder's son at Jon's command. As the son of the King-Beyond-the-Wall, Mance's infant is in danger. Melisandre, the red priestess, might well sacrifice the infant to her god, the Lord of Light, because she believes he possesses king's blood. Gilly agrees to the exchange, leaving her own child at the Wall, and Jon marvels at her passivity. Whereas other women would be outraged by requests that would most likely result in the deaths of their babies, Gilly simply pleads with him and begs him not to go through with this exchange. Jon explains why he must do so: "You saved your own boy from the ice. Now save hers from the fire" (*D with D* 106). Gilly's parting words to Jon, who calls her "my lady," remind him of the huge sacrifice she is making. She asserts her own identity and makes clear her obligation to her child, reminding Jon that she is "a mother, not a lady" (*D with D* 115). Gilly is tormented by Jon's decision to separate her from her son, yet she accepts the duty Jon has given her and carefully nurtures Rayder's infant.

Both mothers and children suffer when they must be separated from each other for political reasons. Martin emphasizes the long-term deleterious effect of such political exchanges on children through his portrayal of Theon Greyjoy, fostered out to the Starks as a child after his father's rebellion. This exchange is intended to keep the Greyjoy family from another rebellion. Although the Starks are kind to Theon, he feels like an outsider. Once he returns to his father's kingdom, he is rejected by his kin. Trying to prove his worth as his father's rightful heir, Theon embarks on an overly ambitious and ultimately self-destructive attempt to regain his status. On the other hand, Lysa Arryn's refusal to foster her son Robert is detrimental to the child, who is coddled and spoiled, and to her kingdom; Lysa prevents possible alliances and thwarts the development of her son when she refuses to foster him.

It would be easy to assume that a society dependent on peace weaving sees only women and children as commodities, bartered according to the political schemes of a patriarchy. However, men, too, could be objects of marital exchange. Stacy Klein argues that Beowulf himself disrupts the social order by not marrying: "Beowulf's failure to marry and reproduce ... disrupts genealogical continuity at a larger cultural level. When Beowulf dies without leaving a son to serve as his successor, he sets in motion a grave anxiety about the Geatish future."[36] The male must participate in these alliances in order to preserve the social order and keep peace among various kingdoms. By (apparently) not marrying, Beowulf does not provide important alliances and leaves no heir. Chaucer's Christian romance "The Clerk's Tale" begins with an account of a marquis who has refused to marry. This marquis, Walter, shows no interest in marriage until the people in his country insist that he do so in order to ensure an heir to the throne. He agrees, but defiantly chooses as his wife the lowborn but virtuous Griselda. The narrative unfolds around Walter's cruel treatment of Griselda, inflicting upon her numerous tests that include leading her to believe that her children have been killed. Ultimately, though, Griselda is reunited with her children, and the subsequent years of her marriage are happy ones.

In Martin's novels, Eddard (Ned) Stark is one example of a successful marital exchange. He is united in marriage to Catelyn Tully in order to seal an alliance between the two families. A substitute for his brother, who dies before he can marry Catelyn, Ned's marriage proves to be long and fruitful, but it is not a marriage that he chooses. Even though this was not initially a love match, the couple grow to love each other, and the marriage successfully unites the two families. Bryndon Tully, however, refuses his brother's attempt to marry him off, causing both familial and political conflict. Hoster Tully, head of the Tully household, cannot forgive Bryndon for refusing a marriage pact to a Redwyne woman. As his older brother and as his lord, Hoster can rightfully dictate whom Bryndon should marry, and he sees Bryndon's refusal not only as politically problematic, but also as a personal affront (*G of T* 789). In one of the more amusing examples of men as objects of marital exchanges, Tyrek Lannister is married off to an infant, an arrangement that may reward him with land and title, but also brings with it humiliation. Tyrik agrees to marry the child Lady Ermesande, yet he is subsequently ridiculed, given the nickname "Wet Nurse" and asked, "what sort of swaddling clothes his bride wore on their wedding knight" (*C of K* 401). Because this marriage offers benefits to his family, both political and financial, Tyrik must hold true to his marriage vows even though the marriage is in name only and causes him much embarrassment.

As Tyrek Lannister realizes, oath breaking, in Anglo-Saxon literature as in Westeros, is a reprehensible offense that often results in war. The marriage of Robb Stark to Jeyne Westerling is a vivid depiction of what happens when a marital pact is broken. Robb reluctantly agrees to a marriage with one of the Frey daughters in order to seal the Freys' allegiance to him. Catelyn is proud when Robb consents to this marriage, recognizing its political importance. She sees this as a sign of maturity for Robb, a transition from childhood to becoming a man and, even more so, a leader: "it took a lord to make a marriage pact, knowing what it meant" (*G of T* 650). Catelyn remembers her own role as a peace weaver, first to Brandon Stark and then to his brother Eddard. She clearly understands the importance and responsibilities of peace weaving as well as the sacrifices. She considers her duty as peace weaver and the effect of her own arranged marriage upon Littlefinger, who loved her. She had willingly agreed to marry Brandon, callously abandoning Littlefinger despite his sincere love for her. Upon Brandon's death, she willingly agreed to marry Ned although she had never met him. She resents that he immediately went off to fight in a war and came home with an illegitimate child. She grew to love him, yet the original marriage was simply "[her] duty" (*C of K* 650). Catelyn knows that the marriage to the Frey girl is a political necessity for her son just as her own marriage had been, and she is pleased with his initial willingness to make the sacrifice.

However, Robb breaks the pact after he sleeps with Jeyne Westerling. Robb finds himself torn between his oath to the Freys and this lady's honor. Frankel explains, "Trapped in a situation with no good choices, he decides to protect another person's honor above his own."[37] Robb's decision to renege on the marital pact with the Freys has dire consequences that affect not only Robb, but all of his followers. Jaime Lannister later comments about Robb's choice to marry Jeyne. He speculates that she must be extremely beautiful, for she has cost Robb "*a kingdom*" (*F for C* 699). To make amends with the Freys, Robb offers his uncle Edmure in a marital exchange. The Freys agree to align Roslin Frey with Edmure. When Edmure asks if he might see her before committing (the Freys are notoriously unattractive), Walder Rivers counters that Edmure can not meet his new bride until the wedding ceremony. He facetiously asks if Lord Tully "feels a need to count her teeth first" (*F for C* 485). He then insists that Edmure must agree to the marriage sight unseen or the marital agreement will be rescinded (*F for C* 485). Edmure has no choice. Although he is pleased with his new bride when he finally sees her, Edmure's marriage to a Frey cannot undo the damage caused by Robb's breach of the earlier marital pact. In a shocking rejection of the rules of hospitality, the Freys slaughter Robb and many of his men at the wedding feast. The Freys demonstrate that, indeed, as Beowulf predicts about the future of the unhappy Freawaru, even the best of wives cannot prevent warfare.

After Robb's death, Jeyne Westerling's family once again considers her value as a peace weaver, using her to re-forge their previous alliance with the Lannisters. The Westerling matriarch Lady Sybell reminds Jaime of his father's promise to arrange a politically advantageous marriage for Jeyne. She tells Jaime that Lord Tywin had promised that both Jeyne and her younger sister would be wed to men of high estate. Jaime responds that Jeyne must wait two years before she weds again to dispel rumors that any offspring belong to Robb Stark. Jaime is wary because he understands that a child of Robb Stark would be a threat to his own family's power. Peace weaving knits a web of potential allies or enemies, so Jaime proceeds with caution.

Perhaps the most vivid example of the political necessity of peace weaving is evidenced by the Boltons' desperate attempts to rise to power and keep their hold on Winterfell through an alliance with the Starks. However, in the novels, no Stark daughters are available. Sansa is missing, and Arya is believed to be dead. This does not deter the power-hungry Roose Bolton and his sadistic (bastard-born but legitimized) son, Ramsay. They simply find a "false Arya Stark," and this girl, Jeyne Poole, is perhaps the most unfortunate peace weaver in Westeros. Roose Bolton, knowing the wedding is a sham, makes an ironic toast to the fake Arya at her wedding. He proclaims that the two great houses will be joined through the marriage and that the longstanding feud between the Stark and Bolton families will end. Roose himself has made a marital arrangement with one of the Frey daughters, a fat one. He brags about the wisdom of his choice of wives when Jaime Lannister wrongly surmises that he has married Fair Walda. He is informed, however, that Roose has chosen Fat Walda because he was offered her weight in silver as dowry. Roose brags that this was his sole motive in selecting her as bride.

With the Freys at his side, the Boltons aspire to keep Winterfell. When word of this marriage reaches Arya's brother Jon Snow, he doesn't realize that the Boltons are using a substitute. He is concerned about his sister, but he also thinks to himself that the real Arya, headstrong and rebellious, will make a difficult bride for the vicious young Bolton. Jon hopes that the priestess Melisandre has seen his sister Arya in her fires, fleeing from this unwanted marriage. Instead, the grey girl on the dying horse who has appeared in the fires is Alys Karstark, who is fleeing from a marriage arranged by her uncle. Upon her arrival at Castle Black, Alys explains to Jon her role as pawn. Her uncle wants her to marry his son, her cousin Cregan, so he can be made Lord of Karstark. This uncle is aware that Alys will inherit if her brother dies. If she marries and has a child with Cregan, he can claim her birthright. She fears that her uncle will dispose of her once this goal is achieved: "He's buried two wives already" (*D with D* 648). At first, Jon refuses to help her. He adheres to the traditions of peace weaving and tells her that marriages should be determined by close kin. However, Alys convinces him to intervene. Jon helps her by arranging a different marriage for her, this one to the Magnar of Thenn.

Meanwhile, the fake Arya, Jeyne Poole, has neither the real Arya's courage, nor Alys Karstark's gumption in escaping. In her desperation, Jeyne looks to Theon Greyjoy for help. Theon is an unlikely rescuer who is weak and broken after suffering from Ramsay's abuse. He does manage to free Jeyne, but her fate remains uncertain. The substitute Stark in the novels more vividly illustrates the necessity of peace weaving than the HBO series in which Ramsay marries an actual Stark, Sansa. The novels better highlight the significance of marital pacts by portraying the desperation of the Boltons to marry a Stark and thereby legitimize their claim on Winterfell.

Peace Weaving and Politics

If the "fake Arya," Jeyne Poole, is the weakest of peace weavers, Daenerys Targaryen has emerged as the most powerful. Readers first see Daenerys as a shy girl, victim of her brother Viserys, who marries her off to Khal Drogo in hopes of aligning himself with the Dothraki and winning back the Iron Throne. This plan backfires for Viserys as Khal Drogo tires of his arrogance and puts him to death. This situation for Daenerys, her husband killing her brother, would seemingly place her in the context of Hildeburh, whose brother is killed by her husband's men. But Daenerys is not a victim to the peace weaving exchange. Spector writes about Daenerys's marriage to Khal Drogo, "…Daenerys understands that being bartered off to a powerful savage, to cement a political and military alliance, is simply part of the role women must play in her culture."[38] Daenerys is not simply playing a role; she comes to love her husband and quickly begins to establish herself as having an important place among the Dothraki. After his death, she asserts her power as a leader and continues her campaign to claim the Iron Throne.

Daenerys finds a voice and uses that voice to wield political power. About Anglo-Saxon women, Bernice Kliman writes, "if [she] may not fight, she can speak."[39] Even the passive narrator of "The Wife's Lament" might be able to wield words as weapons if we read her final words as a curse. Barrie Ruth Straus posits that the last lines of this poem are not a lament, but an active gesture culminating in a curse upon those who have caused her suffering.[40] And John D. Niles agrees that the final lines of the poem, though intentionally ambiguous, are, in fact, the narrator's attempt to take action against her oppressive situation.[41] Likewise, the female narrator of *Wulf* speaks out, probably to her husband, imploring him to hear her words: "Gehyrest þu, Eadwacer?" (Do you hear me, Eadwacer?).[42] In *Beowulf*, Wealtheow also relies upon words as power. She uses her skills at diplomacy to ensure the safety of her sons, to praise Beowulf for his heroism, and to advise her husband. Similarly, Daenerys learns to use words to exert power. She speaks, holding council, negotiating, and making judicial decisions. Frequently falling back on the fact that she is "only a young girl," she manages to outwit many of the men who underestimate her power.

As queen and Mother of Dragons, Daenerys also realizes the importance of a carefully negotiated marriage. She has a number of suitors, many hoping to align themselves with the House Targaryen, but she chooses for herself as second marriage a political arrangement that might benefit her followers rather than a love match. Although she is in love with the sellsword Daario, she marries the nobly born Hizdahr zo Loraq. Her advisor Ser Barristan Selmy admires Daenerys for this difficult choice. He considers Westerosi history and the negative consequences that have resulted when rulers allow themselves to be governed by love. He reminds her of other rulers who chose love to disastrous consequence: Rhaegar's love for Lyanna, Daemon Blackfyre's love for the first Daenrys, and Bittersteel and Bloodraven who competed for the same woman. He also recalls the popular Westerosi love song about the Prince of the Dragonflies and Jenny Oldstone. This song recounts a love so great that the Prince forfeited his crown for his lady. This love had negative consequences for the kingdom of Westeros, which consequently "*paid the bride price*" (*D with D* 959) for their prince's choice. Daenerys's marriage to Hizdahr turns out badly, but her story is not over. Clearly, she recognizes the significance of a political marriage in her quest to gain the Iron Throne.

Daenerys's alliances are critical to the game of thrones, but other minor marital pacts appear throughout the novels. These minor pacts shed light on some of the other nuanced functions of peace weaving. The Blackfish tells Robb of an instance in which a marital exchange becomes a prize for vengeance. He is so determined to exact vengeance on Jaime Lannister that he promises his daughter to the man who can bring him Jaime's head (*S of S* 277). Marital pacts can have far-reaching implications. As emissary for Stannis Baratheon, Ser Davos Seaworth learns of a marital pact between the Manderleys and Freys. The Frey patriarch exploits his numerous children by arranging marital alliances that enhance his own political power. Stannis seeks the alliance of the Manderlys, and Davos realizes that the Manderly/Frey marriage could cost Stannis that alliance. His host, Borrell, gives him the disappointing news. He tells him that Lord Wyman Manderly and Lord Walder Frey have made a pact that will be sealed by a marriage between the two families. Ser Davos also wants an alliance with House Borrell. When Borrell asks Ser Davos why he should follow Stannis, Davos has no good answer but acknowledges to himself that an arranged marriage to a powerful family might suffice to bring Stannis the followers he needs (*D with D* 144). Clearly, marriages are keys to power, as Ser Davos realizes.

Even the unconventional "warrior women" of Westeros, including those who attempt to avoid marriage, cannot overcome their status as potential peace weavers, and at least one, Asha Greyjoy, eventually succumbs to an arranged marriage. Asha, like Daenerys, is a competent and powerful woman. When her brother Theon is fostered out to the Starks as a peace pledge, Asha, who is Balon Greyjoy's only daughter, becomes, in Balon's eyes, his heir apparent. When Theon returns to the Iron Islands and finds out about this arrangement, he tells his uncle that he is well aware of the Ironborn tradition that prohibits women from inheriting when a male heir is living. He insists that he will not be denied his position as male heir (*C of K* 177). Balon, however, sees his son Theon as softened from his time with the Starks and denies him his claim to the Iron Islands. Upon Balon's death, Asha finds herself in contention for the Seastone Chair against her uncles Victarion and Euron. As is the custom for the Ironmen, a Kingsmoot (or Queensmoot, as Asha calls it) is scheduled to determine the next ruler. Asha does not win the vote. Rather, her uncle Euron wins, and she is married off to Erik Ironmaker, an arrangement for which she can't help admiring Euron: "With one stroke Euron had turned a rival into a supporter, secured the isles in his absence, and removed Asha as a threat" (*D with D* 371).

Just as Daenerys would prefer to marry Daario, Asha Greyjoy also has a true love who is unsuitable for marriage, Qarl. She is well aware of the discrepancy between her own social situation and that of the lowborn Qarl, who is grandson to a thrall. Like Thryth of *Beowulf* who acquiesces to her role as peace pledge after her marriage to Offa, Asha accepts her fate. A renowned warrior, Offa surely would have made a formidable enemy to Thryth's kin, and so her conformity in this marriage (whether it is her first or second) benefits both her own kin and her new husband. This "before and after" behavior demonstrates that the success of marital exchanges depends upon the willingness and capability of the woman to assume a diplomatic position in her husband's court. Notwithstanding her marriage to the elderly Ironmaker, Asha remains unconventional, a woman who can lead battles and wield weapons skillfully. Nevertheless, she willingly goes through with the marriage, understanding the political benefits it offers to the Ironmen.[43]

Only the Wildling women beyond the Wall seem free of marital alliances, but they have their own social customs for choosing mates. For the Wildlings, women must be kidnapped, a test of the man's strength and courage. In her book *Beowulf and the Grendel-Kin*, Helen Damico discusses a historical example, King Cnut's legendary kidnapping of Queen Emma. Damico places "the event in the context of medieval Scandinavian marital customs, whereby the bride was first seized, then purchased before the marriage was confirmed."[44] Wildlings have a similar custom. Interestingly, the Wildling women do not see this kidnapping as a sign of subjugation. In fact, Ygritte finds the Westerosi tradition of peace weaving demeaning. She tells Jon that she prefers the Wildling way which ensures that she will have a strong companion rather than "some weakling" to whom her father has assigned her (*S of S* 558). Repeatedly, despite Jon's protests, Ygritte claims that Jon has "stolen" her, and she refuses to see the concept of "stealing women" as degrading. Jon asks what she would do if she were stolen by someone unworthy or cruel, and Ygritte is undaunted. She claims that she would simply cut the throat of the unworthy man as he slept. This action seems so obvious to Ygritte that she follows it with her favorite saying to Jon, whom she finds unworldly and naive: "You know nothing Jon Snow" (*S of S* 559).

Once the Wildlings are allowed to cross the Wall, they will be expected to obey the customs of Westeros. Queen Selyse accuses the Wildling Val of insolence when Val tries to explain the Wildling's customs. She warns Selyse that the Wildlings will neither kneel nor yield. Selyse then threatens Val with a marriage that will make her subservient and informs her that they will find Val a husband who will force her to abide by Westorosi notions of courtesy. Queen Selyse can only view Val as a commodity of exchange because of her marriage to Mance Rayder, King-Beyond-the-Wall. In fact, Val does not have royal blood and is not interested in participating in any marital alliances. However, with Jon Snow's cousin Alys Karstark already married to a Thenn, other marriages with the Wildlings will surely follow. Readers can only surmise how this clash of marital customs might play out, but already, marital exchanges are infringing on customs of the Wildlings.

Peace weavers in Martin's novels have a number of possible responses to marital exchanges. While some women are victimized by the exchanges, others find power within the system, asserting their influence as mothers and diplomats in their new husbands' homes, and still others rebel against the system entirely. Martin shows that peace weaving is not just a woman's issue;

men and children can also be affected by marital exchanges. In fact, peace weaving can affect entire kingdoms, knitting together potential enemies or forging more hostilities, depending on the success of those involved. Christopher Fee sums up what he terms the "fundamental flaw" of peace weaving: "the social cohesion [it provides] is only effective in situations where such cohesion is necessary in the first place."[45] In the game of thrones of Westeros, the contender who best builds cohesion through peace weaving will likely attain the Iron Throne. However, there is no assurance that animosities, old or new, will end as a result. They often reemerge to threaten even the best of alliances. As Beowulf predicts about Freawaru's marriage, "Oft seldan hwær/æfter leodhryre lytle hwile/bongar bugeþ, þeah seo bryd duge!" (Very seldom after the fall of a prince for a short while does the deadly spear rest, although the bride is good.)[46]

Conclusions:
Teaching Westeros

*"Research gives you a foundation to build on, but in the end
it's only the story that matters."*—George R.R. Martin,
www.georgerrmartin.com

The Maze of Terminology

Martin's portrayal of a pseudo-medieval society is detailed and nuanced. The plethora of allusions and the vivid construction of an alternate Middle Ages validate his novels as a rich resource for medievalists. They are also worthy of scholarly consideration because of their adaptation of the chivalric ethos. As a medievalist whose interests have recently moved increasingly towards the field of medievalism, I set out to write a work based on my own scholarship, one that would show the potential scholarly value of works of medievalism such as Martin's novels. When framed in a historical and cultural context, Martin's Westeros can also inform students of medieval literature and students of medievalism. I have used references to Martin's novels and film clips from the series in my own medieval courses, and I have taught a senior capstone course solely devoted to Martin's works. This concluding chapter will detail how Martin's creation of Westeros might be brought into scholarly and pedagogical discussions. I also offer some predictions for how Martin's medievalism, especially his portrayal of the chivalric code, might evolve (or devolve) as he brings the series to completion.

One challenge in bringing medievalism into classroom discussions of medieval literature is helping students navigate the often-hazy distinctions between medievalism and medieval studies. Further, medievalism itself includes numerous subcategories: neo-medievalism, creative medievalism, meta-medievalism, modernist medievalism, and post-modern medievalism.

Working through this almost dizzying maze of terminology is not, however, insurmountable and is, in my view, part of what makes discussions of medievalism provocative. Fortunately, several recent books that grapple with these terms and issues can serve well in the classroom, including Emery and Utz's *Medievalism: Key Critical Terms* and d'Arcen's *The Cambridge Companion to Medievalism*. Students can also consult the website of the Medieval Electronic Multimedia Organization for a handy list of relevant definitions. Discussions of how Martin's novels, the HBO series, and the industry surrounding them might fit into or defy these various definitions can be fruitful.

Martin's world of Westeros vividly illustrates the possibilities for studies in medievalism both because of its popular appeal to a broad audience and also because of its various modes of reception. Books, television programs, products, and blogs that spin off of Martin's novels can be brought into the conversation. Students come to classes on medieval literature with perceptions (and misperceptions) about the Middle Ages that are often based in part (sometimes entirely) on their experience with Martin's novels and with other works of medievalism, such as those by Tolkien and Rowling. Their experiences with recent works of medievalism offer both challenges and possibilities for teachers of medieval literature. Martin's creation of a faux medieval world attracts non-specialists and students to the medieval ethos, but can also cause confusion about what is "authentically" medieval. As with other popular works of medievalism, Martin's novels can sometimes enhance, sometimes hinder, the non-specialist's understanding of the Middle Ages. Placed in the proper context, however, they can become learning tools. Discussions of Martin's Westeros can be an excellent launching point for discussions about authenticity both in works of medievalism and, by comparison, in literature from the Middle Ages itself. How authentic, for example, are depictions of Arthur's court at Camelot? How authentic are accounts of battle in romance? Discussions of questions such as these challenge students' assumptions about what they deem authentic.

For advanced students, prior experience with works of medievalism can inspire more sophisticated discussions about authenticity. In her essay "Authenticity," Pamela Clements describes how the search for medieval authenticity has evolved; ranging from a search for "the historically accurate" and a "search for cultural origins," to "believability or verisimilitude, a sense of the genuineness of the 'medieval' in a modern setting."[1] Martin's medievalism can be used to address these issues of authenticity. Further, his creation of Westeros offers insights about how medievalists re-create the Middle Ages.

The topic of authenticity inspired one of the students in my Martin-themed senior seminar to consult Norman Cantor's *Inventing the Middle Ages* and then to write a philosophical paper about medievalism and authenticity.[2] This student used Martin's Wall as one point of discussion. In an interview with *Rolling Stone*, Martin cites Hadrian's Wall as his inspiration for the massive ice construction that separates the Seven Kingdoms from the horrors that are reported to reside in the northernmost regions.[3] Hadrian's Wall was similarly constructed by the Romans who occupied England as a barrier against perceived threats in the north. Since Hadrian's Wall is in fragments, it can only be fully perceived through the re-creations of medievalists. My student questioned whether, since Martin's Wall is so vividly created and can be so fully visualized, it might be for modern audiences "more 'real' than many historical reconstructions" of Hadrian's Wall.[4] Other students in my class noted Martin's use of history, such as the War of the Roses, and explored the ways writers of medievalism re-shape the past to create their works. My students began to question what we know about historical events and how our knowledge of history is constructed and conveyed.

Westeros in the Medieval Classroom

In his introduction to *Mass Market Medieval*, David Marshall writes about Dan Brown's *The Da Vinci Code*. He explores Brown's use of "extreme elements of the medieval past," such as the self-flagellation of monks. He explains that "Brown's entire novel creates a medieval past that never was by fixating on a small set of iconic images ... to build a fictional Middle Ages devoid of peasant, primogeniture, or pesky details that have no bearing on the desired trajectory of the plot."[5] Martin also creates a Middle Ages that never was and also uses iconic images. His re-creation is in some respects less real than Brown's in that he deliberately crafts an alternate and fantastic Middle Ages. However, Martin does not omit the "pesky details." These details, once sorted out and contextualized, can give a vivid picture of the medieval mindset.

Although Martin's work is classified as fantasy, his medieval re-creation is so vividly constructed that it invites comparison with works of medieval literature. Veronica Ortenburg West-Harling explains the appeal of fantasy fiction with medieval settings: "The origins of the fantasy fiction genre may go back to William Morris, but its real modern roots are in Tolkien's *Lord of the Rings*. Fantasy fiction invents myths, legends, and characters situated in a world before time, doing heroic deeds and achieving impossible tasks with the help of magical creatures (beasts, demons, magicians)."[6] Martin's world, however, is not "before time," but "outside of time." Because Martin does not base Westeros on any one particular time but is rather loosely "medieval," his work can launch discussions of both Anglo-Saxon heroic literature and romance. The values reflected by his characters share similarities with the values of characters in both heroic and chivalric literature. For example, Martin's portrayal of minstrels, detailed in Chapter Two, does not perfectly mirror the minstrel of medieval literature. However, Martin illustrates how varying versions of chivalric and heroic narratives might have developed through his many references to and rich descriptions of the rumors, songs, and legends that circulate among his characters. Likewise, his description of the dissemination of written literature can call attention to the value of manuscripts and to medieval ideas about learning.

While the length of Martin's novels makes problematic their use in a class on medieval literature, teachers can assign passages or show clips from the HBO series to encourage student discussion. Relevant passages from Martin's novels might be paired with other medieval works, such as *Sir Gawain and the Green Knight*, the romances of Chrétien de Troyes, *Beowulf*, and *The Song of Roland*. The inhabitants of Westeros hold as ideals the same attributes depicted in these works. The most worthy among them aspire to heroic acts such as avenging the deaths of loved ones, protecting the realm, showing fealty to a king, demonstrating prowess and courtly love, and honoring oaths and vows. The least worthy serve as negative examples, equally providing a window to chivalric and heroic expectations through their failure to live up to them.

Martin creates a faux history of the institution of chivalry in Westeros, tracing its inception to the Andals. *The World of Ice and Fire*, a compendium of background stories akin to Tolkien's *Silmarillion*, names John the Oak "the First Knight, who brought chivalry to Westeros."[7] The Westerosi are mostly familiar with the pseudo-history of such heroes through legends, songs, and literature. As is common in romance, inhabitants of Westeros look backwards to knighthood of earlier times for their ideals. Martin's portrayal of a chivalric code is especially intriguing because, like Sir Thomas Malory and other romance writers, he shows the contradictions inherent in the chivalric code as the characters in the present-tense of his novels try, and often fail, to live up to these expectations. By emphasizing the struggles of his characters, Martin variously upholds, overturns, critiques, and deconstructs the mores and values that undergird the chivalric code as depicted in medieval literature.

Through his portrayal of concepts such as the importance of bloodline, politically arranged marriages, and reliance on bonds of loyalty, Martin's novels can provide insight into how these same concepts function in medieval literature. Martin, however, teases them out to conclusions far beyond the boundaries of medieval genres. For example, the medieval fabliau illustrates the consequences of social change through typically pithy narratives that expose the flaws of socially liminal characters who attain wealth and title. Through characters such as Ser Davos who has similarly risen through the ranks, Martin is able to portray in full detail the consequences of social ascent on an individual. He explores how Ser Davos sees himself in relation to the true-born nobility, what he expects for his children, and how he is continually influenced by his humble upbringing in Flea Bottom. Such emotional aspects of social climbing are seldom detailed in medieval genres.

Likewise, the peace exchanges that are frequently referenced in medieval genres are played out in full detail in Martin's novels. The Beowulf poet refers to a number of these peace exchanges, and the Anglo-Saxon poem "The Wife's Lament" appears to portray the psychological consequences of an unhappy peace exchange. These Anglo-Saxon works, however, do not reveal in detail the entire stories of the peace pledges. On the other hand, Martin's portrayals of such characters as Sansa Stark and Myrcella Baratheon delve into the emotions of these women and offer up a wide array of responses and consequences that might result from such arrangements. Martin thus explores a range of possibilities left uncovered in medieval literature.

Even the moments of anachronism in Martin's novels can be useful pedagogical tools, for Arthurian literature is also highly anachronistic. In *Sir Gawain and the Green Knight*, for example, which is set in the fictional Arthurian past, the characters are nonetheless dressed in state-of-the-art fourteenth-century armor and finery, surely an appeal to the author's contemporary audience. Martin has similar moments that thrust the present into his fictional past, particularly in his references to other recent works of medievalism. Students may better appreciate the role of anachronism in medieval works by considering the ways Martin similarly interjects modern references into the "medieval" world of *A Song of Ice and Fire*.

Martin, Medievalism and Modern Concerns

As the field of medievalism has gained legitimacy, courses devoted solely to medievalism are rising in popularity. I have had the opportunity to teach such a course: a senior seminar. I sought a theme that would resonate with my students and accommodate a number of critical perspectives. Martin's novels were well-suited for this purpose. While some students came to the class having read Martin's entire series, others had read none of the books. All of the students had watched at least some episodes of *A Game of Thrones* with one exception: a single student had never seen the show nor read any of the novels. To level the playing field, in addition to the books on medievalism discussed at the beginning of this chapter, I assigned Martin's first two novels. I occasionally showed clips from the HBO series, but the course focused primarily on the novels.

A number of students in the class focused their research (which culminated in a senior thesis) on how Martin's works intersect with medieval literature. A few students in the class, however, had never taken a course solely devoted to medieval literature or simply had other interests about which they preferred to write. Their varying interests posed few difficulties as Martin's works not only portray medieval chivalry, but also can be seen as commentary on current issues. David Marshall explains how works of medievalism might respond to contemporary culture: "Recognizing that we cannot 'be' medieval and that any attempt to recreate the medieval amounts to play-acting a dream, producers and participants in … medievalism assert an autonomous expression of the medieval that is contingent upon its own cultural context."[8] Martin's novels, the HBO series, and the industry that has risen around them are popular not only for their reflection of the Middle Ages, but also because they simultaneously reflect a number of modern cultural concerns. Robinson and Clements credit Umberto Eco with one of the first usages of the term neo-medievalism as "an intentional rewriting of medieval social codes and ethics into contemporary aesthetics" that "look[s] back to the past for solutions to the present and the future."[9] Certainly, Martin's works can be viewed in this light, as evidenced by the range and scope of commentary in which bloggers, scholars, and fans discuss the contemporary relevance of his literary and television empire.

Race relations, religion, philosophy, gender issues, and postcolonialism are all subsumed in the pages of Martin's novels. Gregory J. Helmsetter finds in Martin's works relevant social commentary about gay rights, women's rights, and the rights of the physically challenged.[10] Blogger T.J. West claims that the novels and series provide contemporary "commentary on not only the highly precarious position of women–especially those in power–occupy in American society, but also the contradictions and complexities inherent in the representation of sexual and gender violence."[11] John Blake explores ways that "the show reflects contemporary America,"[12] and Charley Carpenter discusses how Martin's novels simultaneously overturn medieval and modern notions about the role of the government to protect its people: "Martin's in-your-face depictions of debauchery, sexual assault, trafficking, forced marriage, and illegitimacy refute the gendered myth that knights and armies exist to protect women and children, just as they refute the political myth that states exist to protect nations from serious external threats."[13]

Thus, Martin's Westeros provides a frame of reference that is simultaneously familiar and remote, allowing students to delve into medieval topics or to explore more recent concerns. My students' papers reflected this versatility. One student in my class used Edward Said's *Orientalism* as a launching point. She looked specifically at Daenerys Targaryen's attempts to colonize in Essos, and she saw in this portrayal a metaphor for current political issues. She argued that medieval "European culture inspired the theme for Martin's saga, but the text also serves a commentary for modern issues, especially the United States' involvement in the Middle East."[14] After reading Helen Young's

Race and Popular Fantasy Literature: Habits of Whiteness, another student was inspired to write about neo-colonialism and attitudes about race conveyed in Martin's depictions of the Summer Islanders.[15] Yet another student looked at Martin's depiction of childhood through the lens of trauma theory to explore how the children of Westeros cope in such a harsh environment, and another student looked at Martin's portrayal of disabled characters through the lens of disability studies. A politically motivated student used Martin's novels as a springboard to discuss the tendency of Americans to create a false sense of nostalgia for a past that never truly existed. She noted as a point of discussion Donald Trump's "Make America Great Again" slogan. The nostalgic view of chivalry in medieval romance, she argued, is similar to the tendency of some Americans to look back to a glorified past that never was: American nostalgia "depends on a similar misremembering and romanticizing." Martin, on the other hand, "does not grieve for the Middle Ages; instead, he calls attention to the elusiveness of true chivalry in order to prevent his readers from becoming nostalgic for a time from which civilization has long progressed."[16] My students submitted their findings to faculty in a mock-conference setting at the end of the semester. Their successes confirmed for me the pedagogical possibilities for Martin's medievalism.

As Richard Utz claims in his recent book *Medievalism: A Manifesto*, "The most exciting new forms of engagement with medievalia … have originated from the confluence of reception studies, feminism, women's studies, and medievalism studies."[17] In sum, Martin's Westeros provides a familiar frame of reference that can launch discussions of literature and literary theory. It can offer a gateway to discussions of medieval topics and also to the burgeoning field of medievalism itself. Bringing Martin's Westeros into my classroom evidenced to me that we can use our students' experiences with works of medievalism productively not only to help them better understand medieval literature, but also to help them better understand the world today.

Predictions

While my focus has been on the pedagogical potential of Martin's novels and the industry surrounding them, fictional Westeros remains foremost a work of fantasy. Notwithstanding the novels' potential as a rich resource for students of medieval literature and medievalism, Martin's primary appeal is as an author of escapist literature; he transfers us temporarily to an intricately fashioned yet fictional, and ultimately magical, world. In heroic and romance literature of the Middle Ages, readers can find monsters, dragons, and frequent supernatural occurrences, but the focus remains on the behavior of the hero, his ability to adhere to a code of conduct that governs honorable behavior.

Thus far in his novels, Martin has kept magic at bay in Westeros, and much of the emphasis has been, as with these medieval genres, on the behavior of his characters. Magic exists primarily north of the Wall and across the Narrow Sea in Essos. The Westerosi are largely skeptical of the fantastic in their pseudo-world. They generally do not believe in dragons, wargs, or the Others. This divide between supernatural and pseudo-reality is one reason Martin's novels work so well as examples of medievalism: he offers more than magic and fantasy. Thus far in the series, much of his emphasis is on the comparatively realistic events in Westeros itself. However, Daenerys Targaryen is poised to return to Westeros with her dragons, and the threat beyond the Wall is growing ever greater. Thus, the divide between the pseudo-reality of Westeros and the doubly fictionalized supernatural threats beyond its borders is poised to be breached.

About fantasy fiction, West-Harling writes that it can "illustrate the importance of man's understanding of, and working with, the natural world, which ultimately brings about wholeness and happiness."[18] Martin himself has indicated that the conclusion of his series will not ultimately bring about "wholeness and happiness": "I've said before that the tone of the ending that I'm going for is bittersweet."[19] Fan theories abound concerning how Martin's game of thrones might be resolved, but most predict an epic battle between ice and fire as Daenerys's dragons confront the white walkers. Such a battle will have obvious appeal to fans of science fiction, yet it may also prove interesting to scholars of medievalism. The ultimate direction of Martin's medievalism will depend on how he manages this ultimate confrontation. Will Jon Snow, who embodies so many chivalric virtues and attributes, emerge as a "once and future king" in the personage of Azor Ahai? Will Daenerys Targaryen, in spite of her attempts to administer justice and mercy, emerge as rightful ruler? Or will she succumb to the madness that cursed her father? Will Bran Stark, who once dreamed of becoming a knight, use his powers as green seer to administer justice and to bring peace to a war-ridden kingdom? Will Jaime Lannister stay on his path to redemption and emerge as a "true knight"? Is Martin's portrayal of chivalric and heroic values ultimately parodic, or will those values serve to save Westeros? Readers and fans must wait and see.

Chapter Notes

Preface

1. Eco, p. 51.
2. Breen, "Why 'Game of Thrones' Isn't Medieval—and Why that Matters."
3. Martin himself makes this claim in a question/answer forum on westeros.org. He maintains that he uses history loosely.
4. Shippey, "Modernity," p. 149–155.
5. Consider, for example, the physical shape of Westeros, the similarities between the struggle for the Iron Throne and the War of the Roses (noted by Martin himself on his website), and the many historical allusions to England such as those detailed in Caroline Larrington's *Winter Is Coming.*
6. Unless otherwise indicated, all translations of Old and Middle English texts are my own. Since Malory's *Le Morte Darthur* poses few difficulties, I have not translated passages from this text.
7. Keen, p. 2.
8. Ackerman, p. 1.
9. "Knight," Westeros.org. This encyclopedic fansite features a compendium of recurring themes and important characters in Martin's novels, and a wiki discussion forum.

Chapter One

1. In recent years, the Popular Culture Association has devoted sessions to Martin, as has the International Medieval Congress. See the bibliography for journal articles and scholarly texts on Martin.
2. *Studies in Medievalism: Medievalism in Europe II* VIII (2006): preface.
3. Shippey, "Medievalisms and Why They Matter," p. 45.
4. D'Arcens, p. 4.
5. D'Arcens, p. 5.
6. Clements, p. 23–24.
7. Emery, p. 83.
8. Robinson and Clements, p. 56.
9. In *Winter Is Coming,* Caroline Larrington explores the many historical and literary medieval references in Martin's series, including various warrior codes.
10. *Beowulf* is preserved in a single manuscript, dated approximately AD 1000. However, scholars have placed the composition of the narrative as early as the sixth century.
11. "Knight," Westeros.org.

12. Saul, p. 38.
13. Martin et al., *The World of Ice and Fire*, p. 208.
14. Keen, *Chivalry*, p. 2.
15. Saul, p. 37.
16. Rovang, p. xiv.
17. Chrétien may, in fact, include some subtle criticism of Lancelot, who is ridiculed for riding in a cart and initially shunned by Guinevere despite his struggles to rescue her. Malory, however, makes obvious Lancelot's struggles by having the affair exposed to the court.
18. Hodges, p. 2.
19. Hackney, p. 132.
20. George R.R. Martin, *A Song of Ice and Fire* 5 volumes (New York: Bantam Books, 2013). Citations will be to individual novels in the series, abbreviated as follows: *A Game of Thrones* (*G of T*); *A Clash of Kings* (*C of K*); *A Storm of Swords* (*S of S*); *A Feast for Crows* (*F for C*); and *A Dance with Dragons* (*D with D*).
21. "Knighthood." Westeros.org.
22. Martin's orders of knights include both secular and religious. Though not relevant to my purpose here, the religious order known as the Faith Militant, who renounce worldly possessions, has an increasingly important role in Martin's most recent novels and in the HBO series.
23. For example Ser Barristan Selmy, while serving Daenerys Targaryen in Essos, trains Meereenese youths to become knights. Across the Narrow Sea, a Warrior Code is certainly already in existence in various forms, as evidenced by the Dothraki and the Unsullied.
24. "George R.R. Martin: *The Rolling Stone* Interview."
25. Robins and Clements, p. 62.
26. Keen, p. 1–2.
27. Keen, p. 47.
28. Lull, p. 114.
29. Malory, pp. 75–76.
30. Martin, *A Knight of the Seven Kingdoms*, p. 98.
31. Blogger RumHam on westeros.org, responding to a chain discussion of Martin's spelling of "Ser."
32. Blogger TheBooksRemember on westeros.org.
33. Hackney, p. 134.
34. Chrétien, p. 295.
35. Malory, p. 649.
36. *Sir Gawain and the Green Knight*, p. 24–27.
37. "George R.R. Martin: *The Rolling Stone* Interview."
38. Zaleski and Zaleski, B13.
39. By "typical" romance, I refer to the twelfth-century works by Chrétien de Troyes and those inspired by them, which feature a single hero, rather than the cycles that assemble Arthurian stories.
40. "George R.R. Martin: *The Rolling Stone* Interview."
41. Jon Snow, bastard of Eddard Stark, joins the Night's Watch ostensibly because he cannot inherit land or title.
42. Many readers predict that Jon will re-emerge as Azor Ahai, legendary hero of prophecy. Jon's fans hope that, like Arthur, he will be "once and future" leader.

Chapter Two

1. Blake "How 'Game of Thrones' Is Like America."
2. "George R.R. Martin: *The Rolling Stone* Interview."
3. Morgan, p. 28.

4. George R.R. Martin, "Knights | George R.R. Martin." Web. http://www.georgerr martin.com/for-fans/knights/.
5. *Beowulf*, ll. 871–874.
6. Lacy and Ashe, p. 1.
7. Malory, p. 717.
8. Martin et al., *The World of Ice and Fire*, p. 169.
9. Unferth is, according to the Anglo-Saxon text, *ðyle*, or orator. Although his motives are sometimes said to stem from jealousy of Beowulf, it is also probable that he is speaking for Hrothgar.
10. *Sir Gawain and the Green Knight*, l. 31.
11. Mance is known for his musical skills, a fact that makes his disguise as minstrel all the more effective.
12. Geoffrey, for example, has Arthur in direct conflict with the Romans, a fact that, as some of his contemporaries argued, surely would have been documented by other sources if true.
13. For an excellent introduction to Arthurian legend, see Norris Lacy's *The Arthurian Handbook*, and also Elizabeth Archibald and Ad Putter's *The Cambridge Companion to Arthurian Legend*.
14. Martin et al., *The World of Ice and Fire*, p. 169.
15. Martin et al., *The World of Ice and Fire*, p. 169.
16. "George R.R. Martin: *The Rolling Stone* Interview."
17. The septon has ulterior motives for telling these tales. The novels suggest (and the HBO series confirms) that The Hound is a penitent on the Silent Isle. Septon Meribald likely seeks to conceal his identity. However, since so many stories have circulated about The Hound, Brienne does not question these accounts.
18. Cole, p. 73–88.
19. Geoffrey of Monmouth, p. 200—201.
20. Scoble, p. 134.
21. *The Anglo-Saxon Chronicle*, p. 55.

Chapter Three

1. Amodio, p. 22.
2. Amodio, p. 15.
3. Lacy, p. 39.
4. Stein, p. 107.
5. Stein, p. 106.
6. *World of Ice and Fire* 10.
7. Stein, p. 125.
8. Saul, p. 157.
9. Caxton, Preface to *Malory's Works* by Sir Thomas Malory, p. 103.
10. *Lull's Book of Knighthood and Chivalry and the Anonymous Ordene de Chevalrie*, p. 22.
11. Shippey, *The Road to Middle Earth: How J.R.R. Tolkien Created a New Mythology*, p. 230.
12. Robinson and Clements, p. 62.
13. Rovang, p. 1.
14. "The Seafarer" expresses the sorrow and loneliness associated with exile although, in this case, the exile of the narrator is self-imposed. He appears to be a sailor, called to his duty at sea yet deeply affected by the isolation that this duty entails.
15. Malory, p. 35.
16. Tom Shippey, "Modernity," p. 154.
17. Martin's novels reflect other works, as well, that aren't necessarily medieval. For

instance, his novels share some motifs with Shakespeare, whose works also often contain medievalisms. Astute readers may note a reference in *A Dance with Dragons* that evokes Act 5, Scene 5 of Macbeth in which Macbeth's enemies carry branches while marching. Macbeth has been warned, "Fear not, till Birnam wood. Do come to Dunsinane." Stannis's men adopt a similar disguise when they march on Deepwood Motte carrying branches in order to take Asha Greyjoy and the Ironmen by surprise. Twice, Martin borrows a motif from Shakespeare's violent play Titus Andronicus, in which the title character bakes the sons of his nemesis into a pie and serves them to her. Martin shapes this motif into the Westerosi legend of the Rat King and again when Wyman Manderly bakes Walder Frey's sons in a pie (*D with D* 544). Yet again, Martin alludes to Shakespeare when Arya recounts mummers' performances, some with titles that may bring to mind Shakespearian plays (*F for C* 725). Martin includes a number of very familiar motifs. Westeros even possesses its own version of a Great Flood story (*D with D* 737). Westeros also has several versions of Trojan Horse (*D with D* 516–51 and *D with D* 975).

   18. Robinson and Clements, p. 63.

Chapter Four

   1. Saul, p. 159.
   2. Saul, p. 172.
   3. Keen, p. 2.
   4. *Ramon Lull's Book of Knighthood and Chivalry*, pp. 51, 102.
   5. *Ramon Lull's Book of Knighthood and Chivalry*, 20.
   6. Keen, p. 2.
   7. E. Perroy, pp. 25–38.
   8. For a detailed discussion of the social implications of the fabliau, see my doctoral dissertation, "The Social Satire of the Medieval Fabliau: A Literary/Historical Approach to the Genre" (University of Georgia, 1993). Typically defined as "short, humorous tales in verse," I argue that a primary purpose of the fabliau is its concern with changing social estates. The corpus of fabliaux consists of approximately 160 Old French and Anglo-Norman tales, and also a handful in English, including six by Chaucer. The tales are typically characterized by their inclusion of a lover's triangle, an elaborate trick, and a character who is the victim of the trick, or dupe.
   9. All references to fabliaux are from the six-volume edition by Anatole de Montaiglon and Gaston Raynaud, *Recuil Général et Complet des Fabliaux des XIIIe et XIVe Siècles*. All translations are my own.
   10. I use the term "royalty" to refer to the ruling family of Westeros; "nobility" refers to the wealthy aristocracy who boast long, impressive lineages, and are often linked to royalty.
   11. Discussions on a Wiki page of Westeros.org offer some theories that posit a noble birth for Daario, after all. However, in the HBO series, Daenerys seems to have abandoned him, refusing to take him along with her to Westeros.
   12. Chapter Eight explores in detail the significance of Martin's marital arrangements.
   13. Hartinger, p. 155.
   14. Garbaty, p. 143.
   15. When Robert Baratheon is introduced in *A Game of Thrones*, he is grossly overweight and drunken, hardly an exemplar of *franchise*. Readers might note that he is strongly reminiscent of the aging King Henry VIII. Both King Robert and King Henry, however, were virile, impressive warriors in their youths.
   16. J.K. Rowling's Harry Potter series also toys with this theme. Although swords do make an appearance in her novels, wands are more clearly paired with particular wizards, perhaps mimicking the destiny of certain swords to be matched with particular owners.
   17. Hartinger, p. 154.

18. Bloch, p. 322.

19. Martin's portrayal of the Middle Ages cannot be pinned to a single time period. Charles Hackney, using armor and weaponry as evidence, correctly observes that "direct comparisons between actual and historical eras and Westeros should ... be handled with a light touch" (132).

20. Montaiglon, Volume III, p, 68.

21. Martin, *A Knight of the Seven Kingdoms*, pp. 6–7.

22. In the HBO series, Littlefinger is on a very different trajectory. Even more ambitious than his literary doppelganger, he proposes marriage to Sansa himself and clearly states his intentions to rule the Iron Throne.

23. Benson, p. 8.

24. The Hound seems to be on the road to redemption in the novels. However, in the HBO series, once the Broken Men are slain, he appears to turn immediately to the task of making a weapon. His intentions in fighting, however, may become more honorable as a result of his experiences.

25. In the HBO series, Samwell reclaims the sword. However, Martin's most recent novels give no hint that Samwell might abandon his plans to become a maester.

26. Some fan theories have posited that Tyrion is actually the son of the Mad King Aerys Targaryen, who feuded with Tywin Lannister and was jealous of his golden twins, Cersei and Jaime. If so, Tyrion may be in line for the Iron Throne through this connection.

27. Jaime's redemption is less clear in the HBO series. He does, however, appear shocked by Cersei's machinations at the end of Season Six.

28. Frankel, *Winning*, p. 59.

29. In the HBO series, Ramsay actually marries a Stark—Sansa—and, after committing numerous egregious acts, is defeated in battle against Jon Snow.

30. In the HBO series, Melisandre sacrifices Shireen, Stannis's own daughter, in an act of desperation as Stannis, whose army is hindered by a snowstorm, tries to battle the Boltons at Winterfell.

Chapter Five

1. Since Martin uses the terms "oath" and "vow" interchangeably to mean "promise," I am doing the same. This chapter discusses, in fact, two different kinds of promises. One form of promise, more properly known as an oath, is part of the sacred ritual that is essential to the dubbing ceremony in which knighthood is granted. It entails verbal statements that generally end with swearing to God. The second, the vow, entails promises to act in response to certain events or situations (by fasting, praying, or seeking vengeance). Both are intricately entwined with the concept of loyalty.

2. Saul, p. 138.

3. *Beowulf*, ll. 2883–2884.

4. Klincke, ll. 29–31.

5. Capellanus, p. 185. In Chrétien's romance, Guinevere claims later that she has only been kidding Lancelot about her anger in his hesitation. It is, however, a true dilemma for Lancelot, one that emphasizes the knight's potential struggles with balancing loyalty for lady and other obligations.

6. *Sir Gawain and the Green Knight*, ll. 1770–1775.

7. Saul, p. 311.

8. Balin is a prisoner in Arthur's kingdom, but his subsequent actions upon drawing the sword indicate clearly his dedication to the king.

9. Malory, p. 75.

10. Kelly, 53.

11. Kelly, 43.

12. Saul, p. 310–311. Saul is here discussing *Sir Gawain and the Green Knight*.

13. "Kingsguard," Westeros.org.

14. Martin et al., *The World of Ice and Fire*, p. 50.

15. Malory, "Caxton's Preface," xv.

16. Martin et al., *The World of Ice and Fire*, p. 8.

17. Martin, *A Knight of the Seven Kingdoms*, p. 98.

18. Spector, p. 180.

19. In the HBO series, Jaime assigns Podrick to be Brienne's squire. This position demands loyalty. In the novels, Podrick's loyalty to Brienee occurs naturally as he comes to respect her.

20. Brienne is on a different trajectory in the HBO series, finding and helping to rescue Sansa Stark from Ramsay Bolton. She does encounter Jaime when he takes Riverrun, but the bond between the two seems to have diminished.

21. A rash boon occurs when a character grants a request in advance of knowing what the request will be. A rash boon motivates the initial action of Chrétien's "Lancelot." Meleagant appears at Arthur's court and promises to release prisoners that he holds if any of Arthur's knights can fight against him and win Guinevere from him. After Meleagant departs, Kay threatens to leave Arthur's court unless Arthur grants him his next request. Arthur agrees, only to learn that Kay wants to take up this challenge. He fails in defeating Meleagant, and both he and Guinevere are taken captive. Chaucer's "The Wife of Bath's Tale" also contains a rash boon. A loathly lady promises a knight the answer to a seemingly unsolvable riddle if he will grant her next request. He has committed a crime, and his life depends upon the correct answer. He agrees to her demands, and his life is spared. To his astonishment, however, she requests that he marry her.

22. Kennedy, p. 99.

23. Hodges, web.

Chapter Six

1. "George R.R. Martin: *The Rolling Stone* Interview."

2. See Charles Hackney, "'Silk ribbons tied around a sword': Knighthood and the Chivalric Virtues in Westeros." Hackney, a psychology professor who has researched the psychology of martial arts, presents an excellent discussion on the ambiguities of chivalry. His focus is on history and chivalric manuals rather than literature.

3. Stein, p. 114. Stein's purpose is to show how the battle scene itself detracts from the political situation inspiring it. However, his description of the scene also highlights the lack of graphic detail.

4. *The Song of Roland*, p. 79.

5. Geoffroi de Charny, p. 95.

6. *Beowulf*, ll. 287–289.

7. French, p. 3.

8. *Ramon Lull's Book of Knighthood and Chivalry*, Epilogue, p. 47.

9. Saul, p. 155.

10. Kelly, p. 43.

11. Kelly, p. 46.

12. *Ramon Lull's Book of Knighthood and Chivalry*, p. 35.

13. *Ramon Lull's Book of Knighthood and Chivalry*, p. 30.

14. *Ramon Lull's Book of Knighthood and Chivalry*, p. 41.

15. Geoffroi de Charny, p. 48.

16. See Chapter Four, "Franchise in Westeros," for a more complete discussion of swords as they help forge familial ties and continuity.

17. The sword bequeathed to Jon should by rights pass to Jeor's son, Ser Jorah Mormont. Ser Jorah, however, has been banished for a crime and deemed unworthy to inherit it.

18. Hackney, p. 135.

19. *Ramon Lull's Book of Knighthood and Chivalry*, p. 64–75.

20. Saul, p. 153.
21. Saul, p. 154.
22. *Ramon Lull's Book of Knighthood and Chivalryl*, p. 97.
23. Malory, p. 306.
24. Lexton, p. 120.
25. Lexton, p. 128.
26. Lexton, p. 124.
27. Malory, p. 615.
28. Geoffroi de Charny, p. 52.
29. Charny, p. 66.
30. *Ramon Lull's Book of Knighthood and Chivalry*, p. 85.
31. *Ramon Lull's Book of Knighthood and Chivalry*, p. 60.
32. *Ramon Lull's Book of Knighthood and Chivalry*, p. 31.
33. See Chapter Four for a full discussion of peasants and their role in chivalric literature.
34. Saul, p. 145.
35. *Ramon Lull's Book of Knighthood and Chivalry*, p. 17.
36. *Ramon Lull's Book of Knighthood and Chivalry*, p. 35.
37. *Ramon Lull's Book of Knighthood and Chivalry*, p. 34.
38. Malory, p. 161.
39. *Ramon Lull's Book of Knighthood and Chivalry*, p. 82.
40. Saul, p. 148–9.
41. Malory, p. 655.
42. Hackney, p. 135.
43. Ser Loras is on a very different trajectory in the HBO series, imprisoned by the High Sparrow for his sins and, in the last episode, brought to a trial that does not end as expected.

Chapter Seven

1. Mapstone, p. 110.
2. Malory, p. 51.
3. Kennedy, p. 205.
4. McClune, p. 100.
5. Malory adapts this story from the *Suite de Merlin*.
6. The HBO series reveals that Lyanna and Rhaegar Tarygaryen are Jon Snow's parents. Lyanna's willingness to be with Rhaegar remains unconfirmed, but many fans suspect that she was in love with Rhaegar and went with him on her own volition.
7. In the novels, Wyman Manderly most likely bakes the Frey sons into the pie, which he serves at Ramsay Bolton's wedding. I discuss this incident in Part Six.
8. In the HBO series, Ellaria Sand poisons Myrcella as Myrcella departs for King's Landing, an assurance that the Lannister/Martell feud will rage on.
9. Daenerys does not feel compelled to avenge the death of her brother Viserys, who has treated her cruelly and obstinately refused to respect her position as wife of Khaleesi.
10. *Beowulf*, ll. 2465–2468.
11. The narrative of one brother killing another and then becoming heir could also be drawn from history. Legends circulated that Henry I killed his brother William Rufus, making the alleged murder appear to be a hunting accident, then ascending to the throne before his other brother and rightful heir, Robert Curthose, could claim it. Richard III is another historical figure accused of kin killing; in this case, his two young nephews for whom he was supposed to serve as protector.
12. McClune, p. 98.
13. Malory, p. 56.
14. Ackerman, p. 125.

15. Malory, *Malory Works*, p. 56.

16. Malory, *Malory Works*, p. 58, p. 59.

17. "Arryk Cargyll," Westeros.org.

18. Again, Martin is likely borrowing from history. The Anglo-Saxon king Edmund Ironsides, who was perhaps as reviled as Tywin Lannister, was reportedly also killed while on the privy. Edmund was murdered by enemies who were not related to him.

Chapter Eight

1. Spector, pp. 187 and 171.

2. "A Very Long Interview with George R.R. Martin." *Oh No They Didn't Live Journal*, Web.

3. West, blog.

4. Frankel, *Women in Game of Thrones*.

5. Westeros: The *A Song of Ice and Fire Domain*, Web.

6. *The Wife's Lament* and *Wulf and Eadwacer* are both elegies that are preserved in the 9th-century Anglo-Saxon *Exeter Book*. The enigmatic "Wulf and Eadwacer," has been variously interpreted. Its placement in the Exeter book before the riddles has led some scholars to assume that it may actually be a riddle. The vague language and presence of *hapex legomena* has inspired a variety of interpretations, although most scholars now concur that the poem is a reflection of female grief. See Carol Jamison, "Traffic and Exile in Germanic Literature," *Women in German Yearbook*. Volume 20 (2004) pp. 13–36.

7. Chance, p. 98.

8. "A Very Long Interview with George R.R. Martin."

9. Although the Anglo-Saxon term appears only once, in *Beowulf*, to describe the rebellious peace weaver Thryth, it has come to be the common designation used by scholars to describe women married off to forge political alliances.

10. Passages from the elegies are based upon editions of the poems in Anne Klinck's *The Old English Elegies: A Critical Edition and Genre Study*. Because of the ambiguous nature of the elegies, I provide my own translations of them unless otherwise indicated. p. 27–28.

11. Klinck, p. 27–28.

12. Klinck, p. 27–28.

13. I argue that Hildeburh's son would likely be an object of exchange, going to live with his mother's kin and forming a close relationship with his maternal uncle. Thus, it is possible that he fights against his father.

14. Martin et al., *The World of Ice and Fire*, p. 169.

15. The HBO series, known for graphic depictions of sex, makes Renly's homosexuality obvious by showing Renly and Ser Loras Tyrell in bed together.

16. George R.R. Martin, Westeros.org.

17. Spector, p. 176.

18. Sklute, p. 539.

19. Cersei grieves for the loss of her son Joffrey, but in the HBO series, she shows less concern for her son Tommen. When she destroys the Great Sept of Baelor, Tommen's wife Margaery is among those who die. Tommen subsequently commits suicide, and Cersei promptly seizes power for herself. Her ruthlessness and callousness at this point could also be her resignation to a prophecy made in her youth that foretold the deaths of her children.

20. Frankel, *Women in Game of Thrones*, p. 73.

21. Cersei's reputation for trickery and subterfuge place her in the tradition of another of Arthur's half-sisters, the vengeful and tricky Morgan le Fey.

22. Lexton, p. 159.

23. Cersei also evokes Signy of the *Volsunga Saga* who sleeps with her brother to produce an acceptable heir since her husband is incapable of doing so. My focus here, however, is on political alliances.

24. Lexton, *Contested Language*, p. 169.

25. Rubin, p. 207.

26. Targaryens traditionally married their own kin, not always to good ends. One possible consequence is the madness that runs through the family.

27. In the HBO series, Cersei uses wildfire to destroy her enemies and then promptly claims the throne.

28. Myrcella's exile to Dorne evokes the exiles, also arranged marriages, of both Constance and Patient Griselda, characters who appear in secular saint's lives told by both Chaucer and Boccaccio.

29. *Beowulf*, l. 1932.

30. Myrcella is killed by the trickery of Ellaria Sand in the series.

31. Mitchell and Robinson, p. 137.

32. *Beowulf*, ll. 2063–2066.

33. Although a popular reading is that the narrator mourns a lost lover, I concur with J.A. Tasioulis in "The Mother's Lament: *Wulf and Eadwacer* Reconsidered" and Marijane Osborn in "The Text and Context of *Wulf and Eadwacer*" that such a reading is unlikely. Tasioulis writes that "The interpretation of the poem does not stand or fall on what can be assumed to be typical or atypical situations in Old English literature, but it is still worth noting that grieving mothers far outnumber adulterous or lovelorn wives" (2). Osborn agrees that interpreting the narrator to be an unhappy lover is unlikely "because most OE loyalty crises occur within the family group" (183). Another scholar who effectively argues that the narrator mourns the loss of a child is Dolorous Warwick Frese in "*Wulf and Eadwacer*: The Adulterous Woman Reconsidered."

34. Osborne, p. 187.

35. Osborne, p. 187.

36. Klein, p. 116.

37. Frankel, *Women in the Game of Thrones*, p. 62.

38. Spector, p. 184.

39. Kliman, p. 39.

40. Strauss, "Women's Words as Weapons: Speech as Action in *The Wife's Lament*."

41. See Niles, "The Problem of the Ending of the Wife's Lament."

42. Klink, p. 27.

43. Asha is portrayed quite differently in the HBO series, where she is named Yara. In the series, Yara is also a skilled warrior, but she has no interest in men. Again, the HBO series does not fully convey the significance of peace weaving with this portrayal.

44. Damico, p. 219.

45. Fee, p. 291.

46. *Beowulf*, ll. 2029–31.

Conclusions

1. Clements, p. 26.

2. Student Matthew Nabors, Armstrong State University, Class of 2016.

3. "George R.R. Martin: *The Rolling Stone* Interview."

4. Student Matthew Nabors, Armstrong State University, Class of 2016.

5. Marshall, Intro. *Mass Market Medieval*, p. 1, 2.

6. West-Harling, p. 1.

7. Martin et al., *The World of Ice and Fire*, p. 208.

8. Marshall, "Haze of Medievalisms." p. 29.

9. Robinson and Clements, p. 59.

10. Helmsetter, Web. http://www.wordandfilm.com/2013/06/whats-the-big-contemporary-deal-%E2%80%98game-of-thrones/.

11. West, Web.

12. Blake, Web.
13. Carpenter, Web.
14. Student Delia Morena, Armstrong State University, Class of 2016.
15. Student Mari Glover, Armstrong State University, Class of 2016.
16. Student S. Taylor Walton, Armstrong State University, Class of 2016.
17. Utz, p. 82.
18. West-Harling, p. 1.
19. "George R.R. Martin Says 'Game of Thrones' Ending will be Bittersweet," Web.

Bibliography

Ackerman, Felicia. "'Always to Do Ladies, Damosels, and Gentlewomen Succour': Women and the Chivalric Code in Malory's Morte Darthur." *Midwest Studies in Philosophy*, vol. 26, no. 1, 2002, pp. 1–12.

Amodio, Mark. *Writing the Oral Tradition: Oral Poetics and Literate Culture in Medieval England*, U of Notre Dame, 2004.

Antonsson, Linda. "The Palace of Love, The Palace of Sorrow: Romanticism in A Song of Ice and Fire." *Beyond the Wall: Exploring George R.R. Martin's A Song of Ice and Fire*, Edited by Elio M. Garcia, Benbella, 2012. pp. 1–14.

Archibald, Elizabeth. "Malory's Ideal of Fellowship." *The Review of English Studies*, vol. 43, no. 171, 1992, pp. 311–328. JSTOR, www.jstor.org/stable/518049, 24 April 2017.

Archibald, Elizabeth, and Ad Putter. *The Cambridge Guide to Arthurian Legend*, Cambridge U P, 2009.

Bartholomew, Barbara Gray. "The Thematic Function of Malory's Gawain." *College English*, vol. 24, no. 4, 1963, pp. 262–267, www.jstor.org/stable/373611.

Benson, David C. "Gawain's Defense of Lancelot in Malory's 'Death of Arthur.'" *The Modern Language Review*, vol. 72, no. 2, 1983, pp. 267–72.

Benson, Larry, editor. Introduction. *The Riverside Chaucer*, 3rd edition, Houghton Mifflin, 1986.

Beowulf. Edited by C.L. Wrenn (fully revised by W.F. Bolton), Harrap Limited, 1971.

Bernthal, Craig. "Review of A Song of Ice and Fire by George R.R. Martin." *The University Bookman*, June 2012, www.kirkman.org.

Bildhauer, Bettina, and Robert Mills, editors. "Introduction: Conceptualizing the Monstrous." *The Monstrous Middle Ages*, MPG Books Ltd, 2003, pp. 1–27.

Blake, John. "How 'Game of Thrones' Is like America." *CNN*, Cable News Network, 14 May 2014, http://www.cnn.com/2014/05/24/showbiz/game-of-thrones-america/.

Bloch, Marc. *Feudal Society*, Translated by L.A. Manyon, The University of Chicago Press, 1977.

Breen, Benjamin. "Why 'Game of Thrones' Isn't Medieval—and Why That Matters" *Pacific Standard*, 12 June 2014, http://www.psmag.com/books-and-culture/game-thrones-isnt-medieval-matters-83288.

Calvino, Italo. *The Nonexistent Knight and the Cloven Viscount*, Harvest Books, 1977.

Cantor, Norman. *Inventing the Middle Ages: The Lives, Works, and Ideas of the Great Medievalists of the Twentieth Century*, William Morrow, 1991.

Capellanus, Andreas. *The Art of Courtly Love*, Trans. John Jay Parry, Columbia U P, 1960.

Carpenter, Charley. "Game of Thrones as Theory." *Foreign Affairs*, Council on Foreign Relations, 29 Mar. 2012, https://www.foreignaffairs.com/articles/2012-03-29/game-thrones-theory.

Caxton, William. Preface to *Malory's Works* by Sir Thomas Malory, Edited by Eugene Vinaver, Oxford U P, 1971, p. 103.

Chance, Jane. "Tough Love: Teaching the New Medievalism." *Studies in Medievalism: Defining Medievalism(s) (2) XVII*, Edited by Karl Fugelso, D.S. Brewer, 2009, pp. 76–98.

Chrétien de Troyes. *Arthurian Romances*, Translated by William Kibler, Penguin Books, 2004.

Clements, Pam. "Authenticity." *Medievalism: Key Critical Terms*, edited by Elizabeth Emery and Richard Utz, D.S. Brewer, 2014, pp. 19–26.

Cole, Myke, "Art Imitates War: Post-Traumatic Stress Disorder in *A Song of Ice and Fire*," *Beyond the Wall*, edited by James Lowder, Benbella Books, 2012, pp. 73–88.

Coleridge, Samuel Taylor. *The Complete Poems of Samuel Taylor Coleridge*, edited by William Keach, Penguin Classics, 1997.

Coote, Lesley. "A Short Essay about Neomedievalism." *Defining Neomedievalism(s): Studies in Medievalism XIX*, edited by Karl Fugelso, D.S. Brewer, 2010, pp. 25–33.

Crossley-Holland, Kevin. *The Anglo-Saxon World: An Anthology*. Oxford U P, 1982.

Damico, Helen. *Beowulf and the Grendel-Kin: Politics & Poetry in Eleventh-Century England*. West Virginia U P, 2015.

D'Arcens, Louise, editor. *The Cambridge Companion to Medievalism*. Cambridge U P, 2016.

Driver, Martha W., and Sid Ray. *The Medieval Hero on Screen: Representations from Beowulf to Buffy*. McFarland, 2004.

Earl, Benjamin. "Places Don't Have to be True to be True: The Appropriation of King Arthur and the Culture Value of Tourist Sites." *Mass Market Medieval: Essays on the Middle Ages in Popular Culture*, edited by David W. Marshall, McFarland, 2007, pp. 102–112.

Eco, Umberto. *Travels in Hyperreality*. Harcourt Brace Jovanovich, 1986.

Emery, Elizabeth. "Medievalism and the Middle Ages." *Studies in Medievalism*, vol. 17, 2009, pp. 77–85.

Emery, Elizabeth, and Richard Utz, editors. *Medievalism: Key Critical Terms*, D.S. Brewer, 2014.

Fee, Christopher. "'Beag' and 'Beaghroden' in *Beowulf*." *Neophilologische Mitteilungen*, vol. 97, no. 3, 1996, pp. 285–294.

Frankel, Valerie Estelle. *Winning the Game of Thrones: The Host of Characters and Their Agendas*. LitCrit Press, 2015.

_____. *Women in Game of Thrones: Power, Conformity, Resistance*. McFarland, 2014.

Fugelso, Karl. "Continuity." *Medievalism: Key Critical Terms*, edited by Elizabeth Emery and Richard Utz, D.S. Brewer, 2014, pp. 53–61.

Flieger, Verlyn. "'There Would Always be a Fairy-Tale': J.R.R. Tolkien and the Folklore Controversy." *Tolkien the Medievalist*, Editor Jane Chance, Routledge, 2003, pp. 26–35.

_____. "Tolkien's Wild Men: From Medieval to Modern." *Tolkien the Medievalist*, edited by Jane Chance, Routledge, 2003, pp. 95–105.

French, Shannon E. *The Code of the Warrior*, Rowman & Littlefield, 2003.

Garbaty, Thomas J. *Medieval English Literature*, Waveland Press, 1997.

Geoffrey of Monmouth. *The History of the Kings of Britain*, Penguin Books, 1980.

Geoffroi de Charny. *A Knight's Own Book of Chivalry*, Translated by Elspeth Kennedy, University of Pennsylvania Press, 2005.

"George R.R. Martin Says 'Game of Thrones' Ending Will Be Bittersweet." Interview by Sean T. Collins, *Observer Culture*, 11 August 2015, http://observer.com/2015/08/george-r-r-martins-ending-for-game-of-thrones-will-not-be-as-brutal-as-you-think/.

"George R.R. Martin: *The Rolling Stone* Interview." Interview by Mikal Gilmore, *Rolling Stone*, 23 Apr. 2014, http://www.rollingstone.com/tv/news/george-r-r-martin-the-rolling-stone-interview-20140423#ixzz3TLrsvtln.

"George R.R. Martin: 'Trying to Please Everyone Is a Terrible Mistake.'" Interview by Adria Guxens, *Adria's News*, 7 Oct. 2012, http://www.adriasnews.com/2012/10/george-r-r-martin-interview.html

Gravdal, Kathryn. *Vilain and Courtois: Transgressive Parody in French Literature of the Twelfth and Thirteenth Centuries*, U of Nebraska P, 1989.

Grewell, Cory Lowell. "Neomedievalism: An Eleventh Little Middle Ages?" *Defining Neomedievalism(s): Studies in Medievalism XIX*, Edited by Karl Fugelso, D.S. Brewer, 2010, p. 34–43.

Hackney, Charles. "'Silk ribbons tied around a sword': Knighthood and the Chivalric Virtues in Westeros." *Mastering the Game of Thrones: Essays on George R.R. Martin's A Song of Ice and Fire,* Edited by Jess Battis & Susan Johnston, McFarland, 2015, pp. 132–149.

Hartinger, Brent. "A Different Kind of Other: The Role of Freaks and Outcasts in A Song of Ice and Fire." *Beyond the Wall: Exploring George R.R. Martin's A Song of Ice and Fire,* Benbella Books, 2012, pp. 153–168.

Haydock, Nicholas. "Medievalism and Excluded Middles." *Studies in Medievalism: Defining Medievalism(s) (2),* vol. XVIII, Edited by Karl Fugelso, D.S. Brewer, 2009, pp. 17–30.

Helmsetter, Gregory J. "What's the Big (Contemporary) Deal, Game of Thrones." *Words and Film: The Intersection of Books, Movies, and Television,* 5 June 2015, http://www.word andfilm.com/2013/06/whats-the-big-contemporary-deal-%E2%80%98game-of-thrones/.

Hodges, Kenneth. *Forging Chivalric Communities in Malory's Le Morte Darthur.* Palgrave Macmillan, 2005.

Ingram, James, translator. *The Anglo-Saxon Chronicle,* edited by James H. Ford, El Paso Norte Press, 2005.

Jauss, Hans Robert. "Modernity and Literary Tradition." *Critical Inquiry,* vol. 31, no. 2 2005, pp. 329–364.

Jauss, Hans Robert, and Timothy Bahti. "The Alterity and Modernity of Medieval Literature." *New Literary History,* vol. 10, no. 2, Winter 1979, pp. 181–229.

Jones, Andrew Zimmerman. "Of Direwolves and Gods." *Beyond the Wall: Exploring George R.R. Martin's A Song of Ice and Fire,* Benbella Books, 2012, pp. 107–122.

Jousstra, Robert, and Alissa Wilkinson. "Think Religion Is Dead? Just Look at 'Game of Thrones.'" *Washington Post,* 7 June 2015. https://www.washingtonpost.com/news/acts-of-faith/wp/2015/06/07/think-religion-is-dead-just-look-at-game-of-thrones/?utm_term=.71a020e6ab70.

Joynte, Irene. "Vengeance and Love in 'The Book of Sir Launcelot and Queen Guinvere." *Arthurian Literature* vol. 3, 1984, pp. 91–112.

Kaufman, Amy S. "Medieval Unmoored." *Defining Neomedievalism(s): Studies in Medievalism XIX,* Edited by Karl Fugelso, D.S. Brewer, 2010, pp. 1–11.

Keen, Maurice. *Chivalry,* Yale U P, 1984.

Kelly, Robert L. "Royal Policy and Malory's Round Table." *Arthuriana,* vol. 14, no. 1, 2004, pp. 43–71.

Kennedy, Beverly. *Knighthood in the Morte Darthur.* D.S. Brewer, 1985.

Klein, Stacy S. *Ruling Women: Queenship and Gender in Anglo-Saxon Literature.* U Notre Dame P, 2006.

Klinck, Ann. *The Old English Elegies: A Critical Edition and Genre Study.* McGill-Queen's U P, 1992.

Kordecki, Lesley. "Prophecy, Dragons and Meaning in Malory," *Medieval Studies,* vol. 1, 1984, pp. 62–72.

Lacy, Norris, and Geoffrey Ashe. *The Arthurian Handbook.* Second edition, Garland, 1997.

Larrington, Carolyne. *Winter is Coming.* I.B. Tauris, 2016.

Lexton, Ruth. *Contested Language in Malory's* Morte Darthur: *The Politics of Romance in Fifteenth-Century England.* Palgrave Macmillan, 2014.

Lull, Ramon. *Ramon Lull's Book of Knighthood & Chivalry & the Anonymous Ordene de Chevalerie,* translated by William Caxton and Brian R. Price, Chivalry Bookshelf, 2001.

Malory, Sir Thomas. *Malory Works,* edited by Eugene Vinaver, Oxford U P, 2004.

Mapstone, Sally. "Malory and the Scots." *Blood, Sex, Malory,* edited by David Clark and Cate McClune, Boydell and Brewer, 2011, pp. 107–120.

Marshall, David W. "The Haze of Medievalisms." *Studies in Medievalism: Defining Medievalism(s) II,* vol. 20, June 2011, pp. 21–34.

___, editor. "Introduction: The Medievalism of Popular Culture." *Mass Market Medieval: Essays on the Middle Ages in Popular Culture,* McFarland, 2007, pp. 1–12.

Martin, George R.R. *A Clash of Kings,* Bantam, 1999.

_____. *A Dance with Dragons,* Bantam, 2011.

_____. *A Feast for Crows*, Bantam, 2005.

_____. *A Game of Thrones*, Bantam, 1996. Print.

_____. *A Knight of the Seven Kingdom*, Bantam, 2015.

_____. *A Storm of Swords*, Bantam, 2000.

Martin, George R.R., Elio M. Garcia, and Linda Antonsson. *The World of Ice and Fire*, Bantam, 2014.

Mason, Eugene, translator. *Aucassin and Nicolette and other Medieval Romances and Legends*. E.P. Dutton, 1958.

Mayer, Lauryn S. "Dark Matters and Slippery Words: Grappling with Neomedievalism(s)." *Defining Neomedievalism(s): Studies in Medievalism XIX*, July 2010, pp. 68–76.

_____. "Simulacrum" *Medievalism: Key Critical Terms*, edited by Elizabeth Emery and Richard Utz, D.S. Brewer, 2014, pp. 223–230.

Mitchell, Bruce, and Fred C. Robinson, *A Guide to Old English*, Sixth edition, Blackwell, 2001.

Moberly, Brent, and Kevin Moberly. "Neomedievalism, Hyperrealism, and Simulation." *Defining Neomedievalism(s): Studies in Medievalism XIX*, July 2010, pp. 12–24.

Montaiglon, Anatole de, and Gaston Raynaud, editors. *Recuil Général et Complet des Fabliaux des XIIIe et XIVe Siécles*, 6 Volumes, Librarie des Bibliophiles, 1872–1890.

Kliman, Bernice. "Women in Early English Literature, 'Beowulf' to the 'Ancrene Wisse'. *Nottingham Mediaeval Studies*, vol. 21, 1997, pp. 32–49.

Moorman, Charles. "Courtly Love in Malory." *ELH*, vol. 27, no. 3, September 1960, pp. 163–176.

Morgan, Gwendolyn A. "Medievalism, Authority, and the Academy." *Studies in Medievalism*, vol. 17, January 2009, pp. 55–67.

Nagy, Gergely. "The Great Chain of Reading: (Inter-)textual Relations and the Technique of Mythopoesis in the Túrin Story." *Tolkien the Medievalist*, edited by Jane Chance, Routledge, 2003, pp. 239–259.

Niles, John D. "The Problem of the Ending of the Wife's Lament." *Speculum*, vol. 78, no. 4, October 2003, pp. 1107–1150.

Nussbaum, Emily. "The Westeros Wing: The Politics of 'Game of Thrones.'" *The New Yorker*, 4 July 2016, pp. 72–72.

Osborne, Marijane. "The Text and Context of *Wulf and Eadwacer*." *The Old English Elegies: New Essays in Criticism and Research*, edited by Martin Green, Fairleigh Dickinson U P, 1983.

Perroy, E. "Social Mobility among the French *Noblesse* in the Later Middle Ages," *Past and Present*, vol. 21, no. 1, April 1926, pp. 25–38.

Peterson, Nils Holger. "Medieval Resurfacing, Old and New." *Studies in Medievalism: Defining Medievalism(s) II*, vol. 20, June 2011, pp. 35–42.

Petrina, Alessandra. "Forbidden Forest, Enchanted Castle: Arthurian Spaces in the Harry Potter Novels." *Mythlore*, vol. 93/94, Winter/Spring 2006, pp. 95–110.

Rekasi, Ester. "Game of Thrones: What a Postmodernist Way of Thinking," 1 December 2012, http://www.academia.edu/3651139/Game_of_Thrones_-_What_a_Postmodern_Way_of_Thinking_.

Risden, E.L. "Medievalists, Medievalism, and Medievalismists." *Studies in Medievalism: Defining Medievalism(s) II*, vol. 18, November 2009, pp. 44–54.

_____. "Sandworms, Bodices, and undergrounds: The Transformative Mélange of Neomedievalism." *Studies in Medievalism: Defining Neomedievalism(s) II*, vol. 19, July 2010, pp. 58–67. Print.

Robinson, Carol L., "A Little History." *Medieval Electronic Multimedia Association*, 31 August 2016, http://medievalelectronicmultimedia.org/.

Robinson, Carol L., and Pamela Clements. "Living with Neomedievalism." *Studies in Medievalism: Defining Medievalism(s) II*, vol. 18, November 2009, pp. 55–75.

Rovang, Paul. R. *Malory's Anatomy of Chivalry: Characterization in the Morte Darthur*. Farleigh U P, 2015.

Rubin, Gayle. "The Traffic in Women: Notes on the 'Political Economy' of Sex." *Toward an*

Anthropology of Women, edited by Raya R. Reiter, Monthly Review Press, 1975, pp. 157–210.

Saul, Nigel. *For Honour and Fame: Chivalry in England 1066–1500*. Pimlico, 2011.

Scala, Elizabeth. "Disarming Lancelot." *Studies in Philology*, vol. 99, no. 4, Fall 2002, pp. 380–403.

Scoble, Jesse. "A Sword without a Hilt." *Beyond the Wall: Exploring George R.R. Martin's A Song of Ice and Fire*, Benbella Books, 2012, pp. 123–140.

Seitz, Matt Zoller. "'Game of Thrones': HBO's Dense, Demanding Epic," *Salon* 14 April 2011. http://www.salon.com/2011/04/14/game_of_thrones_season_1/.

Shakespeare, William. *The Complete Works of Shakespeare*, edited by David Bevington. Seventh edition, Pearson, 2013.

Shippey, Tom. "Medievalisms and Why They Matter." *Studies in Medievalism: Defining Medievalism(s) II*, vol. 17, January 2009, pp. 45–54.

_____. "Modernity." *Medievalism: Key Critical Terms*, edited Elizabeth Emery and Richard Utz, D.S. Brewer, 2014, pp. 149–155.

_____. *The Road to Middle Earth: How J.R.R. Tolkien Created a New Mythology*. Mariner, 2003.

Sims, Harley J. "Is Game of Thrones "Realistic" Fantasy?" *Catholic Exchange*, 08 May 2012, http://catholicexchange.com/is-game-of-thrones-realistic-fantasy.

Sir Gawain and the Green Knight. *The Works of the Gawain Poet*, edited by Charles Moorman, U P of Mississippi, 1977.

Sklute, L. John, "'Freoþuwebbe' in Old English Poetry." *Neuphilologische Mitteilungen*, vol. 71, 1970, pp. 534–554.

The Song of Roland, translated by D.D.R. Owen, Boydell Press, 1990.

Spector, Caroline. "Power and Feminism in Westeros." *Beyond the Wall: Exploring George R.R. Martin's A Song of Ice and Fire*, edited by James Lowder, Benbella Books, 2012, pp. 169–188.

Staggs, Matt. "Petyr Baelish and the Mask of Sanity." *Beyond the Wall: Exploring George R.R. Martin's A Song of Ice and Fire*, edited by James Lowder, Benbella Books, 2012, pp. 141–151.

Stein, Robert M. *Reality Fictions: Romance, History and Governmental Authority, 1025–1180*. U of Notre Dame P, 2006.

Strauss, Barrie. "Women's Words as Weapons: Speech as Action in *The Wife's Lament*," *Texas Studies in Language and Literature*, vol. 23, 1981, pp. 268–85.

Sutter, James L. "The Gray Zone: Moral Ambiguity in Fantasy." *Unbound Worlds*, Nov. 2011, http://www.unboundworlds.com/2011/11/guest-essay-james-l-sutter-the-gray-zone-moral-ambiguity-in-fantasy/.

Tolkien, J.R.R. *Beowulf: The Monster and the Critics*. Houghton Mifflin, 1984.

Toswell, M.J. "The Simulacrum of Neomedievalism." *Studies in Medievalism: Defining Neomedievalism(s) 19*, July 2010, pp. 44–57.

_____. "The Tropes of Medievalism." *Studies in Medievalism: Defining Medievalism(s) II*, vol. 17, January 2009, pp. 68–76.

Tracinski, Robert. "Our Sick National Obsession with *Game of Thrones*," *The Federalist*, 11 April 2014, http://thefederalist.com/2014/04/11/our-sick-national-obsession-with-game-of-thrones/.

Utz, Richard. *Medievalism: A Manifesto*, Arc Humanities Press; New edition, 2016.

_____. "*Medievalitis Fugit*: Medievalism and Temporality." *Studies in Medievalism: Defining Medievalism(s) II*, vol. 18, November 2009, pp. 31–43.

_____. "Speaking of Medievalism: An Interview with Leslie J. Workman." *Medievalism in the Modern World: Essays in Honour of Leslie J. Workman*, edited by Richard Utz and Leslie J. Workman, Brepols, 1998, pp. 433–450.

Vaught, Susan. "The Brutal Cost of Redemption in Westeros Or, *What* Moral Ambiguity?" *Beyond the Wall: Exploring George R.R. Martin's A Song of Ice and Fire*, edited by James Lowder, Benbella Books, 2012, pp. 89–106.

Verduin, Kathleen. "The Founding of the Founder: Medievalism and the Legacy of Leslie J. Workman." *Studies in Medievalism: Defining Medievalism(s) II*, vol. 17, January 2009, pp. 76–98.

"A Very Long Interview with George R.R. Martin." - *Oh No They Didn't!*, 8 Oct. 2012, http://ohnotheydidnt.livejournal.com/72570529.html.

West, T.J. "*Game of Thrones* and Contemporary American Culture." Web log post. *Queerly Different*, 3 June, 2014, http://tjwest3.com/2014/06/03/game-of-thrones-and-contemporary-american-culture/.

West-Harling, Veronica Ortenberg. *In Search of the Holy Grail: The Quest for the Middle Ages*. Hambledon Continuum, 2006.

_____. "Medievalism as Fun and Games." *Studies in Medievalism: Defining Medievalism(s) II*, vol. 18, November 2009, pp. 1–16.

Westeros: The A Song of Ice and Fire Domain, 2016, http://www.westeros.org/.

Whitney, Erin. "'Game of Thrones' Showrunners Wanted That Awful Death to Raise Morality Questions." *The Huffington Post*, 8 June 2015, http://www.huffingtonpost.com/2015/06/08/game-of-thrones-shireen-death_n_7535126.html

"A Wiki of Ice and Fire," 2017, http://www.westeros.org/.

Zaleski, Philip, and Carol Zaleski. "Oxford's Influential Inklings: C.S. Lewis and J.R.R. Tolkien." *The Chronicle Review*, vol. 61, no. 35, 15 May 2015, pp. B10–13.

Index